Traditions of the Osage

Traditions of the Osage

Stories Collected and Translated by Francis La Flesche

EDITED AND INTRODUCED BY **GARRICK BAILEY**

University of New Mexico Press
Albuquerque

© 2010 by the University of New Mexico Press
All rights reserved. Published 2010
Printed in the United States of America
Book design and composition by Karen Mazur

First paperback printing 2023

ISBN 978-0-8263-4850-0 (cloth)
ISBN 978-0-8263-4851-7 (paper)
ISBN 978-0-8263-4852-4 (e-book)

Library of Congress Cataloging-in-Publication Data
Traditions of the Osage : stories collected and translated by Francis la Flesche /
edited and introduced by Garrick Bailey.
    p. cm.
 Includes bibliographical references and index.
    ISBN 978-0-8263-4850-0 (cloth : alk. paper)
    1. Osage Indians—Folklore. 2. Osage Indians—Rites and ceremonies. I. La Flesche,
Francis, 1857–1932. II. Bailey, Garrick Alan.
  E99.08T74 2010
  398.0897′5254—dc22
                              2009035342

Photographs courtesy: Osage Tribal Museum
Jacket design: Karen Mazur

In memory of my good friend Wy-e-gla-in-kah
(James Lacy Red Corn)

Contents

PART TWO: FOLK STORIES

Illustrations

Preface

As a graduate student researching Osage culture I read George Dorsey's *Traditions of the Osage*. This work, originally published in 1904, was and still is the only major work on Osage oral traditions available. I found these stories disappointing in that they gave the reader little insight into Osage culture and society. Later, when I was involved in field research, I thought about trying to collect additional traditional stories. However, I quickly discovered that I had arrived too late. During the first two decades of the twentieth century the vast majority of Osage traditionalists had converted to the Peyote church, a fusion of Christian and traditional Osage beliefs and practices. Not wanting their children to be burdened by the past, most Osage peyotists took the position that traditional teachings were best "put away" and forgotten, and they focused on preparing their children to live in the white world. To this end they emphasized the learning of English and at the same time attempted to extinguish the knowledge of the past.[1] One of the many cultural casualties of this new ideology was knowledge of their traditional stories. Assuming that the stories collected by Dorsey were a true reflection of the nature and content of traditional Osage stories, I gave little additional thought to the subject and made no attempt to pursue the topic.

In 1992 I was a senior fellow at the Smithsonian researching Francis La Flesche's studies of Osage religion and religious ritual. In the course of studying his papers[2] in the National Anthropological Archives I came across a thin file labeled "Osage Ethno: Myth, Legends and Stories." On reading them, I was immediately struck by the difference between these Osage stories and those collected and published by Dorsey. The Osage stories recorded by La Flesche were important cultural documents clearly illustrating various aspects of Osage cultural beliefs and social behaviors. In comparing these stories to those published by Dorsey I could not help but think of La Flesche's remarks given in Philadelphia in 1903 at the dedication of the statute of the Medicine Man. In his speech La Flesche talked about the misconceptions the white man held about the Indian. In speaking of academic research he remarked:

> The myths, the rituals, and the legends of the race have been frequently recorded in such a manner as to obscure their true meaning and to make them appear as childish or as foolish. This has been in a large measure due to linguistic difficulties. The Indian tongues differ widely from the English language, not only in the construction of sentences but in general literary form. Moreover, the imagery of the Indian speech conveys a very different meaning to the mind of the Indian from that which it conveys to the mind of the white man. The Indian looks upon nature, upon all natural forms, animate and inanimate, from a different standpoint and he draws from them different lessons than does one of the white race. So when scholars give a literal translation to an Indian story, both its spirit and its form are lost to the English reader. Or when the myth is interpreted by an Indian who has picked up a scanty and colloquial knowledge of English, even if by chance he has himself a comprehension of the meaning of the myth he translates, his rendition will be one that no intelligent Indian can accept as a true presentation of the mythic story. It is from translations such as these that the mental capacity of the Indian has been judged.[3]

Were it not for the fact that *Traditions of the Osages* was published in 1904, a year after La Flesche delivered this speech, one might think that his remarks were directed at Dorsey's work.

At the time I thought that it was unfortunate that La Flesche had not collected more such stories. However, as I pursued my study of his papers and publications, I soon discovered that only a small number of the stories that he had collected were to be found in this thin file. Scattered throughout his other notes and published works were still other stories. By combing La Flesche's notes and publications, I was eventually able to assemble the collection of forty-nine Osage traditional narratives published in this book. What makes this collection of stories both interesting and important in the understanding of early American Indian oral literature is that they were collected in their original language (Osage) by a scholar who not only spoke a mutually intelligible language (Omaha) as his native language but who was highly educated and articulate in English as well.[4] In terms of the quality of translations, this collection of Native American stories has few, if any, equals. In these stories, particularly the ones I categorize as "folk stories," the early Osage come alive as individuals exhibiting the full range of human emotions and behaviors. These are stories of exceptional individuals both noble and evil and of events comic, mysterious, and tragic. Their stories tell of individuals capable of great love, courage, generosity, sacrifice, and wisdom, as well as of others capable of jealousy, selfishness, deceitfulness, vindictiveness, and foolishness. Collectively these stories put a human face on traditional Osage life that cannot be found in the academic studies of Osage history and anthropology. It is this quality of humanness that makes these stories important in not just understanding the Osage past but the Native American past in general.

Acknowledgments

My research on the Osage has now covered a period of over forty years. During this time I have had countless formal and informal discussions with members of the Osage community. All of these discussions have not only contributed to but have been the basis for my understanding of Osage culture and history. To these individuals I am forever indebted. Since most of them are no longer with us, I can only hope that their descendents can gain something of value from this book and my other studies.

In addition I would like to individually thank some members of the Osage community who have directly contributed to this volume. Katherine Red Corn, director of the Osage Tribal Museum, was very supportive. Rhonda Kohnle, secretary of the Osage Tribal Museum, searched through the extensive photograph collection of the museum identifying photographs for possible inclusion in this volume. Louis Burns has worked hard to identify campsite locations and map the hunting trails used by the Osage. He kindly supplied me with drawings of his maps, the information from which was incorporated into the map in this volume.

The archival research for this study was done while I was a senior fellow at the National Museum of Natural History at the Smithsonian Institution in 1992. I would like to thank the late William Sturtevant, who acted as my sponsor, the staff of the Department of Anthropology, Carole Lee Kim, Karen Moran, Joyce Sommers, and Lawan Tyson as well as the staff of the National Anthropological Archives, Mary Ruwell, Kathleen Baxter, and Paula Fleming.

Justin Brown, a student in graphic design at the University of Tulsa prepared the illustrations.

Finally, and most of all, I would like to thank my wife, Roberta, who for years has supported my research. Without her encouragement, none of it would have been accomplished.

Chapter 1

Introduction

One cannot fully appreciate the importance of the Osage stories in this volume without first understanding the background of the individual who recorded and translated them. Francis La Flesche was a truly exceptional individual. Born in Nebraska in 1857, he was the son of a traditional Omaha chief. As a boy and young man he attended a mission school on the reservation. On vacations from school he participated in tribal buffalo hunts and rituals. In 1881 he accepted a job as a copyist for the Indian Service and moved to Washington, D.C., where he became involved with members of the local anthropological community. He studied linguistics informally while also taking degrees in law—an LLB (1891) and an LLM (1893)—at National University (later George Washington University). His early anthropological research concerned the Omaha and was done in collaboration with Alice Fletcher. Their joint research culminated in the publication of *The Omaha Tribe* by the Smithsonian Institution's Bureau of American Ethnology.[1]

While *The Omaha Tribe* was still in press, the Bureau of American Ethnology approached La Flesche with the proposition that he do a comparable study on the Osage. La Flesche was the ideal person to study the Osage because the Osage and the Omaha spoke mutually intelligible languages and shared similar cultural traditions. The proposition appealed to La Flesche, and in 1910 he resigned from the Indian Service to become an ethnographer with the Smithsonian. In September 1910, La Flesche arrived in Pawhuska, Oklahoma, to begin his new career. For the next thirteen years he traveled regularly between Washington and Oklahoma collecting data on the Osage. In 1914 he finished the first of six major book-length manuscripts on the Osage.[2] In the summer of 1923 he made his last field research trip to Oklahoma. His close friend and collaborator, Alice Fletcher, had died that spring and by this time most of the Osage who he had worked with had also died. Between 1923 and his retirement from the bureau in 1929, he finished his last five manuscripts. He returned home to Nebraska, dying there in 1932. The last of his manuscripts, *A Dictionary of the Osage Language* (1932) and *War Ceremony and Peace Ceremony of the Osage Indians* (1939), were published posthumously.[3]

Oral Traditions

Osage oral traditions fall into three distinct categories: 1) sacred teachings, which were part of the tribe's sacred knowledge and under the control of formally organized priesthoods, 2) folk stories, which were stories concerning memorable people and events that were known to and told by the public as a whole, and 3) animal stories, which were stories told to educate and entertain children. Of the three types of stories, the sacred teachings were the most important and the most complex.

One of the last Osage priests, Saucy Calf, remarked to La Flesche that "our ancestors knew not the art of writing, but they put into ritual form the thoughts they deemed worthy of perpetuation."[4] Osage religious rituals were not merely supplicatory appeals to the supernatural for assistance but were also extremely complex and sophisticated mnemonic devices by which the Osage recalled and transmitted sacred knowledge. "Sacred" included a broad range of subjects for the Osage. In their religious teaching they spoke both of Wa-kon'-da and Wa-kon'-da's creations and of their own social and political institutions and how these institutions, blessed by Wa-kon'-da, had come into being.

Major rituals took the form of enactments of sacred stories similar to pageants found in other societies. Each ritual was divided into varying numbers of ritual elements, the particular elements used depending on the purpose of the ritual. These elements included participants who symbolically represented some aspect of the cosmos, sacred objects (pipes, war standards, medicine bundles, etc.), ritual performances (involving symbolic participants and sacred objects), songs, poetic recitations called *wi'-gi-e*, and sometimes sacred instructions.[5]

There were two main forms of sacred teachings: 1) *wi'-gi-e*, which were spoken in an archaic form of Osage and which made use of metaphors and other semantic devices to hide their full meanings, and 2) sacred instructions, which were spoken in everyday Osage.

The core element in any ritual was the recitation of a particular set of *wi'-gi-e*. All other ritual actions merely served to more fully explain or convey the meaning of the *wi'-gi-e* recited. *Wi'-gi-e* were highly redundant poetic recitations that varied in length from a few dozen to over fifteen hundred lines of text. Each *wi'-gi-e* was a fragment of Osage sacred knowledge. It is difficult to estimate the total number of *wi'-gi-e*. La Flesche collected at least partial information on over fifty *wigi-e*.[6] The total number probably exceeded five hundred. A *wi'-gi-e* was not in itself a narrative or story but rather the factual outline of a story. It was a poem in which key factors were noted in a particular order. However, knowledgeable priests could, and did, convert *wi'-gi-e* into a narrative form.

As important as they were, *wi'-gi-e* were not public property. Every *wi'-gi-e* was the property of a specific priesthood or group of priesthoods. All together there were twenty-four clan priesthoods and three tribal priesthoods, each of which was the custodian of a particular set of *wi'-gi-e*. Only the initiated priests of that particular clan or tribal priesthood had the authority to recite their *wi'-gi-e*. The *wi'-gi-e* made extensive use of archaic words and metaphors in a attempt to disguise their true meanings. Thus, even if or when they heard it, uninitiated Osages would have had little idea as to the actual meaning of a particular *wi'-gi-e*, and even priests from other clans would have only a general idea as to its meaning. Just as every ritual was a fragment of the story, so every *wi'-gi-e* itself was also a story fragment. Collectively the *wi'-gi-e* of all of the priesthoods told of the nature of the cosmos, of Wa-kon'-da, of the origins of the tribe and clans, and of how over time the religious leaders of the Osage changed the tribal organization in order to secure Wa-kon'-da's continued blessings and to survive in their conflict with other humans. In other words, collectively they constituted what were in effect the encyclopedia of knowledge as well as the history of tribal organization.

In response to a particular question, a priest could draw on segments from one or more his clan's *wi'-gi-e* to frame an answer in the form of a narrative story. In other words, *wi'-gi-e* were mnemonic devices that allowed individuals to remember and recall large bodies of important factual information.

No individual priest had the knowledge, let alone the authority, to fully explain the stories contained in the *wi'-gi-e*. Each priesthood was entrusted to retain and transmit only portions of this knowledge. Even to create the basic outline of the origin story of the Osage recorded in story 1.1 ("Allegorical Story of Tribal Organization"), La Flesche had to piece together narratives collected from four different clan priests. *Wi'-gi-e* narratives that La Flesche later collected from these and other priests expanded on many of the points noted in this general story. For example, in the first part of story 1.1 we learn that the Water, Sky, and Earth peoples came to earth from the sky. In stories 1.2 ("Origin

Story of the Wolf Clan") and 1.8 ("Haircut of the Gentle Sky Clan"), we discover that the people took the form of eagles to descend to earth. Stories 1.2, 1.3 ("Origin Story of the Black Bear Clan"), and 1.8 tell us that they were scattered when they first reached the earth, some landing in various trees and others on rocks of different colors. In story 1.9 ("Finding of the Four Colors"), the reason why they landed on trees and rocks becomes clear: the earth was covered with water. As a result the people sent a man to look for land on which the people could live. In story 1.5 ("Earth Names and Sky Names") we learn that the "man" was of the Hon'-ga, or Earth, people and was actually two men, Wa'-tse-gi-tsi (the Bear clan) and Wa-tse-ga-wa (the Puma clan). In story 1.9, we find that the Bear and Puma discovered people already living on earth. First they discovered the Crawfish people, who joined them and became a clan of the Hon'-ga division but could not help them find land. Later, according to stories 1.5 and 1.9, the Bear and the Puma discover the Elk people, who join them as the Elk clan and create the land. If we had all of the relevant *wi'-gi-e* of the other clans, we could greatly expand on this part of the story of the origin of the Osage. As said, story 1.1 is an extremely brief outline of the full story.

The priests could also draw on the information represented in one or more *wi'-gi-e* to answer more specific questions. In stories 1.2 and 1.3, for example, *wi'-gi-e* are converted into narratives to explain why certain names are given to members of these two clans. In story 1.8, a *wi'-gi-e* is converted into a narrative to explain why the clan cuts its children's hair in a particular style. In 1.7, Charles Wah-hre-she drew on information from a number of different *wi'-gi-e* to explain the origin of tattooing and the meanings of the tattooing designs.

The sacred teachings drawn from the *wi'-gi-e* exhibit several characteristics that sharply distinguish them from folk stories. In the sacred teachings, individuals are never mentioned. What appear to be "individuals" are in reality designations for clans or groups of clans. Secondly, specific geographical places are never mentioned. The stories tell only of directions of movements and geographical features—water, hills, forest, rivers, and so forth—never specific places.

Sacred instructions were standardized lectures made by one of the priests during the ritual and were spoken in everyday Osage. In a sense they were an addendum to the ritual in that the information they conveyed, while sacred, was not directly derived from the *wi'-gi-e*. There were two categories of narrative ritual statements: instructions to women and the listing of the war honors. Women were not initiated as priests, yet they nonetheless frequently had critical sacred roles they had to fill. The first role was that of a mother. During the child-naming ritual the presiding priests would deliver a standardized lecture, story 1.10 ("Instructions to the Mother"), to the mother on her duties as a mother.

The wife of a priest had certain ritual responsibilities regarding the bundle in her husband's keeping. As part of an initiation ceremony, the presiding priest would lecture the wife on her new sacred duties (story 1.12, "Instructions to the Wife of a Priest"). As part of the initiation rite for the Ni'-ki degree[7] of a priesthood, the wife (together with some of her female relatives and friends) would be given the authority to paint the sacred robes for children. The presiding priest would lecture these women on their new authority (see story 1.13, "Instructions in the Painting of the Sacred Robes"). There are many unanswerable questions concerning sacred instructions to women. Were these same instructions given in other rituals, and were there still other sacred instructions given to women in other rituals? Unfortunately, we will never know.

Most warriors were young men who would never become candidates for the priesthoods. Yet at the same time it was important for them to know what constituted a war honor. During certain ceremonies, an individual who had won all thirteen of the different war honors, or o'don, was asked to publicly list them. This man, called a wa-don-be, would name each of the war honors in order and tell how he had earned them. Story 1.14 ("Counting the O'don") is Shun-kah-mo-la's reciting of the list of honors he had won when acting as a wa-don-be.

Unlike sacred teachings, which were controlled by and known only to the priests and priesthoods, folk stories were public property. Any Osage, man or woman, could know, tell, and hear such stories. This is not, however, to say that there were no restrictions on the telling of folk stories. The Osages made a distinction between stories that were u'tha-ge, or true, and stories that were hi'-go, or fictional. Hi'-go could only be told during the winter months, when snakes were hibernating. Snakes were the guardians of truth, and the telling of a story that was untrue was thought to anger snakes. Folk stories also differed from sacred teachings in their subject matter, form, and purpose.[8]

Whereas sacred teachings were religious in nature, folk stories ranged widely in subject matter. Most folk stories fall into a number of broad subject categories: histories (stories 2.1, 2.6, 2.7, and 2.8), captive narratives (stories 2.6, 2.9, and 2.10), war stories (stories 2.4 and 2.12), ghost stories (stories 2.26, 2.27, and 2.28), stories of the supernatural (stories 2.17, 2.18, 2.19, 2.20, and 2.21), stories of family conflict (stories 2.11, 2.13, and 2.15), mysteries (stories 2.25, 2.29, and 2.30), love stories (stories 2.27 and 2.28), stories of noble individuals (stories 2.11, 2.12, and 2.13), and stories of good versus evil (stories 2.18, 2.19, and 2.21). Most folk stories combined several of these and other themes.

Sacred teachings were always educational, whereas folk stories served a variety of purposes. In most there was a strong entertainment value. Some were humorous and others frightening, but all were interesting stories. This is not to say that folk stories did not serve an educational purpose. The primary educational purpose of folk stories was to instill in the hearer an appreciation for the proper social norms and values of the Osage.

The characteristic that distinguished animal stories from other folk stories was that animal stories were intended for children. This distinction is clear in two of the stories collected by La Flesche. "The Vision of a War Leader" as told by Charles Wah-hre-she (story 2.26) appears to be the adult form of the story "The Hawk and the Horned Owl" told by Tho'-xi Zhin-ga (story 3.2). In telling the story for children, Tho'-xi Zhin-ga retained the emphasis on the basic ideal of courage but simplified it by eliminating the strong religious overtones. La Flesche showed little interest in recording Osage children's stories and recorded only these five. In contrast, the vast majority of stories recorded by Dorsey in his *Traditions of the Osage* were children's animal stories. Unfortunately, Dorsey's translations are poor and as a result the stories are difficult to analyze. The main purpose of the animal stories appears to have been to provide entertainment. However, there was an educational purpose as well. The stories illustrate Osage norms and values as well as convey information about the behavioral and physical characteristics of the different animals.

Editorial Changes

Some minor changes have been made to the stories. As noted, La Flesche began his fieldwork among the Osages in 1910 and continued collecting materials until 1923.[9] His first major publication on the Osage was not finished until 1914. La Flesche published some of the stories contained in this volume, while others are found only in his field notes. La Flesche's field notes are interesting in that they exist in two forms. First, there are his handwritten notes, which were taken in the field during the interviews. These notes are in English, meaning that La Flesche was translating the interview from Osage as he was taking notes. At a later time, La Flesche made typescripts of some of his field notes. In typing up his field notes, La Flesche polished and refined the text—many of these changes are apparent since he made them on the typed pages themselves. However, we cannot recover all of the changes he made, since it appears that after typing up his field notes, he would discard his handwritten notes. It also appears that after preparing his notes for publication he would then discard the relevant typed field notes. Thus for each of the stories I have indicated if the source is handwritten field notes, typescript field notes, or a published work.

During his research and writing La Flesche increasingly standardized his phonetic transcriptions for Osage words and refined his translations of Osage terms. One of the major changes I have had made in these stories is the standardization of the words and terms. The spellings of Osage words and terms, as well as their translations, have been standardized so that they correspond to the spellings and translations in his dictionary of the Osage language.[10]

Personal names have been treated in a number of different ways. When possible, in the stories I have usually translated the name into English. The reason for this is that it is easier for the reader to identify the characters and follow the plot. It was not possible to translate all of the names found in the stories. For the informants and individuals living at the time of La Flesche's work, I have used their names as they appear on the 1906 allotment roll.[11] Unfortunately, it was not possible to fully identify all of La Flesche's sources.

I have corrected the spelling of English words, and, to ensure readability and flow, I have made minor changes in punctuation and grammar to the stories following contemporary conventions of American English. I also made one change in La Flesche's word usage. La Flesche used the terms *gen* and *gentes*; I have substituted "clan" and "clans." Changes I made in titles and titles I created for untitled stories are noted in the footnotes. More substantive changes and guesses at words that could not be deciphered or were missing have been indicated by the use of brackets, which indicate a word or words inserted into the texts, and by footnotes, which indicate deletions and changes in the sentence or paragraph order of the text.

Finally, it has to be noted that clan names and the frequently used terms *hon'-ga* and *wa-xo'-be* are confusing. Clans did not have actual names. Every clan symbolically represented a number of different manifestations of Wa-kon'-da. A clan could be noted by reference to any of these "life symbols." Not all of the life symbols of every clan are known; thus in a number of cases in the texts clans are referred to that cannot be identified.[12] *Hon'-ga* has several meanings. In one sense it means the earth in its entirety. Thus *hon'-ga*, referring to the moiety, means all of the clans of the Hon'-ga (dry land) and Wa-zha'-zhe (water) peoples. However, it also can be used to just refer to the dry-land portion of the earth, as in the case of the Hon'-ga phratry. In addition the term *hon'-ga* also refers to an object that is inherently sacred.[13] *Wa-xo'-be* means any object that had been created by humans for sacred use. It is not inherently sacred but rather has been made sacred. In most cases in the texts the term *wa-xo'-be* is used in reference to a clan or tribal sacred bundle. However, it can also refer to another object made for ritual use.[14]

Chapter 2

History and Culture

The stories in this volume were stories told by Osages to other Osages. As a result they have to be understood in the context of Osage culture and history. For example, each of the sacred teachings addresses one or more aspects of the tribe's socioreligious organization: the chiefs, the clans, the sacred objects, the war organization, and so forth. Unless one understands the overall socioreligious structure of the Osage, these stories will be incomprehensible. A similar problem exists with understanding the folk stories. Osage folk stories are about exceptional, not ordinary, events and people. The exceptional nature of these people and events can only be understood within the context of the normal daily life of the Osage. Finally, European contact brought major changes to Osage life, particularly in the annual cycle of economic activities. Most of these events could have occurred during any period; others, however, could have occurred only during a particular period in Osage history. In this brief overview of Osage history and culture, reference is made to some but not all of the stories. It is important to realize that these stories frequently raise many questions concerning Osage beliefs and practices that cannot today be fully answered.

Historical Context[1]

In 1673, French explorers reported that the permanent villages of the Osage were located along the banks of the Osage River and its tributaries in what is today southwestern Missouri. Near these villages, the women planted small fields of corn, beans, and squash and gathered large quantities of wild plant foods; nuts, berries, persimmons, wild potatoes, and chinquapins. The men were hunters, hunting deer and a wide variety of other game in the woodlands and prairies near the villages most of the year. In the early summer and fall, the villagers would move to temporary hunting camps in the prairies of western Missouri and eastern Kansas for communal bison hunts. In the winter, many families would move to small, widely scattered hunting camps in the northern portions of the Ozark Plateau area of Arkansas, where they hunted bear, deer, elk, and other game. How long the Osages had occupied this region of mixed prairies and woodlands is unknown. Story 2.1 ("Tradition of the Omaha Departure from the Osage") tells of how in earlier times the Osage, together with the Omaha, Ponca, Kansa, and Quapaw, had, as a unified tribe, migrated down the Ohio River and crossed Mississippi before dispersing. Since these tribes, called the Dhegiha Siouans, speak mutually intelligible languages, the migration could not have long predated French contact.

Initial contact with French traders occurred almost at the same time that the Osage acquired their first horses from the Plains tribes. The introduction of guns and horses quickly changed the balance of power among the tribes. To acquire guns, metal weapons, and other desired trade goods from the French, the tribes needed trade items in the form of captives, horses, hides, and furs. The result was a rapid escalation in warfare as the tribes in trade contact with the French began raiding the more distant tribes in search of captives and horses. The major targets of Osage raids were the more numerous horse-rich but poorly armed Caddoan-speaking villages of the middle Arkansas River valley.[2] By the 1770s, the Osage had succeeded in driving the Caddoan peoples out of the valley. Some of these people, the Pawnee, fled north, although they continued to raid the Osage until both tribes were placed on adjoining reservations in Indian Territory. Others moved south and west to the Red River, where they became known as the Wichita.

In 1763, following the French and Indian War, France ceded Louisiana to Spain. Soon after the first Spanish governor of Louisiana arrived in 1769, numerous changes were made in that territory's Indian policy to reduce the number of destructive wars between the tribes. Traders now had to be licensed. Indian slavery, and thus the trade in captives, was outlawed.[3] Trade in horses[4] by the tribes was also prohibited and the trade in firearms was limited. Although the new Spanish government could not fully enforce its regulations, it did greatly lessen the importance of captives and horses in the trade.

In the last decades of the eighteenth century, the Osage substantially expanded the range and the intensity of their hunting and trapping. Using horses to transport people and goods, the summer and fall bison hunting parties now ventured further west, beyond the Arkansas River onto the Great Plains.

Only the old, the young, and the ill would remain behind in their villages. The small family hunting parties that went out during the winter months in search of deer, bear, beaver, otter, and other small game became increasingly scattered in a wide arc stretching from the northern Ozarks south to the Ouachita Mountains. It was the hides and pelts of the game animals taken on the winter hunts that were the tribe's main trade items. In the 1750s and 1760s, the Osage and the Missouri tribes together were reported to have annually traded 80 packs of skins and hides.[5] By 1800, the Osage alone were trading 950 packs a year, and the Osage trade was the most valuable in Spanish Louisiana.[6]

Throughout the early and mid-eighteenth century, the Osage had primarily been in conflict with the tribes to the west. At first this had been with the more settled Caddoan tribes. However, as they ranged further west on the plains they had come into increasing conflict with the Kiowa, Comanche, and Cheyenne. At the same time, conflict along the eastern margins of their territory grew. Following American independence in 1783, Anglo-American settlers began flooding westward, displacing the tribes of the Ohio Valley and the Southeast. With the encouragement of the Spanish government, growing numbers of small refugee bands of Sac and Fox, Delaware, Shawnee, Illini, Ottawa, Cherokee, Choctaw, Creek, Chickasaw, and other eastern tribes began settling west of the Mississippi and so ended up directly competing with the Osage for game resources. Small-scale raiding of hunting camps by both sides became common. By the 1790s, the Osage were virtually surrounded by hostile tribes and were put on the defensive along their eastern border. No small party of Osage hunters or travelers was safe. Whether they were on one of their bison hunts or in their winter hunting camps, they had to be constantly on the alert for enemy raiders.

As the numbers of the emigrant eastern Indians swelled,[7] the Osage found themselves being forced to slowly relinquish the easternmost portions of their hunting and trapping territories. By the turn of the nineteenth century, their permanent villages had been relocated to the western headwaters of the Osage River and to the Verdigris and Neosho rivers in present-day eastern Kansas and Oklahoma. Here they were closer to the bison range and further removed from the hostile eastern tribes.

In 1803, the United States purchased Louisiana with the intent of using portions of the region for the resettlement of eastern tribes, and in 1808, the Osage signed a treaty ceding virtually all of their lands in what are today Missouri and Arkansas. Immigrant eastern Indians as well as Anglo-American settlers poured into the ceded area, and conflict between the Osage and eastern tribes increased. In 1817, a party of Cherokees, Creeks, Choctaws, and Shawnees attacked Claremore's village on the lower Verdigris while most of

Osage Territory

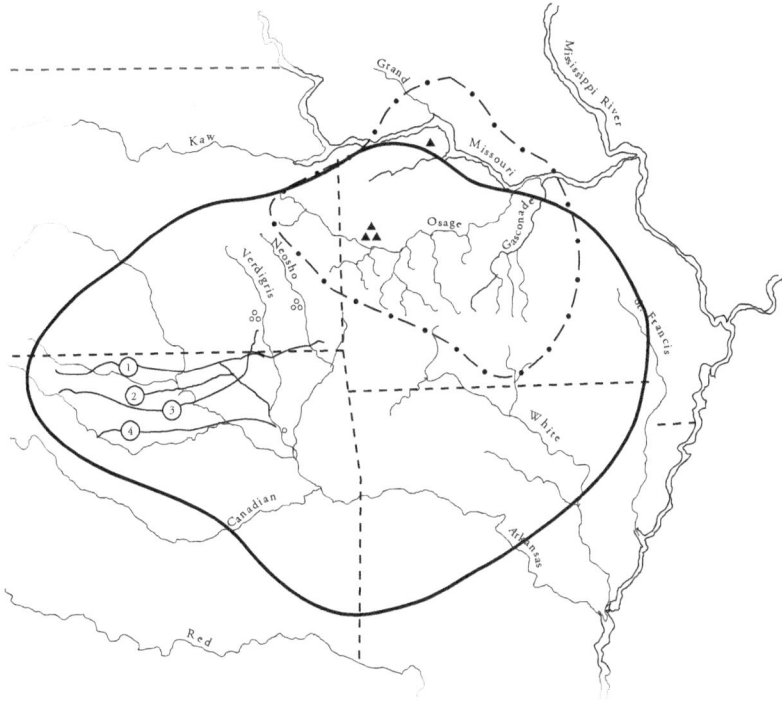

Legend:

— ● — Mid–18th Century
—— Early 19th Century
▲ Villages–Middle 18th Century
○ Villages–Early 19th Century

1. Black Dog and Heart Stays Trail
2. Bird Creek Trail
3. Two Little Hills and Upland Forest Trail
4. Cimarron Trail

0   50   100   150

the men were away on their summer bison hunt, killing or capturing about two hundred. In 1818, the Osage ceded a small portion of eastern Oklahoma, but the raids continued. In 1821, the Cherokee again attacked Claremore village, during which both sides incurred losses. In 1825, a treaty was signed in which the Osage ceded all of their remaining lands except for a reservation fifty miles wide that stretched from eastern Kansas west to what was then the undefined border of Mexico. However, Claremore and the other Osages on the lower Verdigris were not party to this treaty and refused to move to their newly defined reservation.

The Treaty of 1825 prepared the way for the passage of the Indian Removal Act of 1830, the purpose of which was to resettle the remaining eastern tribes in an area designated as the "Indian territory."[8] This territory was initially defined as the area west of the line between the Red and Missouri rivers that formed the western boundaries of Missouri and Arkansas. Between 1830 and 1839, in excess of seventy-three thousand eastern Indians were settled on reservations just west of this line.[9] The Osage, whose population had by this point been reduced to only about fifty-five hundred owing to war and disease, now lost their rich eastern hunting and trapping areas in the Ozark and Ouachita mountains.

By the 1830s, the Osage were in an increasingly desperate situation. A trader, Pierre Chouteau, wrote that "these [eastern] Indians . . . are now overrunning the former hunting grounds of the Osage."[10] In 1839, the tribe's hunting grounds having been destroyed, Claremore and the other Osage leaders on the lower Verdigris signed a new treaty and moved north to their reservation.

Fortunately for the Osage, the loss of their eastern hunting and trapping areas coincided with a change in trade. The market for bearskins, deer hides, and beaver and other pelts declined as a new market for buffalo robes emerged. Still having access to the vast bison herds on the plains to west, the Osage very quickly became robe traders. Not only did they increase their hunting of bison and their making of robes, but in 1837 or 1838, they made peace with the Comanche, trading their annuity goods for horses and mules and still more robes, which could be traded to Anglo-American settlers. In the 1850s, the Osage were trading twenty thousand buffalo robes annually.[11]

In 1854 Kansas Territory was created out of the northern part of what had been Indian Territory, and portions were opened for Anglo-American settlement. Pressure to open still other Indian reservations was temporary relieved by the Civil War. However, with the end of the war in 1865, demands grew to remove the remaining tribes out of what had become in 1861 the state of Kansas. In the Treaty of 1865, the Osage agreed to sell their lands in Kansas and to use part of the proceeds to purchase a new reservation, with title in fee simple, in Indian Territory. In 1871, the Osage abandoned their villages in Kansas when they left on their fall bison hunt. When they returned from the hunt in early 1872, they settled on their new reservation. In the summer of 1874, just as the Osage were beginning their summer hunt, the Red River War involving the Kiowa, Comanche, Cheyenne, and Arapaho broke out. To avoid getting drawn into the conflict, they returned to their reservation early and short of meat.[12] There were no bison hunts in 1875. In 1876, they held their last bison hunt. It was a failure, as there were few bison left on the southern plains.

Fortunately, not all of the funds from the sale of their Kansas reservation had been needed to purchase the new reservation in Indian Territory. The surplus was deposited in a trust fund with the U.S. Treasury. By the 1880s the Osage had over $8 million in this fund on which they received 5 percent interest a year. As hunting fell off, the agency, using money from the trust fund, began issuing rations. In 1878, the agency was making quarterly per-capita cash payments to the Osage. In 1890, Special Agent E. E. White stated that, based on the value of their land holdings and their trust fund, the Osage were, per capita, "the richest people in the world."[13] In 1897, the tribe signed its first lease for oil exploration. The Osage Allotment Act was passed 1906, which divided reservation lands equally among tribal members while retaining the mineral rights for the tribe. Development of oil reserves during the teens and early 1920s made the richest people in the world far richer.

The sacred teachings, and most likely the animal stories, predate European contact. A few of the folk stories, such as story 2.21 ("The Cruel Medicine Man and the Orphan"), probably date to before French contact. At least one story, story 2.6 ("Origin of the Hair Bundle"), concerns an event that occurred after contact but before 1770. The great majority of these stories are from the period between about 1770 and 1870. This was a time of increasing conflict with other tribes and growing reliance on bison hunting. Not surprisingly, many of the stories are directly or indirectly concerned with warfare and/or events that occurred during the bison hunts. Few stories seem to concern events that occurred after the move to Indian Territory in 1872.

Cultural Background

Religious Beliefs[14]

Osage culture was based on and reflected their religious beliefs. The cosmos was the creation of a mysterious invisible force termed Wa-kon'-da and controlled by it. Everything, all the different animals, birds, trees, grasses, celestial bodies, and other natural phenomenon found in "visible world," was a visible manifestation of this mysterious and invisible force. The cosmos was a logically integrated system; every living, moving thing within it had been created for a purpose. Humans were unlike other creations of Wa-kon'-da in that they had the power of reason[15] and the ability to create. Consequently, Wa-kon'-da made humans responsible for their own actions and own survival. Only by gaining a greater understanding of Wa-kon'-da through the study of Wa-kon'-da's visible manifestations could a group enhance its chance of survival.

Based on their empirical observations of the visible world, the Osage defined the basic structure of the cosmos. There was the sky and the earth. All living things existed on the surface of the earth, which they conceived of as a lens, called the ho'-e-ga, or snare, that existed between the sky and earth. The earth was nourishing of life and considered maternal; the sky, the source of life, was paternal. Life was brought forth on the surface of the earth through the interaction of the forces of the sky and the earth. On death one's spirit left the ho'-e-ga that held it and passed back into the invisible world.

Within this lens between sky and earth were a seemingly infinite number of living, moving things. Each of these things created by Wa-kon'-da had a meaning and purpose. Some creatures, such as animals and plants, had qualities that were directly beneficial to humans. Some animals had flesh that could be eaten. Others had skins that could be used for clothing. Some plants could be eaten; others could be used to make tools or cure illness. Still other phenomenon, such as storms, lightning, heavy rains, and tornadoes, could be dangerous to humans. Many had qualities that could be both beneficial and dangerous.

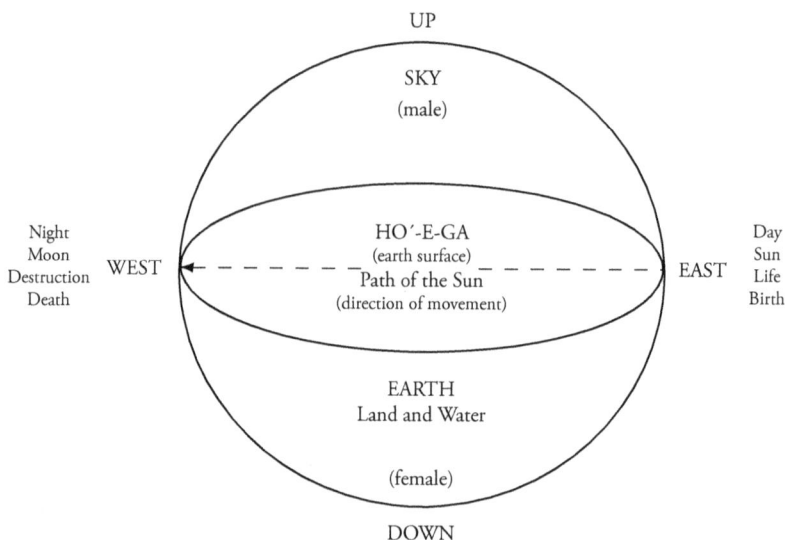

Figure 1. The Structure of the Cosmos

The greatest of Wa-kon'-da's gifts was fire. Controlled, fire could be considered the most beneficial of Wa-kon'-da's creations in giving life-sustaining warmth. Uncontrolled, as in a prairie fire, fire was the most dangerous of all of Wa-kon'-da's creations. Still other creations represented forces of Wa-kon'-da that could aid humans in their survival if they emulated them, such as hawks for their courage, bears for their ferocity, otters for their swimming abilities, and wolves for their tenacity. The Osage did not claim to know the meaning and purpose of all of Wa-kon'-da's manifestations; there were many mysterious forces and powers they did not understand. Feeling that their collective survival was dependent on all members of the tribe increasing their understanding of the creations of Wa-kon'-da, they constantly studied and analyzed the world around them. To the Osage, knowledge was power.

The greatest of all mysteries to the Osage was the cycle of life. Everything born will eventually die. They saw this in the cycle of the day: the birth of the sun at sunrise, its maturity at midday, and its death at night. The movements of sun showed the ever-recurring and relentless path of life as it passed from east to west. They saw this cycle in the seasons of the year—in the birth of the year in the spring and its death in winter. Every living, moving thing is born and will die. This was true of not just every individual but of every group of living, moving things. The Osage as a people followed the symbolic path of life from east to west and someday would eventually die as a people. Why or when this would happen they did not know. What they did know was that the survival of a group of people depended upon the continued blessing of Wa-kon'-da in the form of children, another generation of life.

Tribal organization was structured in such a manner as to reflect the structure of the cosmos. This cosmic model was the basis for Osage clan organization, village arrangement, political structure, and religious ceremonies. Within this cultural model everything the Osage did collectively had to have meaning and purpose. In organizing their lives in this manner the Osage were attempting to show respect for Wa-kon'-da and Wa-kon'-da's creations. In essence their lives were structured as an unending symbolic prayer for the continued blessings of Wa-kon'-da. However, as many Osage leaders stressed, the sacred structure of the tribe, as well as their sacred objects and rituals, was the creation of human beings, not Wa-kon'-da. They were merely human created symbols of the sacred, having no mystic power or force of their own.[16]

Finally, the Osage noted that the universe was constantly changing. New enemies and threats to their collective well-being were constantly emerging. As human beings it was their responsibility to adapt to these threats by making changes in their tribal organization. Some of the major changes they made in their tribal organization over time are the subjects of story 1.1 ("Allegorical

Story of Tribal Organization"). "Creation of the Houses of Mystery" in story 1.1 tells of the creation of tribal war parties. Eventually they found that these large, slowly organized tribal war parties were inadequate to meeting the constantly recurring dangers they faced from small enemy raiding parties. "Origin of the Clan, or Hawk, Bundles" tells how they created the clan bundles that allowed them to more quickly organize smaller moiety- and/or clan-based war parties to respond to more immediate threats. Later still, they discovered that they needed some form of secular government and so established the positions of chiefs, or ga-hi'-ge. The creation of the chiefs and their duties are the subject of "The Creation of the Ga-hi'-ge, or Chiefs" of story 1.1. Finally, "Vision of the Sky Chief" and "Vision of the Earth Chief" tell of the visions of the two chiefs and creation of two new sacred bundles, wa-xo'-be ton-ga, or great bundle, and the mon-kon ton-ga wa-xo'-be, or great medicine bundle. These two bundles were associated with health and long life.

Tribal Structure[17]

CLANS

The primary social and religious units of the Osage were their twenty-four patrilineal clans. Every clan was associated with and symbolically represented a specific set of manifestations or forces of Wa-kon'-da. These were referred to as the zho'-i-the, or life symbols, of the clan and included specific animals, plants, and other visible natural phenomenon. The name for the clan was taken from one or more of its life symbols.[18] Clans were divided into subclans,[19] which had a more specific relationship with particular life symbols of the clan. Collectively the clans symbolically represented the cosmos in its entirety. Just as the cosmos was divided into Sky and Earth, so the clan were grouped into two large divisions, or moieties: the Sky peoples, or Tsi'-zhu, and the Earth peoples, or Hon'-ga. Nine clans belonged to the Sky people moiety and collectively represented the forces of the sky. Fifteen clans were grouped as the Earth people moiety, collectively representing the forces of the earth. Just as the earth was divided into land and water, so the Earth people were further divided in two phratries of seven clans each known as the Water (Wa-zha'-zhe) and Land (Hon'-ga) phratries. The fifteenth clan, called the Isolated Hon'-ga, stood alone. "Allegorical Story of Tribal Organization" in story 1.1 tells of the origin of the Isolated Hon'-ga and of how they came to join the Osage. The nine clans of the Sky people were divided into two phratries. Seven clans belonged to the Sky phratry that was collectively symbolic of the sky. Two clans, the Tho'-xe (Buffalo Bull) and Ni'-ka Wa-kon'-da-gi (Men of Mystery) clans, formed a second phratry called the Last to Camp. The joining of these two is discussed in "Origin of the

Clan, or Hawk, Bundles" in story 1.1. It was said that these clans were not true Sky people and that they were only symbolically placed there to maintain the balance between the Earth and Sky peoples.

Every clan had its own origin myth, which was recorded in a *wi'-gi-e*, or

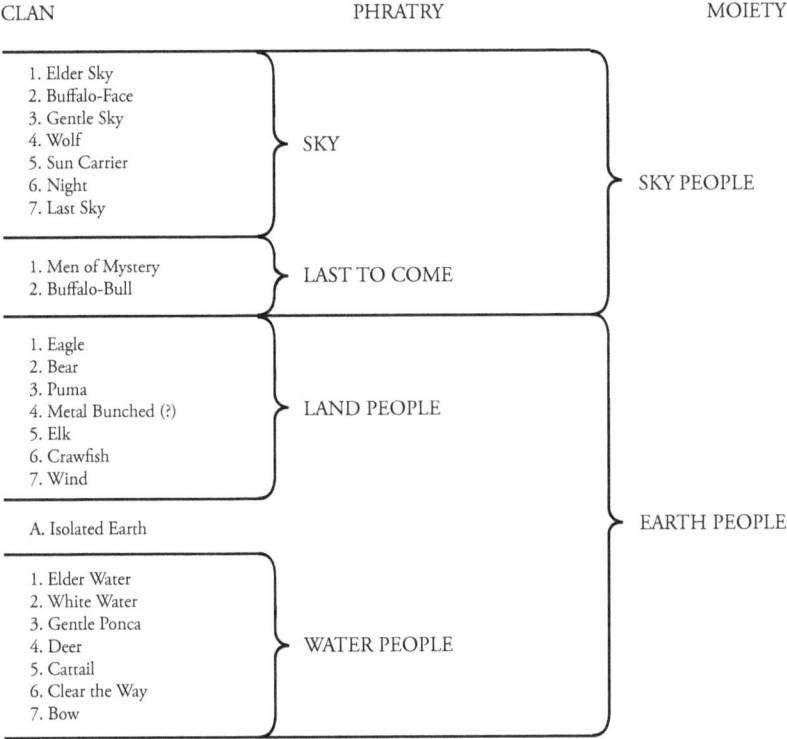

CLAN	PHRATRY	MOIETY
1. Elder Sky 2. Buffalo-Face 3. Gentle Sky 4. Wolf 5. Sun Carrier 6. Night 7. Last Sky	SKY	SKY PEOPLE
1. Men of Mystery 2. Buffalo-Bull	LAST TO COME	
1. Eagle 2. Bear 3. Puma 4. Metal Bunched (?) 5. Elk 6. Crawfish 7. Wind	LAND PEOPLE	EARTH PEOPLE
A. Isolated Earth		
1. Elder Water 2. White Water 3. Gentle Ponca 4. Deer 5. Cattail 6. Clear the Way 7. Bow	WATER PEOPLE	

Figure 2. Clan Organization

prayer, that discussed the clan's life symbols and their symbolic meanings. Story 1.2 ("Origin Story of the Wolf Clan") and story 1.3 ("Origin Story of the Black Bear Clan") are only two of the twenty-four clan origin myths. Fragments of other clan origin myths are found in still other sacred stories. Every clan also had its own separate set of priests called *non'-hon-zhin-ga*, or little old men, who had custody of and authority over the use of the clan bundles, associated ritual objects, and sacred knowledge of the clan.

BANDS AND VILLAGES

The Osage were divided into five permanent named bands. According to tradition, originally the Osages had all lived together in a single village. However, a great flood, sometime in the distant past, had caused the people to become separated. One group found refuge on the top of a hill and became known as the Pa-ciu'-gthin, or Big Hills. Another group fled to a wooded hillside and became known as the Con'-dse'-u-gthin, or Upland Forest. A third group stopped at the base of hill and became known as the I-u-dse'-ta, or Dwellers Below. Over time this third became known as the Little Osages. Still another group found shelter in a thicket and were called the Wa-xa'-ga-u-gthin, or Thorny Thickets. Finally, one group remained near the flooded village and were henceforth called the Non'-dse-wa-cpe, or Heart Stays.[20] During the early historic period, each band may have occupied a single village, but by the early 1800s these villages had become fragmented into about fifteen or so settlements.[21] Even still, band identity persisted, and each village identified with one or another of five bands. Although they frequently occupied several separate residential villages, the villages of the band would come together and function as a single band-village during the summer and fall bison hunts.

Each village was physically arranged in such a manner as to represent a symbolic model of the cosmos. There was a main east-west street, the symbolic "path of the sun" or "path of life," that divided the village into two approximately equal halves. Situated along and back from the street on the north side were the longhouses, or wigwams, of the families of the Sky clans. Each of the Sky clans had a specific location for the dwellings of its families along this north side. On the south side were the Earth clan families, and once again each clan occupied a specific location.

Osage wigwams were usually rectangular structures consisting of a framework of poles bent over and tied together and covered with woven cattail mats, bark, hides, or some combination of these materials. These dwellings were usually about twenty feet wide, forty to fifty feet long, fifteen to eighteen feet high, and oriented along an east-to-west axis. The typical Osage house had two doors on the south side, one toward the east end, and one toward the west end and two interior fireplaces, each with its own smoke hole in the roof.

The permanent villages were fully occupied for only part of the year. In preparing for the summer and fall bison hunts the Osage would strip off the mat, bark, and hide coverings of the wigwams, leaving only their pole frameworks. House coverings were either piled at one end of the village and covered and tied down with poles or cached in bundles in trees. Other personal belongings not taken on the trip were cached in hidden pits. Similar preparations were made for the fall hunt. The elderly, the sick, and women with babies and young

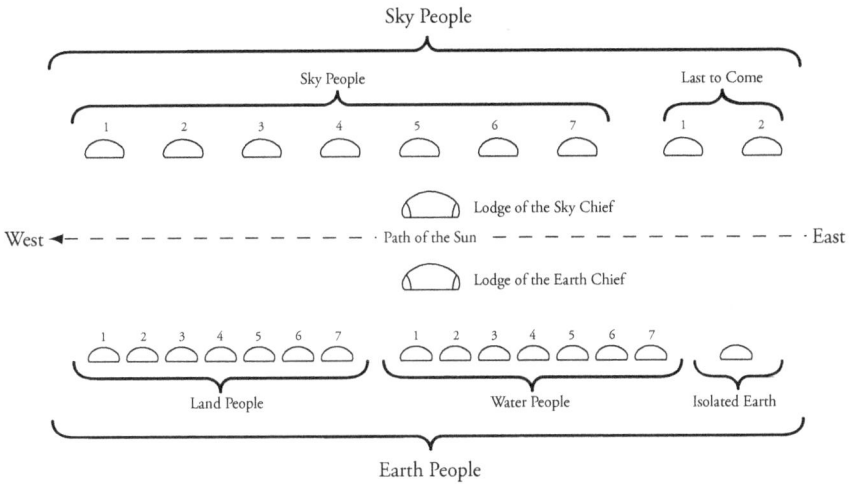

Figure 3. Village Arrangement

children usually remained in their wigwams in the partially deserted village during the summer hunt but went along for the fall hunt, which occurred following harvest. Families would usually build small camps hidden in the woods, some distance from the village, where they would cache their stored crops and leave the individuals not going on the hunt.

Hunting camps used for the summer and fall bison hunts were different from the village camps. When traveling to the plains, the Osage made use of regular named trails and campsites that were usually ten to twelve miles apart.[22] The dwellings in the camps consisted of simple small frameworks of poles about 15 feet long by 7 feet wide and about 4 1/2 feet in height. When using them for the night, they would cover the framework with hides, leaving them open at either end. The frameworks were left standing and used by the same family on hunt after hunt. The main difference in the organization of these hunting camps from that of the permanent village was that the Isolated Hon-ga clan families were located at the west end in the hunting camps, whereas they resided in the east end in their permanent village. The symbolic meaning of this shift is unknown.[23]

The Osage used a slightly different village arrangement during ceremonies. For the performance of major rituals Isolated Hon-ga clan families were located in the middle of the south side, between the families of the Water and Land clans. Once again the symbolic meaning of this arrangement is unknown.[24]

POLITICAL LEADERSHIP

The Osage made a distinction between secular and religious leaders. Secular leaders called *ga-hi'-ge*, or chiefs, were tasked with preserving harmonious relationships between individuals and families and with ensuring the daily economic well-being of the people. Religious leaders, *non'-hon-zhin-ga*, or little old men, were concerned with the external relationships of the people, both human and supernatural.

Bacon Rind (Wa-tse-mon-in), ca. 1895, showing a tattooed chest and wearing an otter-skin hat, indicators of an Osage leader. Osage Tribal Museum P01-607. (Photo by Delancy Gill, Bureau of American Ethnography. Courtesy of the Osage Tribal Museum.)

Each of the five bands had two *ga-hi'-ge*; a Tsi'-zhu *ga-hi'-ge*, or Sky chief, and a Hon'-ga *ga-hi'-ge*, or Earth chief. "The Creation of the *Ga-hi'-ge*, or Chiefs," in story 1.1 recounts how these chiefs were appointed and describes their authority. These positions were hereditary within specific clans and lineages. The chiefs would appoint ten men, called *a'-ki-da*, or soldiers, to assist them in their duties. These men were chosen from ten specific clans, five Sky clans and five Earth clans. In the very middle of the village, across the street from one another, were the houses of the two chiefs. The houses of the chiefs were different in physical form as well as symbolism from other houses. These houses had east- and west-facing doors and a single fireplace in the middle, symbolic of the passage of the sun from east to west. The houses of the chiefs were also sacred and symbolic of life. The house fires in the village were kindled with coals taken from one or another of the chief's houses. As symbols of life, no blood could be shed in these houses. An enemy could take refuge in one of these houses and be protected. Clustered near the houses of the chiefs were those of their soldiers.

Each band's two chiefs had identical authority over all of members of the village, not just their division. The major duties of these two chiefs and their soldiers was to settle disputes between village members and to organize and direct the summer and fall bison hunts. On alternating days during the hunt, from the time the party left the village until they returned, one or the other chief and his soldiers were in charge. The chiefs made use of certain men in the village called *wa-je-pa-in*, or criers,[25] who would walk through the village calling out the instructions of the chiefs. On special occasions, such as weddings, other individuals also made use of these criers.

PRIESTS AND THE PRIESTHOODS
The real power within the tribe rested not in the hands of the chiefs but rather in the collective hands of the *non'-hon-zhin-ga*, the little old men. The priesthoods were not only the intermediaries between the Osage people and the supernatural world; they also controlled the relationships between the Osage and the visible world. The decisions of peace and war were the exclusive prerogative of the priests.

The little old men are spoken of as a single group, but there were important distinctions among them. The main division was between the clan priests who were the custodians of clan bundles and ritual knowledge and those who were the custodians of the tribal bundles and ritual knowledge. The clan priests were by far the most numerous.

Every clan had its own *wa-xo'-be zhi-ga* ("little sacred objects"), or clan bundles. There was no fixed number of clan bundles or priests. If needed, new bundles could be created. However, sometimes special new clan bundles were created. Stories 2.6 ("Origin of the Hair Bundle") and 2.7 ("Origin of the Whistle Bundle") concern the creation of such clan bundles. Each of the five bands seems to have had a complete complement of priests from all twenty-four of the clans.

In addition to the twenty-four clan priesthoods, there were three tribal priesthoods: the great bundle priests, the great medicine bundle priests, and the pipe priests. The origins of these two tribal bundles are the subject of the visions of the Sky and Earth chiefs in story 1.1. There are no known traditions concerning the origin of the pipe priests. Although information is lacking, it is thought that every band had its own great bundle priest and great medicine bundle priest. In addition every band had a number of pipe priests.

Not every man wanted to be a priest, and only a minority of men became priests. To become a clan priest, a man first had to find a priest from his clan to act as his sponsor. If the priest agreed, there was a short ceremony in which he was formally accepted as a candidate. Becoming a candidate was a serious commitment. The man took a vow that within seven years he would acquire all of the items needed for his formal initiation into the clan priesthood. First, the candidate had to hunt and take the skins of seven specific sacred animals, which would then be used in the initiation ritual. Second, the candidate had to collect adequate food and gifts to feast and pay the participants in the ceremony and their families. An initiation ceremony required a complete representation of priests from all twenty-four clans. There were still other priests and individuals who performed particular parts of the ritual. All of these individuals and their families had to be fed for the four days of the ceremony. Finally, all of the participants had to be paid with gifts of clothing, horses, trade goods, and other items. It was an extraordinary economic burden on a family to have a man become a priest. That is why they were given seven years to stockpile the food and gifts.

Becoming a member of one of the tribal priesthoods was different. A man could not present himself as a candidate; instead, he had to be chosen. There were a limited number of great bundle priests and great medicine bundle priests. When one of these priests became too ill or aged to perform the necessary rituals, he would then ask another man, undoubtedly one of the clan priests, to assume his position. Since the old priest was ailing, once a man agreed, the initiation ceremony was held in short order. As in the case of clan priests, to be initiated as tribal priest was costly to the family of the initiate. However, the initiation ceremonies for these priesthoods lasted only one day.

There was no initiation ceremony as such for the pipe priests, and there was no set number of pipe priests. A pipe priest would simply ask a man to sponsor the peace ceremony. Once again it was costly. To sponsor the ceremony meant that an individual and his family had to feed and give gifts to the participants. After a man had sponsored four such peace ceremonies, he became a pipe priest and did not have to sponsor any others. It is thought that most bands had only a single great bundle priest and a single great medicine bundle priest. However, each band would have had a number of pipe priests at any one time.

Individuals called *sho'-ka* were used as official messengers between priests. They carried a pipe as the symbol of office, and, according to story 1.6 ("Origin Story of the *Sho'-ka*"), ideally they were captives.

Collectively the priests formed what was a de facto village or band council. Possibly the most important authority conferred on these men was the authority to control warfare.

RELIGION AND RITUAL PRACTICES

Since only a few of the major ceremonies are mentioned in the stories, our discussion will be brief. The clan priest controlled and conducted the ceremonies concerned with the visible world. These rituals included those relating to weather, hunting, burial, the naming of children, and warfare. The most frequently mentioned of these ceremonies are those having to do with war. Warfare was organized and conducted as a religious ceremony. From the time a war party was organized until the men returned to the village and claimed their o'don, or war honors, the members of the war party were participating in one continuous religious ritual. There were three basic types of war parties: tribal war parties, clan/moiety war parties, and mourning dance war parties. All were sanctioned by the clan priesthoods, and they were similar in their basic organization, although the rituals performed during each of them were somewhat different. All such parties were led by a *do-don'-hon'-ga*, who acted as the ritual leader of the party. There were between two and eight *xthe'-tsa-ge*, or commanders, who organized and led the men in the attack. Finally, there were a varying number of *tse'-xe-k'in non-non*, "kettle carriers" or privates. All of these parties used ritually prepared black charcoal paint to paint their faces before attacking the enemy. A man on one of these parties could not claim a war honor (o'don) for killing an enemy unless he was wearing this paint at the time. This is not to say that there were not unsanctioned war parties. At least four of the stories concern what appear to be unsanctioned war parties: stories 2.6 ("Origin of the Hair Bundle"), 2.7 ("Origin of the Whistle Bundle"), 2.12 ("The Woman War Leader"), and 2.16 ("The Two Young Men Who Mourned Their Living Father"). At other times, Osage hunting parties might be attacked. Not being part of a war party, they would not have charcoal paint on their faces. Shun-kah-mo-lah in story 2.23 ("Dreamers") tells of capturing a Wichita and letting him go. He could claim a war honor in this incident, but since he did not have black paint on his face, he was not obligated to kill the man to earn it.

The three tribal priesthoods controlled the ceremonies concerned with the invisible world. Of the three, least is known about the great medicine bundle and its priests.[26] Although the Gentle Sky clan was the symbolic keeper of the bundle, the priest himself could be from any of the clans. The main elements of the bundle were the "man plant" and it female counterpart. These plants are more popularly known as ginseng root. The origin of this bundle is told in "Vision of the Sky Chief" in story 1.1. Rituals using this bundle were concerned with healing.

The origin of the great bundle is told in the "Vision of the Earth Chief" in story 1.1. The Gentle Ponca clan was the symbolic keeper of this bundle. However, a great bundle priest, or *ton'-won a-don-be'* (village guardian), could be a member of any clan.[27] Bundles consisted of tattooing needles in a cormorant skin encased in the skin of a pelican.[28] The pelican was a symbol of long life, and tattoos were symbolic prayers for long life and fertility. The great bundle priest was in charge of the spring, or new year, ritual and also tattooed individuals.

By far the tribal ceremony most frequently performed was the *wa'-wa-thon*, or peace ceremony.[29] Various forms of this ritual, frequently called the calumet dance or pipe dance, were found among the other prairie tribes as well. The ceremony was usually performed to celebrate the formal visit of the members of either another Osage band or a friendly tribe. The pipe was symbolic of the unity of the participants in the prayer for Wa-kon'-da's help and was an acknowledgment of the peace and friendship that existed between the groups. Although it could be performed at any time of the year, during the nineteenth century this ceremony was most commonly performed on the plains following the summer bison hunt. With plenty of food, Osage bands and other friendly tribes visited each other's hunting camps. A full complement of twenty-four clan priests was required for this ceremony to be performed, but the central figures were a candidate for the pipe priesthood and a sponsoring pipe priest, or *ni'-ka don'-he*.

The most basic religious rite was that of an individual appeal for Wa-kon'-da's guidance and blessing. This rite, called the *non'-zhin-zhon*, or rite of vigil, was performed daily. Every morning, just before the sun broke the horizon, all of the people of the village—men, women, and children—would place earth upon their foreheads and, standing before their doorways, would weep and pray aloud for Wa-kon'-da's blessing. This daily individual ritual was the most basic form of the rite of vigil. At other times, particularly in times of crisis or danger, specific individuals would undertake a longer form of the rite, during which they would fast and pray for up to six nights and seven days, hoping to receive some guidance or sign of a blessing from Wa-kon'-da. These longer forms of the rite were sometime called "fasting rites" by La Flesche and are similar to the "vision quests" found in other Native American societies. Because almost every significant undertaking of the Osage was initiated with a rite of vigil, they are frequently mentioned in Osage narratives. In four of the fourteen sacred stories and in ten of the thirty folk stories a rite of vigil is an important element. In story 1.1 ("Allegorical Story of Tribal Organization"), after the Osage named the two *ga-hi'-ge*, the newly appointed chiefs take the rite of vigil for six nights and seven days, seeking Wa-kon'-da's blessing. When a man was appointed the *do-don'-hon'-ga* of a tribal war party, his first act was to seek guidance through six nights and seven days of fasting and prayer before the party left the village. He would then proceed to observe the rite during the entire journey. After the death of a close relative or friend, an individual would usually take the rite of vigil for six nights and seven days and then continue to observe it in an abbreviated form for a year or more. A man in search of supernatural guidance or power might take the rite of vigil for six nights and seven days. In most cases we do not know what, if anything, was revealed to the individual during these rites. However, in other cases what is revealed is an important, if not core, element of the story. We have already discussed the visions of the Sky chief and Earth chief and the resultant creations of two tribal sacred bundles. Similarly story 2.8 ("Origin of the Mourning Dance") relates how a man taking the rite of vigil in mourning for a relative heard the voice of the deceased man ask him to kill an enemy to accompany him on his journey. This led to the organizing of the first mourning dance. In preparing to lead a war party, the appointed *do-don'-hon'-ga* took the rite of vigil. Story 2.4 ("The Vision of a War Leader") is about the vision of such a *do-don'-hon'-ga* and the meaning of courage. Story 2.18 ("Strange Medicine Man") tells of a man of supernatural power and how that power was revealed to him in his rite of vigil. Story 2.22 ("Wah-ti-an-kah) tells of a man who fasted for eight nights and nine days and how it was revealed to him that his village was going to be attacked.

Life Cycle

The Osages were not egalitarian. On the contrary, their society was one with marked differences in social status. Some differences in status were ascribed, determined by birth order and family, clan, and subclan affiliations. Still other social statuses were the result of individual achievements, war records, and social behavior.

Children were considered by the Osage to be the greatest of Wa-kon'-da's blessings, since they were an indication of Wa-kon'-da's wish for them to survive as a people. Thus every family strove to have a large number of children. The relative status of an individual was influenced by their birth order. The eldest son was called *in-gthon*, the second son *kshon'-ga*, and the third and all additional sons *ka'-zhin-ga*. Similarly the first daughter born was called *mi-na*, the second *wi'-he*, and the third and all subsequent daughters *ci-ge* or *a-cin-ga*.

CHILDHOOD AND ADOLESCENCE

Children belonged to their father's clan, and naming was the first important event in the life of an individual. A child was not considered to be a clan member, and thus not an Osage or even a human, until formally named. Each clan had its own particular naming ceremony, although all followed the same basic pattern. The ceremony was an elaborate and expensive event for the family, since it involved a presiding priest from the child's clan as well as priests from a number of other clans and also guests.[30] All present had to be fed, and the priests had to be compensated with gifts. Every clan had its own set of personal names, which were related to the life symbols of the clan.[31] The origin of some of the names of the Wolf clan are discussed in story 1.2 ("Origin Story of the Wolf Clan"), while some of the names of the Black Bear clan are discussed in Story 1.3 ("Origin Story of the Black Bear Clan"). Naming ceremonies were held only for the first three children of each sex, and the names given these children were called "sky names." The ceremony for the third son and third daughter sufficed for the fourth and all additional children of that gender. A special set of names called "earth names" were given to these additional children in a very simple ceremony involving only the appropriate clan priest.[32]

The naming ceremony ended with the presiding clan priest reciting story 1.11 ("Instructions to the Mother"). This naming gave the child a place within the family, clan, and tribe, the name publicly signifying both his or her clan as well as his or her birth rank within the family. It also served as a prayer for the long life and health of the child.

The eldest son and daughter of the family occupied privileged positions. It was assumed that the eldest son would eventually be a leader, and he was trained from birth for this role. His younger brothers and sisters were conditioned as children to defer to his wishes. Later, as a young man, the eldest son assumed the position of family head in the absence of his father. Hereditary offices within the tribe were usually filled by the eldest son. There were exceptions. In Story 2.7 ("Origin of the Whistle Bundle"), the youngest brother asks for and is given the position of leader.

Likewise much attention was bestowed on the eldest daughter in the family. In fact, *mi'-na*, the term for the eldest daughter, is translated as "the favorite" or "the favored." Some Osages say that the eldest daughter was always spoiled by the family and that less work was demanded of and more gifts and attention given to her than the other daughters.

After a child was named, the child was given a special haircut. Every clan had its own style of haircut for children. The style in which a child's hair was cut was related to one of the life symbols of their clan.[33] This is the subject of story 1.8 ("Haircut of the Gentle Sky Clan").

Although the eldest son and daughter were favored, all children were usually well treated by their parents.

Unidentified young woman and child, ca. 1895. The trade-cloth blouse and skirt, with a silver brooch, were the typical style of dress for Osage women throughout the nineteenth century. The child's haircut indicates her clan. Osage Tribal Museum P01-886. (Courtesy of the Osage Tribal Museum.)

Fathers paid particular attention to their sons, making them toys when they were small and teaching them how to hunt and ride as they grew older. Teenage boys usually assisted their father by taking care of the family horses. Mothers made dolls and other toys for their daughters, and as they grew older, daughters helped their mother with such tasks as taking care of younger siblings, sewing, and cooking. Storytelling was still another way to educate children. During the winter months, *hi'-go*, or fantasy stories, about animals were told, including the five stories in part 3. The lessons varied. Story 3.1 ("The Squirrel Maidens") taught the children of the pitfalls of arrogance, while story 3.3 ("The Hawk and the Horned Owl") gave them an example of real courage. Ideally, parents did not verbally or physically abuse their children. However, story 2.11 ("The Boy Driven from Home") is about a father who abused his son.

Most parents gave to their children all that they could afford, but significant wealth differences existed between families. Families depended primarily on kinsmen for support. War and accidents took a tremendous toll on the young adult male population of the tribe. Sometimes the husband or father was badly crippled. There were widows without close relatives, and there were children who were orphans. Thus there were families and individuals without property or horses who at times had to depend on the largess of the community. Story 2.12 ("The Woman War Leader") is the story of a widow without close relatives.

If a family could afford it, they would have one or more of their children, always the eldest ones, made *zhin-ga' o-xta*, or honored little one. This was extremely costly in food and gifts because it involved hosting five ceremonies over a period of years. In the first ceremony a special cradle board was made and paid for with horses and blankets. Second was a special feast held when the child took his or her first step. The third ceremony was the piercing of the ears of the child, at which guests were feasted and given gifts. The most costly was the fourth ceremony, the *wa-ton' wa-ku-be*. Numerous guests were invited to a large corn feast. Among these guests were four special individuals called *wa-ton'-ga*, two men and two women who were themselves "honored little ones." As part of this ceremony, a special dance called the *da'-gthe wa-tse'*, or captive dance, was performed. The fifth and final ceremony was a second naming ceremony in which the child received a new clan name.[34] The special status of these honored children is noted in Story 2.2 ("Making the Buffalo Come").

Although not a religious ceremony, marriage was a socially important event for Osages. Two factors played an important role in the choice of a spouse. The individuals had to be from different divisions. A member of one of the Sky people clans had to marry an individual from one of the Earth people clans. Just as all life was the creation of the interaction of the sky and the earth, all children had to be the product of parents from both the Sky and Earth peoples. The second factor was the relative social status of the individuals and families. Ideally, an eldest son would marry an eldest daughter and vice versa. And, since marriages affected not only the status of the bride and groom but also that of their parents and their future children, ideally, they were arranged. Girls were considered eligible for marriage after they reached puberty, and many were married by the time they were thirteen or fourteen years old. A boy was not considered eligible for marriage until he was in his late teens or early twenties. Adolescent girls and boys were not allowed to speak to or socialize with each other. It was the responsibility of a boy's father to find him a suitable wife, and they frequently initiated a marriage without the boy's knowledge. Story 2.16 ("The Two Young Men Who Mourned Their Living Father") concerns a father who would not arrange marriages for his sons. After a suitable girl had been chosen, the groom's family asked four men who held the title *ni'-ka don-he* (good man)[35] to negotiate the marriage and the number and value of the gifts to be presented by the boy's family.

The girl's parents then contacted the other relatives of the girl to discuss the agreement. Of particular importance were the girl's maternal uncles. If these maternal uncles agreed to the marriage, then the other relatives would concur. If the extended family gave its consent, then the parents of the girl sent word to the boy's parents, and the day was set.

The Osage had three categories of marriage. A marriage between two previously unmarried individuals was called a *mi'-zhin* and was the ideal form of marriage. The marriage of two individuals who were either widowed or divorced was called an *o-mi'-hon*. While *o-mi'-hon* marriage was a socially approved form, such marriages were arranged between the two parties with little formality.[36] However, in story 2.12 ("The Woman War Leader"), the widow is remarried following the all of the formalities of a *mi-zhin* marriage.

Sometimes individuals who feared that their parents would not agree to their marriage ran off together. Such "marriages" were termed *ga-shon'-the mi'-ghon-ge* and were not approved of and carried a social stigma. The term itself refers to a natural or animal state. Such a liaison affected not only the status of the couple and their parents but that of their children as well. No matter what the husband achieved or how he behaved later in life, he would never be a *ni'-ki don-he*. The children born of such a marriage were not considered to be real people but the products of an animal-like sexual union, and no respectable family would agree to one of their children marrying one of these individuals.

After the marriage, the bride and groom lived with the bride's family. Moving into the house of his in-laws, the new husband became the primary economic support for the family. It was his responsibility to hunt and supply the meat not only for his wife but for her parents as well. Because residence was matrilocal, polygyny usually took the form of sororal polygyny. The husband of the oldest daughter had the right to marry the younger sisters in the family as they came of age and frequently did. Osage couples were like any other couples in the world. Some couples were deeply in love with each other, such as those in story 2.27 ("The Young Warrior and His Dead Wife") and story 2.12 ("The Woman War Leader"). Sometimes couples would have bitter fights with each other as in story 2.5 ("Death of an Old Warrior"), which has disastrous consequences. A husband had some degree of authority over his wife or wives. Sometimes wives were unfaithful to their husbands and a husband could, if he desired, kill an unfaithful spouse and her lover. Such is the case in story 2.14 ("The Adulterous Wife"). However, in story 2.15 ("Mourning Dance for Yellow Ears"), the husband chooses not to kill his wife but rather her lover's favorite horse, Yellow Ears. The husband's authority was not, however, absolute. A wife could leave an abusive husband and remarry, such as in story 2.13 ("The Youngest Wife"), if strongly supported by her maternal uncles. Divorce could take place even if both parties did not consent. If the husband died, it was expected that the widow(s) would remarry their deceased husband's brother.

THE ROLES OF MEN AND WOMEN

The Osage saw the roles of men and women in the family as distinct, complementary halves. To the Osage, protecting and destroying life were masculine qualities, while bringing life into the world and nurturing it were feminine qualities. This dichotomy was the basis for defining the roles of husbands and wives. The husband was the protector of the family from human enemies who might destroy them. The husband was also the provider of meat for the family, which also involved the destruction of life. Thus the two major roles of a man were those of warrior and hunter. A woman was expected to bring of life into the world and to nurture it. Thus the roles of the wife was as mother, gardener, and gatherer of wild plant foods. Just as a man risked pain, suffering, and even death in defending his family and his community from their enemies, so did a woman risk pain, suffering, and even death in bringing new life into the world, and in so doing, she added strength to the family and community. The roles of warrior and mother were equal, as were the roles of hunter and gardener/gatherer.

Charles Me-she-tsa-he, ca. 1895, with his hair cut in the traditional roach worn by Osage men. Osage Tribal Museum Alt PO-180. (Bureau of American Ethnography photograph. Courtesy of the Osage Tribal Museum.)

HUSBANDS

All men could attempt to achieve recognition on three fronts: as family heads, as warriors, and as priests. Every man was expected to be an ideal husband and father. And men were judged as to how well they performed the various tasks involved in being a family head. Was he a good enough hunter not merely to feed his family but to provide them with luxuries as well? Did he treat his wife or wives fairly and provide for their comfort? However, the main criterion in judging a man was how good of a father he was. Did he have his children named properly? Was he able to have one or more of his children made a "little honored one"? Was he successful in training his children for adulthood and in instilling in them the proper respect for others and the community? The major test was in his children's marriages. Were they all married properly? In others words, did they all have arranged *mi'-zhi* marriages? If not, he had failed, since it would indicate that he had failed to instill in them respect for himself, their families, and tribal traditions. Only after all of a man's children were married and had children of their own could he be judged as successful or not. If he was successful in these respects, then he might be judged a *ni'-ka don-he*, "a good man," a respected elder.

The Osages were surrounded by enemy peoples. During the eighteenth and early nineteenth centuries, the Osage were in a constant state of war with most of their neighbors. The most intractable of their enemies were the Pawnee. Warfare usually took the form of small enemy raiding parties attacking isolated families or hunters. To this end enemy war parties would commonly lay in ambush along one of the frequently used hunting trails. This is the case in story 2.5 ("Death of an Old Warrior") and in story 2.10 ("Captive of the Pawnee"). At other times raiders would attack families who remained behind when most of the villagers were gone on a buffalo hunts, such as in story 2.7 ("Origin of the Whistle Bundle"). At no time nor in any place were the Osage completely safe from enemy attacks. As a result, every man was expected to be a warrior and defender and protector of the women and children of the village.

The symbol of the warrior was the hawk, and the sacred object encased in clan bundles was the body of a hawk painted blue. To the Osage, the hawk was the most courageous of birds. A small hawk would fight a much larger bird in defense of its nest. Like the hawk, the warrior had to fight, even to the death, to protect the women and children of the tribe.

Osage warriors and war parties did not attack enemy tribes merely for the sake of horses, captives, or glory. Any attack on a neighboring tribe had to have a purpose and serve the interests of the village or tribe. Thus, as we noted, the Osage, attempted to organize all warfare as a religious ritual controlled by the clan priests.

As warriors, every man strove to gain war honors, or *o'-don*. There were thirteen named war honors. These honors are listed in story 1.14 ("Counting the *O'don*"). Osage war honors differed from those of the Plains tribes in that a warrior could not earn them by taking horses or carrying out individual acts of bravado. Most war honors could only be acquired by men while serving as

Early Risen, 1874. A young man dressed in typical men cloths of the nineteenth century: a trade-cloth shirt, leggings, and breech cloth. The porcupine roach on his head was only worn on formal occasions. Osage Tribal Museum PO1-868. (Courtesy of the Osage Tribal Museum.)

members of formally organized war parties, and then only if their faces were painted black with charcoal. However, the most prestigious of the war honors was the one that was awarded a man who killed an enemy within the village (that is, an enemy who posed a direct threat to the women and children). In these cases the man was not part of a war party and did not have black paint on his face. Only a man who had earned all thirteen *o'don* could be tattooed.

WIVES

Every woman was expected to become a wife and mother. As a wife, a woman was the keeper of the hearth or fireplace, symbolic of the home in general. Although patrilineal in descent, the Osage were matrilocal. Ideally, the family resided with her band and lived in her clan's section of the village. The dwelling and all of the food and household goods within it were hers—or at least under her responsibility and control. Although her children belonged to her husband's clan, she had the primary responsible for their nurturing. In story 1.11 ("Instructions to the Mother") the basic role of the mother is defined. She must protect her child from harm, symbolized by the robe. She must also provide her child with nourishment, symbolized by the sacred foods of corn and water lily roots. Her corn has to be planted in a sacred manner and the water lily roots have to be collected in a sacred manner. In story 1.13 ("Instructions in the Painting of the Sacred Robes") the mother, or mother to be, is told how to paint a robe for her child to make it sacred. In story 2.13 ("The Youngest Wife"), the

Figure 4. Tattooing of Women

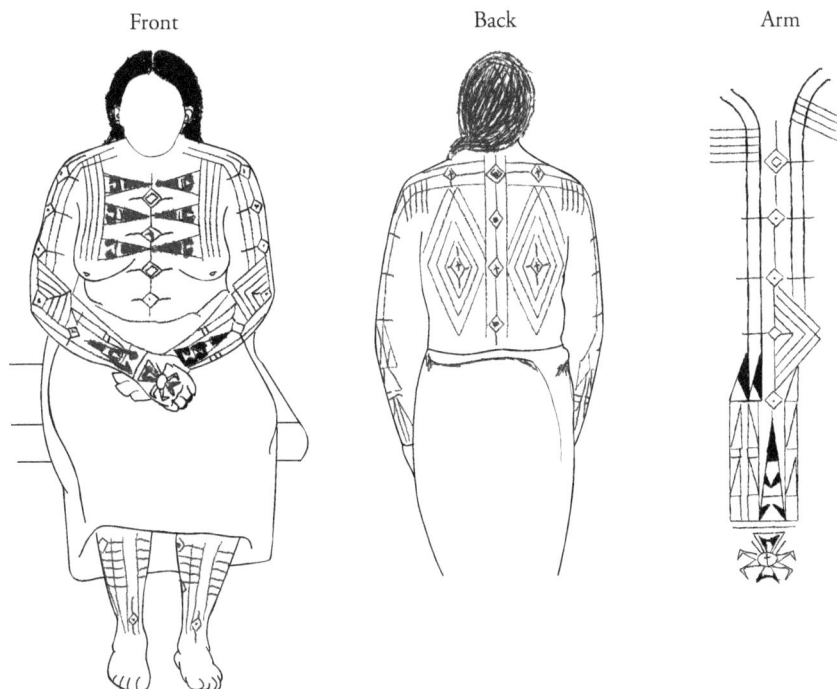

wife Wa-zha'-xa-in is presented as the ideal wife and mother, she having borne eight children, four boys and four girls. As noted, children were the greatest of Wa-kon'-da's blessings because they were the future and because they indicated Wa-kon'-da's desire that the Osage as people continue to survive.

Being the wife of a priest accorded a woman great social status. Thus a wife would be willing to endure the economic cost of having her husband become a priest. It also, however, imposed certain ritual obligations on the wife. The sacred bundle was not just entrusted to the husband but to the wife as well. When a man came to their house to ask for the clan bundle to be taken on a war party, it was the wife, not her husband, who ritually presented the bundle. While the war party was absent, it was the wife, not the husband, who had to perform certain ritual acts. Story 1.12 ("Instructions to the Wife of a Priest") makes the wife's new ritual responsibilities clear. On the death of a clan priest, it was common for his wife to be made an honorary priest and for her to participate in the tribe's ceremonies. During the ceremonies, these women would sit behind the priest and symbolically represent the voice of the people.

Since every man was a warrior, special recognition was only accorded to the wives of what might best be termed honored warriors; men who had earned all thirteen o'-don. However, it must be remembered that only members of the priesthood could earn certain o'-don. Unlike other women, only the wife, or wives, and daughters of a man who had earned all thirteen o'-don could be tattooed. These tattoos accorded them honor and respect, and they were also prayers for long life. See story 1.7 ("The Tattooing Custom").

Although women did not participate in warfare, there was one famous exception, the subject of story 2.12 ("The Woman War Leader"). In this case a widow organized and led as a do-don'-hon'-ga a mourning dance party for her deceased husband.

EXCEPTIONAL MEN AND WOMEN

The Osage never claimed to fully understand the supernatural world. There were among the Osage both men and women who were not members of the priesthoods who had exceptional supernatural powers.

Some of these men were termed wa-kon'-da-ge, or medicine men. In most cases it appears that at some point in their life they had experienced direct contact with some supernatural being who had given them power. Some of these men used their powers for the good of the people, some for evil purposes, and still others for both. All were considered dangerous, at least potentially. Among these men were individuals who could turn themselves or objects into animals, heal the sick, bring the dead to life, kill others by magically "shooting" them with objects, or see the future in their dreams. Not surprisingly there are a large number of stories concerning such men: story 2.17 ("The *Wa-kon'-da-gi*, or Medicine Men"), story 2.18 ("Strange Medicine Man"), story 2.19 ("The Death of Village Maker"), story 2.20 ("Big Bear and Runs-to-meet-men"), story 2.21 ("The Cruel Medicine Man and the Orphan"), story 2.22 ("Wah-ti- an-kah"), and story 2.23 ("Dreamers").

Finally, there were some women with mysterious supernatural powers that sharply distinguished them from other people. Story 2.25 ("Spirit Woman") concerns a mysterious woman of unknown origin found by a war party who was able to heal the minds of people gone mad. There were also women who were prophets or dreamers, who predicted the future and warned the people of pending dangers. Perhaps the most famous of these women was Wa-zhi'-xa-win, the subject of story 2.24 ("The Woman Dreamer").

DEATH AND BURIAL

At noon on the fourth day following death, the deceased was buried. They were dressed in their best clothes and seated facing east, and then a stone mound was constructed over them. With them in their grave was food as well as some of their treasured possessions. Sometime a horse was killed. At the burial a priest from the Wind clan burned cedar fronds, and members of the mourning party would pull smoke over their heads and bodies to spiritually cleanse themselves. A feast was held, and gifts were given by relatives of the deceased to the mourners.

The period of mourning varied. Husbands and wives usually performed the rite of vigil. Some would go for seven days into the hills or woods to fast and pray. Others would stay at home but seclude themselves and then fast and pray during the day. How long one continued his or her mourning depended upon the individual. Story 2.12 ("The Woman War Leader") offers a good description of mourning customs.

If a family chose, and if they could afford it, they would have a mourning dance for the deceased. This took place sometime after the burial of the individual. A mourning dance consisted of organizing a war party with the intent of killing an enemy whose spirit could then accompany that of the deceased. The war party was organized like any other war party, having a leader, commanders, and common warriors, or kettle tenders. The party would travel west and kill the first enemy it encountered and return home with the scalp, which would be scattered on the grave. The mourning dance was not a traditional Osage religious practice. The origin of it is told in story 2.8. During the nineteenth century, mourning dances became increasingly common, and thus many of the war stories concern this type of war party. Story 2.12 ("The Woman War Leader") is about a woman who once led such a party. There are also two humorous stories about mourning dance parties. The family who sponsored a mourning dance for a favorite horse is the subject of story 2.15 ("Mourning Dance for Yellow Ears"), while story 2.16 ("The Two Young Men Who Mourned Their Living Father") is the story of a mourning war party held to shame a living man.

Traditional Osage beliefs concerning ghosts and the spirits of the dead are not clearly understood. At death, the spirit of the individual passed from the visible into the invisible world. There are several folk stores that speak of ghosts. Two of these stories, story 2.26 ("The Flute Ghost Story") and story 2.28 ("Return of the Dead"), were told as a *u'-tha-ge*, or true stories.

Part One

Sacred Teachings

1.1 Allegorical Story of Tribal Organization[1]

In the beginning the peoples of the *wa-zha'-zhe* [water], the *hon'-ga* [earth], and the *tsi'-zhu* [sky] came from the sky to the earth [see also stories 1.2, 1.3, and 1.7].[2] After these three groups of people had descended, they started forth to wander over the earth, observing, as they marched, the sequence in which they had reached the earth; first the Wa-zha'-zhe, then the Hon'-ga, and last the Tsi'-zhu. One day, after they had wandered for a great length of time, the Wa-zha'-zhe suddenly halted, and the leader looked back over his shoulder to his followers, who had also halted, and in an undertone said: "We have come to the village of a strange people." The leader of the Hon'-ga looked back over his shoulder and in the same manner passed the word to the Tsi'-zhu.

Overhearing the words cautiously spoken by the Wa-zha'-zhe leader and his followers, the people of the village sent a messenger to inquire who these strangers were and what their mission was. On the invitation of the messenger the Wa-zha'-zhe alone entered the village, for the Hon'-ga and the Tsi'-zhu declined to follow because they had noticed with revulsion that the bones of animals and of men lay scattered and bleaching around the village. It was the village of death to which they had come, when they had been seeking life.

The Wa-zha'-zhe leader was conducted to the house of the leader of the strange people, and there the two men exchanged words in friendly terms. The Wa-zha'-zhe presented a ceremonial pipe to the leader of this strange village, who in turn gave a pipe[3] to the Wa-zha'-zhe, and then the two leaders conversed freely about the life and customs of their people. In the course of their conversation the Wa-zha'-zhe said that he belonged to a people who called themselves Hon'-ga,[4] whereupon the stranger said: "I also am a Hon'-ga." He then told the Wa-zha'-zhe the manner in which his people destroyed life wherever it appeared on the earth, using for their weapons the four winds, and [said] that whichever way the people turned the winds, the animals and men stricken by them fell and died. It was at this point that the Wa-zha'-zhe leader made known to his host that the Hon'-ga and the Tsi'-zhu desired to dwell with him and his people but did not like their habit of destroying life. The Wa-zha'-zhe leader then suggested that his host and his people move to a new country, where the land was pure and free from the signs of death. The Hon'-ga U-ta-non-dsi (the Isolated Hon'-ga), as the Wa-zha'-zhe called these strangle people, willingly accepted the invitation and moved with the Wa-zha'-zhe to a "new country,"[5] where they joined the Hon'-ga and the Tsi'-zhu.

All the four groups, the Wa-zha'-zhe, the Hon'-ga, the Tsi'-zhu, and the Hon'-ga U-ta-non-dsi, thereupon moved to a new country, where the land was undefiled by decaying carcasses and where there were no visible signs of death. There they united themselves in friendship, each pledging to the other its strength and support in resisting the dangers that might beset them in the course of their united tribal life.

[Creation of the Houses of Mystery]

At the beginning the affairs of the tribe were under the control of the Hon'-ga U-ta-non-dsi, a division representing the earth.[6] During this period the tribe was in a continual state of confusion from external and internal disturbances. In order to preserve the tribal existence, a movement toward reorganization became necessary, and in time such a movement was initiated by the Wa-zha'-zhe, a subdivision of the great Hon'-ga division.[7]

It was at this time that the dramatic incident took place between the Wa-zha'-zhe and the Hon'-ga. The Wa-zha'-zhe offered to the Hon'-ga a symbolic pipe,[8] but before accepting it the Hon'-ga asked, "Who are you?" The Wa-zha'-zhe replied:

> I am a person who has verily made of a pipe his body,[9]
> When you also make of the pipe your body,
> You shall be free from all causes of death, O, Hon'-ga.

The Hon'-ga took the pipe and said in response:

> I am a person who has made of the red boulder his body,[10]
> When you also make of it your body,
> The malevolent gods in their destructive course,
> Shall pass by and leave you unharmed, O, Wa-zha'-zhe.

It was thus that the two groups, the Wa-zha'-zhe and the Hon'-ga, pledged support to one another in times of danger so long as tribal life should last.[11]

At the time of this council the people of the three groups gave to the Hon'-ga U-ta-non-dsi [the Isolated Hon'-ga] a house which they called *tsi' wa-kon'-da-gi,* house of mysteries. Both the house and its fireplace they consecrated to ceremonial use, and [they] made them represent the life-giving earth. To this house of mysteries were to be brought all the infants of the four groups to be ceremonially fed upon the sacred foods of life that they might arrive safely at the age of maturity,[12] and the children were here to be given their clan names in order to take their established places in the tribal organization.

The council at this time also established another house, *tsi' wa-kon'-da-gi,* house of mysteries, which they called *hon'-ga tsi'* [earth house], and placed it in the keeping of the Wa-ca'-be [Bear] clan of the Hon'-ga group. In this house were to be performed the ceremonies that pertain to war. Within its fireplace, which was called *ho'-e-ga* (snare), were placed four stones, arranged at the cardinal points, one for each of the four winds. Upon these four stones was placed the *tse'-xe ni-ka-po*,[13] a caldron for the boiling of certain plants that represented certain persons belonging to enemy tribes.[14]

When the *tsi' wa-kon'-da-gi* [house of mysteries] of the Bear clan and its fireplace had been consecrated, each of the clans of the four groups placed within the house its life symbol(s).[15]

These four warrior groups conducted both the war and hunting movements of the people, and no one group could act independently of the others. A war party thus ceremonially organized by all of the four[16] groups was called *do-don'-ton-ga*, war party in great numbers.

[Origin of the Clan, or Hawk, Bundles]

The reorganized government proved effective in maintaining peace and order within the tribe and in upholding the dignity of the people as an organized body, but it was burdened with ceremonial forms that did not admit of the prompt action often necessary for moving against aggressive and troublesome enemies.[17]

The *non'-hon-zhin-ga* [little old men], becoming conscious of this defect, again made a "move to a new country" to bring their organization to final completion. In this second move the various clans of the tribe were empowered to organize war parties in three classes:

1. A war party composed of the warriors from the clans of one of the two great divisions.
2. A war party made up of two or more of the clans of one of the two great divisions.[18]
3. A war party organized by one clan.

War parties of the first two classes were called Tsi'-ga-xa Do-don'.[19] War parties of the third class were called Wa-xo'-be U-kon-da [Isolated Hawk]. War parties of these three classes were not required to observe the tedious ceremonial forms prescribed for the war parties organized under the rule of the four divisions. Under this new movement each clan of the tribe was given a hawk, *wa-xo'-be*, for ceremonial purposes. This was the second stage in the development of the military branch of the tribal government.[20]

The *wa-xo'-be* were made of hawk skins and symbolized the courage of the warriors of each fireplace. The choice of the hawk to symbolize the courage and combative nature of the warrior proved satisfactory to all the people, for the courage of the hawk was considered as equal to that of the eagle, while the swift and decisive manner in which the smaller bird always attacks its prey ever excited the admiration of the warrior.[21]

The *non'-hon-zhin-ga* sat within their longhouse as they worked on the *wa-xo'-be*. Their heads were still bent over one when they were startled by the angry bellowing of an animal. All eyes turned upon the *sho'-ka* [ritual servant], who hastened to the door and quickly threw aside the flap. There stood an angry buffalo, with his head lowered and his tail trembling in the air, pawing the earth and throwing clouds of dust toward the sky. Stricken with fear, the *sho'-ka* asked with unsteady voice, "Who are you?" The bull answered, "I am Tho'-xe, lift ye your heads!" At that moment there came a crash of thunder that seemed to issue from the end of the ridgepole of the house. In an excited manner the *non'-hon-zhin-ga* gathered up all of the *wa-xo'-be* [bundles][22] and threw them toward the bull, who at once lowered his tail, ceased pawing the earth, and became friendly.

These two angry visitors, the bull and the thunder, were representatives of the Tho'-xe [Buffalo Bull] and the Ni'-ka Wa-kon'-da-gi [Men of Mystery or Thunder] clans. It was in this dramatic manner that these two clans were jointly given the office of caring for the *wa-xo'-be*.[23] It is said that all the *wa-xo'-be* belong to these two clans because the *non'-hon-zhi-ga* had given them to the two clans through fear.

[The Creation of the Ga-hi'-ge, or Chiefs][24]

In the progress of time the *non'-hon-zhin-ga* made a third [or fourth?] "move to a new country." At this time the civil branch of the tribal government was instituted. It was then agreed that the people should be governed by two men, one for each of the two great tribal divisions, who should bear the official title of *ga-hi'-ge* (chief). The duties assigned to these two chiefs were:

1. When two men quarrel, come to blows, and threaten to kill each other, the chief shall compel them to cease fighting.
2. When a murder is committed and a relative of the person slain threatens to take the life of the murderer in revenge, the chief shall compel the relative to keep the peace.
3. If the relative persists in his effort to take the life of the slayer, the chief shall expel him from the tribe.
4. If the relative takes the life of the slayer when the chief had already offered him the sacred pipe to smoke, the chief shall give the order for him to be put to death.

5. The chief shall require the murderer to bring gifts to relatives of the man he has slain as an offering of peace.
6. If the murderer refuses to do this, the chief may call upon the people to make the peace offering and then expel the murderer from the tribe.
7. If a man's life is threatened by another and he flees to the house of the chief, he shall protect the man.
8. If a murderer pursued by the relatives of the slain man flees into the house of the chief, he shall protect the man.
9. If a stranger, even if he be from an enemy tribe, enters the house of the chief for safety, the chief shall protect him.
10. When a war party comes home with captives, the chief shall give them their lives and have them adopted into the tribe.

When the tribe goes out for the annual buffalo hunt it shall be the duty of the chief to designate the route to be taken and the site in which the camp is to be pitched, and the order shall be proclaimed by a crier. The two chiefs shall taken turns each day in conducting the journey, both when going forth and when the returning to the home village.

For the enforcement of their orders the two chiefs shall be empowered to select and appoint ten officers, one from each of the following clans:

On the Hon'-ga side: Wa-ca'-be [Bear] or In-gthon'-ga [Puma]; Ta I-in-ka-shi-ga [Deer]; O'-pxon [Elk]; Hon'-ga A-hiu-ton [Winged Earth]; Hon'-ga U-ta-non-dsi [Isolated Earth].

On the Tsi'-zhu side: Ni'-ka Wa-kon'-da-gi [Men of Mystery]; Tho'-xe [Buffalo Bull]; Tsi'-zhu Wa-non [Elder Sky]; Mi-k'in Wa-non [Elder Bow]; Tse-do'Ga-indse [Buffalo Bull Face].

These officers shall bear the title *a'-ki-da* (soldier) and shall be chosen because of the military honors that they have won as well as for their personal friendship for the chief. The chief in selecting his officers shall not be restricted to his own division, but he may, according to his own preference, choose his officers from any of the designated clans of the opposite division. These officers shall have their houses close to that of the chief.

The officers selected from three of these designated clans were honored with special titles, which afterward became part of these clans' personal names. These titles, and later the names, were *a'-ki-da ton-ga* (great soldier) for the officer chosen from the Wa-ca'-be [Bear] clan or the related In-gthon'-ga [Puma] clan; *a'-ki-da zhin-ga* (little soldier) for the one chosen from the Ta' I-n-ka-shi-ga [Deer] clan; and *a'-ki-da ga-hi'-ge* (chief soldier) for the one from the Ni'-ka Wa-kon'-da-gi [Men of Mystery] clan.

It was agreed at this time that the office of the chief shall descend to the lineal male heirs. In case the heir is disqualified for the office owing to mental infirmity or indifference to the customs held sacred by the people, the *a'-ki-da* [soldiers] in council shall determine who of the nearest kin to the former chief shall succeed to the office.

The clans from which the two *ga-hi'-ge* (or chiefs) were chosen were the Wa'-tse-tsi [Ponca] clan (the people who descended from the stars) of the Wa-zha'-zhe [Water] subdivision of the Hon'-ga [Earth] great division; and the Tsi'-zhu [Sky] clan of the Tsi'-zhu [Sky] great division. The title, Wa-shta'-ge, Gentle, was at that time added to the names of these two clans, so that in speaking of them both the name and the title were mentioned, as Wa'-tse-tsi Wa-shta'-ge [Gentle Star] (sometimes called the Pon'-ka Wa-shta'-ge [Gentle Ponca]) and the Tsi'-zhu Wa-shta'-ge [Gentle Sky]. This clan was sometimes called Tsi'-zhu Wa-bin' I-ta-zhi, the Tsi'zhu-who-do-not-touch-blood, because the people of that clan are supposed to refrain from shedding of blood. The rule that required the chief to protect a man fleeing to his house for refuge applied to all the families of this clan.

It was also agreed that the house of the chief should be held as sacred as it represents two life-giving powers—the earth and the sun. The house stands for the earth and must have two doors, one opening toward the rising sun and the other toward the setting sun. The fire that is placed midway between the two doors represents the sun, whose pathway symbolizes endless life, and thus passes through the middle of the house that stands for the earth. The fireplace was also consecrated, and the fire taken there from by the people to start their home fires was thought of as holy and as having power to give life and health to those who used it. It was also declared that the two doors, which represent the continual flow of life, shall be closed to the man who approaches them when contemplating murder.

The ceremonial position of the chief's house in the village was also established at this time.

Some time after the creation of the office of chief for each of the two great divisions and the men chosen had been inducted into their office, the two chiefs went out separately to seek for some sign of approval from the supernatural. For seven days and six nights the men fasted and cried to Wa-kon'-da.

[Vision of the Sky Chief][25]

As the darkness of evening spread over the land, on the sixth day of his vigil, the Tsi'-zhu Wa-shta'-ge [Gentle Sky] chief removed from his face the sign of vigil and sat down to rest for the night. While he was yet awake and in deep thought he heard approaching footsteps, and as he looked up he beheld a man standing before him, as though in the light of day. The stranger spoke, saying: "I have heard your cry. I am a person who can heal all the pains and the bodily ailments of your people. When the little ones make of me their bodies they shall always live to see old age. In the morning when the mists have cleared away go to yonder river, follow its course until you come to a bend, and there, in the middle of its bank, you will see me standing in the midst of the winds."

When morning came the chief followed the course of the river, as the stranger bade him, until he came to a sharp bend, where the waters had washed away the earth, leaving a high bank. The chief looked up and there, in the middle of the bank, he saw the stranger, who was *mon-kon ni'-ka-shi-ga*, the man medicine *(Cucurbita perennis)*.[26] The chief removed from its place the strange man-shaped root, being careful not to break any part of it. As this was the seventh and the last day of his fast, the chief then started toward his home, following the course of the river. He had not gone far when he came to another bend of the stream where there was a high bank. In the middle of it he beheld another root, which he examined and found to be of the female sex. The chief carried home these two roots, which afterward were used to cure bodily ailments.[27]

[Vision of the Earth Chief][28]

On the evening of the sixth day of his vigil the Wa'-tse-tsi [Wa-shta'-ge] [Gentle Ponca] chief removed from his face the sign of vigil and sat down to rest for the night. While he was yet awake there appeared before him a very aged man, who spoke to him, saying, "I have heard your cry and have come to give myself to your people. I am Old Age. When the little ones make of me their bodies they shall always live to see old age. When morning comes, go to yonder river, and in a bend where the water, sheltered by a high bank, lies placid you will find me. Take from my right wing seven feathers. Let your people make of them their bodies, and they shall always live to see old age." In the dawn of the morning that was the seventh day of his vigil, the chief arose and again put upon his face the sign of vigil. He went to the river, and in a bend where the water was sheltered from the winds by a high bank he saw, on the water's edge, a white pelican so old that he could not move. In this bird the chief recognized his visitor of the night before. From the right wing of the bird the chief plucked seven feathers and started for home. As he was approaching a brook he met an eagle, who gave him a downy feather as a symbol of old age. When he was nearing home he beheld lying on the ground a piece of black metal, which he also took as a symbol of old age.

On his return to the village the chief assembled the people of both great divisions, to whom he told the story of vigil. The people were well pleased and formally consecrated the pelican to be thenceforth their sacred symbol of old age, and it thus became wa-xo'-be [sacred]. The portable shrine that held the sacred symbols and the symbols themselves are spoken of collectively as *wa-xo'-be*.[29]

1.2 Origin Story of the Wolf Clan (Pah-nee-wah-with-tah)[30]

The people, whose abode was in the heavens, assembled that they might mediate upon the means by which they would descend to the earth to come into bodily existence. They decided that the eagle was the only person who could safely conduct them to the earth. They, therefore, appealed to him and he led them downward. The people, led by the eagle, came to the earth and alighted upon seven trees: *pon'-ton-ga-hiu*, the full-grown shagbark hickory; *pon'ton-ga-hiu zhin-ga*, the young shagbark; *pi-ci'* [acorn] or *zhon'-zhi-hi* [redwood], the red oak; *ca'-ghtu-hi ha shu-ga*, the thick-barked hickory; *ca'-gthu-hi*, the smooth-bark bitter hickory; *thiu'-xe*, the willow (the old man said seven trees, but he gave the names of only six).

The people found that in the willow tree there was a mystical power—a power for resisting the forces inimical to life.[31] They wished to cut the tree to make a part of its body a *wa-xo'-be*, a sacred article for ceremonial use. They sent their *sho'-ka* (official messenger) to find the material out of which to make a knife. Four times he went out to make search but without success. The fifth time he brought home a knife he had made out of a stone of a grayish color. He had made for it a handle that was round. The people accepted the knife, consecrated it for ceremonial use, and called it *mon'-hin-i-ba-btho-ga*, the round-handled knife. With this sacred knife they cut out of the body of the tree four small pieces, which they threw into the air as sacred offerings, one to each of the four winds. Blood flowed from each of the four wounds made with the ceremonial knife.

Then the people, using their sacred knife, proceeded to cut down the tree, to shave the trunk to a proper size, and to shape it for a club. This club they called *wa-xo'-be* (sacred) and consecrated it for ceremonial use. The natural color of the wood did not satisfy the people and they regarded the sacred article as incomplete. Then, as though by a common understanding and consent, they hastened to gather leaves and dry twigs. These they placed in a great pile to which they set fire, and the smoke and flames tinged the darkened heavens with a reddish hue—a color pleasing and satisfying to the minds of the people.

It resembled the color cast upon the eastern sky as it rises and that the people always hailed with joy with uplifted hands. It was this color they put upon the symbolic club to add to it the life-giving power of the sun.

The weapon was thus finished, and there remained nothing more to do with it but to test its magical power. For this purpose the people sent their official messenger [*sho'-ka*] to a far-off country to search for some creature upon which to make the test. The messenger returned in the evening of the day, weary and footsore, to report that he had been to a valley where he saw nothing worthy of notice. Again he went out and returned from a second valley to report that he had found nothing. He was bidden to go again, and in the evening of that day he came home to report that he had been to a third valley, where he had seen the footprints of a person (a buffalo bull). The footprints showed the person's feet to be cloven, and the grasses upon which he had trodden were crushed. To commemorate this event, the people agreed to name their children Non-xthon'-zhe, Crushed-with-his-feet. For the fourth time the messenger was sent out, and in the evening of the day he came home to report that he had been to a fourth valley, where he saw the person of the footprints, whom he described as a person of formidable appearance and bearing upon his head curved horns. To make this report memorable, the people agreed to name their children He-thi'-shi-zhe, Curve Horns. The messenger gave a graphic description of the face of the person, and from this the people agreed to name their children Tse-do'-ga-in-dse, Buffalo Bull Face.[32]

Upon hearing the last report, the keeper of the new weapon picked it up and caressed it with four downward strokes of his hand. At each stroke he uttered a word: *we'-tsi-pi-zhi*, mysterious weapon; *we'-tsin-zhin-ga*, little weapon; *we'-tsin-hu-ton*, weapon that cries out; *we'-tsin-don-a-thin*, possessor of a good weapon. These words also became sacred names given to the children of the clan.[33]

Then speaking to the messenger, the keeper of the sacred weapon said, "That is the very person for whom we have been in search. Whoever he may be, we shall send him to the abode of spirits." "What course shall we take in approaching that person?" the people asked, and the keeper of the sacred weapon replied: "We will take the path always taken by the sun."

The people approached the person, moving in a westerly direction in imitation of the sun.[34] They made four ceremonial pauses on their way. At the fourth pause the keeper of the sacred weapon lifted the club, brandished it in the air, and the bull suddenly bellowed as though stricken instantly with pain. Again the keeper brandished the weapon, and the animal started to flee. A third time the keeper brandished the club, and the beast was stricken with mortal pain in the hindquarters. At the fourth brandishing of the weapon the bull whirled around and fell in death, his blood gushing from his mouth.

The people hastened to the fallen animal. They made a slight cut in its skin, using the sacred knife, that with which they had cut the willow tree, and from the cut fat protruded. They tasted of the fat and said: "It is good, it shall be food for the little ones; they shall seethe it in boiling water to prepare it for use." Out of the skin of the left hind leg they cut a round piece, which they called *mon'-ge-tse-ha-wa-gther*, breast shield; also two long narrow straps, which they named *we'-thin-zhu-dse*, red strap, and *we'-thin-ca-gi*, strong strap, which names they subsequently used as personal names.[35] From the skin of the left side of the body they cut seven narrow straps, which they painted red. The straps thus cut they called *mon'-sha-kon*, and these served as the original types of similar straps to be ceremonially made whenever the warriors are about to go to war and to be used by them for tying their captives should they succeed in taking any. The round piece of skin called breast shield, which symbolized the sun, they also painted red, and it too served as a type for similar shields to be ceremonially made for the warriors and worn by them as symbolic shields as well as as charms. At the same time that they made these sacred articles they dedicated the tails, the bladders, and the heart sacks of buffalo bull to ceremonial use and made them sacred types.

1.3 Origin Story of the Black Bear Clan (Bacon Rind)[36]

The people came from above. When they reached the earth they alighted upon seven great rocks. Two were [?], one black, and the other(s?) red. The people started from the seven rocks to go over the earth. All was strange, and they were afraid. They had no weapons, nothing but their hands.

In their wanderings they came across a white swan; they approached it stealthily to get near enough to kill it. They had killing powers in their index fingers. When they came near the swan the leader pointed his index finger at it and it fell dead.

From that incident the children of the (Black Bear) people were named White Swan and White Feather and after the habits of the bird.

The people went on again wandering over the earth. They came across a dark object lying on the ground; it was a strange animal. They approached it stealthily as they did upon the swan. When they came near they found it dead. It was a buffalo. From that incident they named their children after the buffalo.

Going on again they came across a man. This was strange to them for they thought that they were the only people on the earth. They approached him stealthily intending to kill him. When the man found that he was being approached by these people he spoke to them and told them he was a Hon'-ga [Earth person], that his name was Wa'-tse Ga-hi'-ge, Star Chief.[37] His life was spared, and he was permitted to join the party, who went on. From this incident the children are named Zhin-ga Ga-hi'-ge [Little Chief] and similar names referring to chief.[38]

The people went on and found another man. They approached him for the purpose of taking his life, when he called to them and told them that he was their benefactor. In his hand he carried a bit of black earth. He said that he was Hon'-ga Mon-in-ka-zhin-ga (Little Earth).[39] "I am the one who separated the earth from the waters." So, instead of killing him, they made friends with him, and he became a part of the people. To this day he is the one who, at the ceremonies of the Osage people, distributes the five symbolic soils of the earth: dark, blue, red, and yellow.[40]

The dark soil is used in the rite of fasting [vigil]. It must be taken and used before sunrise. It is put on the face and body, and the man taking the rite fasts until sundown and then removes from his face the sign of fasting.

1.4 Creation of the House of Mystery (Charles Wah-hre-she)[41]

When the people came to the earth from above they began to wander about. The people of the Wa-zha'-zhe division were the first to come, and so they went forth ahead of the other divisions. In their wanderings they came upon the village of a strange people. They were a people who made use of the winds to kill the animals upon which they lived, and the whitened bones of these animals lay scattered all around the village. The stench of the village was so great that the Wa-zha'-zhe people could not stand it.

The Wa-zha'-zhe desired to make friends with these strange people, and so the leader introduced himself to them and said, "I am a Wa-zha'-zhe Hon'-ga.[42] Who are you?" "I also am a Hon'-ga," the leader of the strange people replied. Then the two exchanged pipes, and their people became as one. These strange people became known as the Hon'-ga U-ta-na-dsi, the Hon'-ga-who-dwell-apart. Because of the great stench of the village of the Hon'-ga U-ta-na-dsi, the Wa-zha'-zhe suggested that the people of the two tribes move to a new location. The suggestion was accepted by all of the people, and so they moved to a new place where they were joined by the other divisions of the Wa-zha'-zhe people,[43] who had also come to the earth from above.

After the meeting of all the people of the Wa-zha'-zhe, it was agreed at a general council held by them that a new house of gathering should be built and that the Black Bear and Puma people[44] should build it. The house was built and it was covered on one side with a black bear skin and on the other with a cougar skin. The house when finished was called *tsi' wa-kon'-da-gi,* or sacred house. The house symbolized the cave of the black bear.

Upon completion of the *tsi' wa-kon'-da-gi,* the Black Bear and the Puma people furnished a pot, which they placed in the fireplace, first putting at each corner of the fireplace a stone, one for each of the four winds. The pot, which was called *tse-xe ni-ka-pu,* was placed upon these four stones.

When the pot had been placed upon the fireplace, a man was sent out to find some food to cook in the sacred pot. The man came to a lake, and along its shallow edges he found a plant he thought would be good for food. This he pulled up by its roots and brought to the people assembled at the *tsi' wa-kon'-da-gi.* The plant was carefully examined and tested and was declared to be unfit for food. This plant was then and is now known by the name of *ho'-xthon ta-xe.*[45] Although the plant was declared to be unfit for food, it was given a place in the sacred rites.

When the *ho'-xthon ta-xe* was declared to be unfit for food, another man was sent out. He also came to a lake and along its shallow edges found a plant he thought would be good to eat. He pulled it up by its roots and hastened back to the *tsi' wa-kon'-da-gi* with it, and there it was examined and tested and found to be unfit for food. Nevertheless this plant was given a place in the sacred rites. It was then and is now known by the name of *cin-mon-non-ta.*[46]

A third man was sent out when the *cin-mon-non-ta* was found to be unfit for food, and he also came to a lake, and there along its shallow edge he found a plant he thought would be good to eat. He pulled it up by its roots and hastened back with it to the *tsi' wa-kon'-da-gi.* It was examined and tested and was found to be good. It was a food that could be used for a short season but could not be depended upon for a great length of time. It was declared to be a nourishing food, and it was also given a place in the sacred rites. This plant was then and is to this day known by the of *cin.*[47]

When the *cin* was declared to be good for food but not altogether satisfying, a fourth man was sent out to find a food that could be depended upon for its abundance and its persevering qualities. This man went out, and as he wandered in the woods he found a plant that he thought was the right one for food. He pulled it up by its roots and hastened back to the *tsi' wa-kon'-da-gi,* where the people sat awaiting is return. The plant was examined and tested and it was declared to be a food that could be depended upon at all times. It was nourishing and pleasing to the taste. The plant was given a place in the sacred rites, and it was then and is now known by the name of *hon-bthin'-cu.*[48]

These things, the house, the four stones for the fireplace, the pot, and the four different plants enumerated became a part of the paraphernalia of the rites pertaining to war. While these four plants were each given a place in the sacred rites as symbols of life of the people, they also stood as the supernatural destroyers of the enemies of the people. Thus, while the *ho'-xthon ta-xe* gave to the people, it took from the enemy (supernaturally) the life of a youth who has not yet reached his puberty, a life that has a potential power of reproduction. The *cin-mon-non-ta* gave life to the people and at the same time took from the enemy the life of a maiden who has not yet reached her puberty, also a life having a potential power of reproduction.[49] The *cin* gave life to the people, and at the same time it took from the enemy the life of the warrior enjoying the honors conferred upon him, a life that was in its full power of reproduction. The *hon-bthin'-ciu* as it gave life to the people took from the enemy the life of a woman who for the first time gave birth to a child, a life that was in its full power of reproduction.[50]

When the *tsi' wa-kon'-da-gi* was completed, and the sacred pot was put upon the four stones, a representative of each one of the various clans brought a brand [live coal] from his fireplace and gave it to the sacred fire of the *tsi' wa-kon'-da-gi*. The only clans that did not contribute a brand to the sacred fire were the Tsi'-zhu Wa-shta'-ge [Gentle Sky] and the Pon-ka Wa-shta'-ge [Gentle Ponca] because they were a people of peace.

1.5 Earth Names and Sky Names (Charles Wah-hre-she)[51]

When the Hon'-ga people were coming from the sky to the earth they chose two persons (clans) to act as official messengers. One of these persons was called Hon'-ga Wa'-tse-gi-tsi, The-sacred-one from-the-stars, and the other Hon'-ga Wa-tse-ga-wa, The-sacred-radiant-star. These messengers were expected to find some way of dispersing the waters that submerged the earth and of exposing the ground beneath so as to make it habitable for all living creatures.

Wa'-tse-gi-tsi and Wa'-tse-ga-wa, the two messengers, found on the still waters the water spider, the water beetle, the white leech, and the dark leech, whom they asked for aid, which they could not give, but [they] promised to help the people to reach old age. The two messengers went on, and they met *o'-pon ton-ga*, the great elk, and appealed to him for aid. The great elk threw himself upon the waters four times and splashed about until the ground was exposed and ready to receive men and animals. He then called to the four corners of the earth for the life-giving winds to come. Next he threw himself upon the ground and rolled about; then, as he arose, the hairs of his body clung to the soil and became the grasses of the earth.

The two messengers then led the people over the dry land of the earth, when suddenly Hon'-ga Wa'-tse-gi-tsi, The-sacred-one-from-the-stars, came upon *in-gthon'-ga*, the puma. The messenger then changed his name from Wa'-tse-gi-tsi to In-gthon'-ga [Puma]. In like manner the Hon'-ga Wa'-tse-ga-wa, The-sacred-radiant-star, came upon *wa-ca'-be*, the black bear. The-sacred-radiant-star then changed his name from Wa'-tse-ga-wa to Wa-ca'-be, Black Bear.[52]

1.6 Origin Story of the *Sho'-ka* (Saucy Calf)[53]

At the beginning when the Osage had organized, they sent a young man to explore the country. This young man in his wanderings came to the head of a valley. He saw old footprints of the buffalo. He went further and came to the head of still another valley and saw still fresher signs of buffalo. He went on and came to the head of still another valley and saw still fresher signs of buffalo, [and] there were some fresh droppings. He went on and came to the heads of three other valleys with increasing freshness in the signs of buffalo. When he came to the head of the seventh valley, instead of seeing buffalo as he expected to do, he saw seven villages. He returned to the village and reported to the people what he had found. A council was held and the question discussed as to whether to go and make war upon the people of the seven villages. After much discussion the Hon'-ga U-ta-na-dsi were consulted. These people said: "We have told you that you would always by our council be successful in war. Go now and make war on these people." The Osage moved against the people of the seven villages and captured them all. They put to death the people of five of the villages and saved those of the other two. They bound the arms of the captives so they could not escape, and after further discussion the Osage determined to make servants of the captives. To make them contented with their situation they made them Osages by slitting the tips of their noses. In this way their own blood flowed out of them and Osage blood was infused into their bodies by feeding on Osage food. Then they were released from their bonds, but they did not run away. They became contented and became *sho'-ka*, or slaves, to the Osage.[54]

1.7 The Tattooing Custom (Charles Wah-hre-she)

When all of the Osages had united they were camped in a place that they thought was not suitable for the raising of their children, and so, after some counseling, they agreed to search for some land in which they could "grow" their little ones with more safety and comfort. After a search they found some land, well watered and timbered and pleasing to them. When they had moved to this new country of their choice and had settled down, they felt that the people could be the better governed if they had leaders, and so they chose two men to be their chiefs, one from the Tsi'-zhu Wa-shta'-ge [Gentle Sky] clan and the other from the Wa'-tse-tsi Wa-shta'-ge [Gentle Ponca] clan.[55] For a long time these two men counseled, one with the other, as to how they could best lead the people, but they were unable to come to any definite plan of action. They were sorely perplexed when suddenly both were struck with the thought of seeking supernatural guidance through the ancient rite of *non'-zhin-zhon* [rite of vigil]. And so it was that the two went, separately, far away from the village, where, undisturbed by any human influences and the petty thoughts of daily life, they could stand in wistful supplication before Wa-kon'-da, the All-knowing.

Sky Chief [56]

When the Tsi'-zhu Wa-shta'-ge man had come to a lonely place, he took a bit of the soil from the earth and moistening it with his saliva rubbed it upon his head, not only as a token of extreme humiliation and unworthiness but also as a [sign of] recognition of the earth as one of the dwelling places of Wa-kon'-da. For five days he cried to Wa-kon'-da without ceasing, without eating, drinking, or sleeping. On the evening of the sixth day, at the time of the day when faces become indistinguishable in the dark shadow, the supplicant fell to the ground, overcome with exhaustion and the desire for sleep. Then, when he was deep in this sleep of weariness, there came to him a strange man who spoke to him and said:

"Your cry has been heard, and your sufferings have become known, and I have come to give myself to you and to your people as a medicine that will give them long life and that will heal all their sickness. When, in the morning, you awake from this sleep, and the mists have cleared away, go to yonder river where it bends, where waters strike the earth, and there you will find me standing against the bank exposed to the air and the wind." When morning came, which was the seventh day of his *non'-zhin-zhon* [rite of vigil], and the mists had cleared away, the man arose and went to the river, and there he saw the man of his dream standing against the bank. He was *ni'-ka-shi-ga mon-kon*, the Man Medicine (*Cucurbita perennis* [plant]). As instructed in the dream, the man took the Man Medicine without breaking any part of him and carried him away. Further down the river he found the wife partly exposed and along the same bank. The man took both the male medicine and the female medicine home with him and the Osages have ever since used them for healing purposes. They made a *wa-xo'-be* [bundle] of the two first.

Earth Chief[57]

The Waʼ-tse-tsi Wa-shtaʼ-ge man, when he had come to a place of seclusion, also put moistened earth upon his head and cried to Wa-konʼ-da and fasted for five days. On the evening of the sixth day he fell asleep. In that sleep there came to him a strange man who spoke to him and said:

"I have heard your cry and know of your sufferings, and I have come to offer you help for your people. You see that I have reached the extremity of old age. My feet are wrinkled with old age, my legs are wrinkled with old age, my body is wrinkled with old age, my face is wrinkled with old age, and my head is whitened with age. If your people will carry me enfolded in their arms, in their life journey, their children shall live in the midst of the life-giving air without hindrance and become aged like me. Now, when the morning comes and the winds have blown away the mists, arise and go to yonder river, and in a bend where the waters, sheltered by a high bank against the violence of the winds, lie placid, you will find me. Take from my right wing seven feathers. Let your people in their life journey carry them enfolded in their arms and by them their lives shall be lengthened so that they will reach old age without hindrance."

When morning came, which was the seventh day of his vigil, and the breezes had carried away the mists, the man went to the river, and there in a bend, where the bank was high and the water was still, sat a pelican, bowed and enfeebled with old age. This the Waʼ-tse-tsi Wa-shtaʼ-ge man recognized as the man he saw in his dream of the night before. He caught the bird and plucked from its right wing seven feathers and started for his home thinking that nothing further would be revealed to him in answer to his supplication. He had not gone far when an eagle (honʼ-ga) came to him and gave him a downy feather that would be a help to his people in their life journey. Further on he came to a piece of black metal that offered its help to the people in their desire to secure long life.

When the Waʼ-tse-tsi Wa-shta-ge man got home he called together the people of all the clans and told them of the gifts he had received in answer to his supplications, and all were pleased and accepted them as sacred gifts. They made a wa-xoʼ-be and into it they put the seven feathers of the pelican, the downy feather of the eagle, and the piece of black metal to be kept as sacred treasures. They also put into the wa-xoʼ-be all their clan totems.

[This last part is rather confusing. Each clan symbolically placed their clan symbols into the wa-xoʼ-be by reciting their clan wiʼ-gi-e that named the symbols. This part is called the wa-theʼ-the, or ceremony of sending. All of the priests recite the wigi-e of their clans simultaneously. The following are short narratives of some, but not all, of the clan wiʼ-gi-e.[58]]

Wa-zha'-zhe[59]

First to place their totems in the *wa-xo'-be* were the Wa-zha'-zhe clan and sub-clans. In placing their sacred symbols in the *wa-xo'-be* each clan spoke as though in one person. "I am Ni'-ni-gka-shi-ga (a Water people)," said the Wa-zha'-zhe. "[?] of me your bodies, out of the life-giving water and the life-giving cedar [?] made my body." Speaking as the water, he said: "I am a person who knows no death. The little ones who, in their life journey, carry me enfolded in their arms shall be hardened against death." Speaking as the cedar, he said: "I am a person who knows no death. The children who, in their life journey, carry me enfolded in their arms shall be hardened against death. The white fish, the red fish, the blue fish, and the black fish I also carry, and the little ones who, in their life journey, carry these in their arms shall be hardened against death."

Elder Water Clan[60]

Speaking as the turtle, the *ke-k'in* said: "I also am a person. I am the turtle with the spotted breast. The spots on my breast are of the life-giving sun, the force of the day. I am hardened against death, and if the little ones, in their life journey, carry me enfolded in their arms they too shall be hardened against death."

White Water Clan[61]

"I also am a person," said the mussel, "hardened against death, and if the little ones, in their life journey, carry me enfolded in their arms they too shall be hardened against death. The hollows of my wings that are like the hollow of the sky are the shelter of my life. The little ones who, in their life journey, carry me enfolded in their arms shall be equally well protected by the sky. The sky is the cavity of my mouth (*i-u'-thu-ga*[62])."

Bow Clan[63]

"My name is E-non' min-dse-dton [Sole-owner-of-the-bow[64]]," said the Bow clan. "I am he who carries enfolded in his arms the bow and arrow by which these little ones shall procure food in their life journey. These also shall take part among those who offer their help to prolong the lives of these little ones."

Deer Clan[65]

The Dta' I-ni-gka-shi-ga, Deer clan, spoke and said: "I am the deer. Black is the color of my hoofs, my eyelids, and the tip of my nose. These I made charcoal of.

This color shall be a symbol of me, and the little ones who, in their life journey, carry me enfolded in their arms shall use charcoal to make this symbol when in their distress they appeal to me. My fleetness has enabled me to escape death. My life is prolonged by my fleetness. I escape the missiles that are hurled at me by those seeking to slay me. So shall these little ones escape death when they appeal to me."

Eagle Clan[66]

Hon'-ga, the mottled eagle spoke and said "I am *hon'-ga*. The color of my feet, my feathers and my beak is black (of this I make charcoal). This color shall represent me and the little ones who carry me enfolded in their arms, in their life journey, shall use charcoal to symbolize me. This shall be a protection to them and preserve their identity as a people."

Elk Clan[67]

"I am *o'-pxon*," said the Elk clan. "My name is Mon-zhon'-ga-xe (Earth Maker). The identity of these little ones as a people shall be preserved. I have a *ho'-e-ga* in which all living creatures are ensnared. This I give to the little ones. It shall be a help to them in their search for food. In warfare it shall be a help to them, and they shall live long. My buttock is the earth out of which all living things spring and in which they dwell. My tail is the forests in which abound all kinds of animals. My backbone is *the a'-thin*, the ridges among which dwell all kinds of animals. My body is the earth. In it dwell all kinds of animals. The hollow of my neck is the sides of the hills or the [?] valleys where all kinds of animals feed. The protuberances on the base of my horns are the rock that shelter all kinds of animals. My nose is the *bpa-he'*, the round hills among which all kinds of animals browse. My forehead is the *ho'-e-ga* that is a snare for all living things. It is the place that draws to it all living things. This the little ones shall use in their search for food. A handful of grass shall represent a handful of hair from my forehead. The little ones in searching for food shall take a handful of grass from the earth and raise it in the direction where they wish to hunt, and there they shall find game in abundance. It shall also be a help to them in warfare. All these shall be for the prolonging of the lives of the little ones."

This is what is symbolized by the straight lines tattooed on the arms of the women. The lines represent the animal paths, all leading to the *ho'-e-ga*, or the earth, that ensnares all living things and from which none can escape.

———

Gentle Sky Clan [?][68]

Tsi'-zhu then spoke as the red eagle and said: "My name is Hon'-ba Tha-gthin (Beautiful Day). My life is in the midst of the clear sky that is beautiful. My life is hardened against death, for I live in the midst of the life-giving sky. If these little ones carry me enfolded in their arms, in their life journey, they shall live long. They shall dwell in the midst of the life-giving sky, as I do, and their lives shall be hardened against death, and they shall live long."

Then speaking as *gkon-ha-u-thishte* (meaning unknown),[69] the Tsi'-zhu said: "My walk is in the midst of the life-giving perspiration (moisture) of the air and the earth. I move about in the midst of the *xtha-cka*,[70] the white blossoms of the spring. I move about in the midst of the *xtha-ci*,[71] the yellow blossoms of the autumn. I am deathless. The little ones who carry me enfolded in their arms in life's journey shall be hardened to death, and they shall live long. Their walk shall be in the midst of the life-giving moisture of the earth and of the sky. They shall move about in the midst of the white blossoms of the spring and the yellow blossoms of the autumn."

Speaking as the sun, the Tsi'-zhu said: "I am the force of day. There are seven *ga-gthe'-ce* (rays) on my left side. These shall be for the little ones, for the destruction of their enemies. Seven *o'-don* (honors) shall each one count to correspond to the number of these rays. And thus shall their lives be hardened against death and be prolonged. Six *ga-gthe'-ce* (rays) are on my right side. These shall be for the little ones, for the destruction of their enemies. Six *o'-don* shall each one count, equal in number to the rays on my right side. And thus shall their lives be hardened to resist death. If these little ones carry me enfolded in their arms, in their life journey, they shall live long, for of all the forces I alone am hard to die." Speaking as the star, he said: "I am Little Star, and if these little ones carry me enfolded in their arms, in their life journey, they shall live long." Speaking as the moon he said: "I am also the moon. If these little ones carry me enfolded in their arms, in their life journey they shall live long."

Night Clan[72]

Speaking as *hon*, or night, he said: "I also am *ni-ka-shi-ga* [a people[73]], I am night and darkness. I am also *wa-ca-be*, the black bear. If these little ones carry me in their life journey, they shall be hardened against death and they shall live long. The *wa-ca-be*, the black bear, the *in-gron-ga*, the puma, and the *mi'-xa*, the swan, are associated. With them are also four sacred woods: *zhon-sha-be*, dark wood or the Judas tree; *mon-ca-hi*, or dogwood or arrowwood; *thus-xe-ts'a-zhi*, or evergreen willow; and the *xon-dse*, the cedar. *Bpe-dse*, the fire, is also associated with all these."

Men of Mystery and Buffalo Bull Clan[74]

Last to come were the Ni'-ka-Wa-kon'-da-gi [Men of Mystery] and the Tho'-xe [Buffalo Bull]. Ni'-ka-Wa-kon'-da-gi said: "I have seven *wa-xo'-be*. These I offer to the little ones." The Tho'-xe said: "I have four varieties of corn, and four varieties of squashes. These I offer to the little ones." The *non'-hon-zhin-ga* rejected the *wa-xo'-be* but accepted the offer of the corn. They consecrated the corn and the squashes to the use of the little ones. The white ear of corn they entrusted to the keeping of the O'pxon, the Elk people [clan], the blue to the keeping of the Ni-ni'-ka-ski-ga, or Water people [Elder Water clan?], the red ear to the keeping of the Xu-tha Zhu-tse, or Red Eagle people [Gentle Sky clan], and the speckled ear to the keeping of the Gkon-ha-u-this-shti, or Flower people [unidentified clan]. The wish that goes with the corn, in its planting, for its growth and successful development is accompanied by the wish for the securing of game. One kind of animal is wished for each varied of corn planted.

When all the totems were thus consecrated to the new *wa-xo'-be* the people said: "There are four persons, four great forces, that surround us. Let us call them together so that the little ones in their life journey may appeal to them for aid for long life. First let *hon-ba*, the day, come to whom the little ones may look for long life. Next let *mon'-xe*, the sky, come so that the little ones may live in its midst and in its protective care. Next, younger brothers, let *mon-zhon'*, the earth, come so that the little ones may walk upon it and live upon it. It will yield to the little ones all nourishing foods by which they will be strengthened and their lives prolonged. Last of all, younger brothers, let our grandfather *mi*, the sun, come. He will look down upon the little ones which watchful care."

When the various clans put their totems in the tattooing *wa-xo'-be*, the Hon'-ga U-ta-non- dsi put its totem in, the *dtse-xo-be* (spider). A conventional design of the spider is tattooed on the hands of the women. This design is called *tse-xo-be wa-ga-xe*.[75] It is said to symbolize the Hon'-ga U-ta-non-dsi's house, which is the earth. When all the various clans of the Wa-zha'-zhe[76] came down from the sky they found Hon'-ga U-ta-non-dsi. The Hon'-ga U-ta-non-dsi people had no weapons, but they killed with the four winds, and the ground around their houses lay strewn with the bones of the animals they had killed.

In performing the ceremony of the tattooing only the story of the finding of the aged pelican is recited in ritual form. The story of the finding of the man and woman medicine is omitted, as to recite both stories would make the ceremony too long. The house of the Hon'-ga U-ta-non-a-dsi was called *tsi-pi-zhi*, bad house, also *tsi'-wa-kon'-da-gi*, mysterious house, because of its mysterious power of killing with the winds. The lines marked on the breasts of the men represent the seven and six rays of the sun. Every warrior is required to strive to win *o-don*, or war honors, equal to the number of the thirteen rays of the sun,

1.8 Haircut of the Gentle Sky Clan (Shun-kah-mo-lah)[77]

In the beginning the Tsi'-zhu people came down in the form of eagles, from the upper to the lower world. As they came in sight of the earth they beheld a large red oak tree. They soared down to it and alighted upon its topmost branches. The shock of their weight set to the ground a shower of acorns, which scattered around the foot of the tree, whereupon they said: "We shall make of this tree our life symbol; our little ones shall multiply in numbers like the seeds of the oak that fall to the earth in countless numbers." The eagles that crowded upon the top branches of the oak became a people whose thoughts dwelt upon war, but two of the eagles found no resting place on the outspreading branches of the great oak and were obliged to drop to the earth. One alighted on a larger elder tree, and his people became known as the Ba'-po, people of the elder tree. The other eagle alighted upon the ground in the midst of a patch of little yellow flowers, which his people made to be their life symbol and their emblem of peace. The people cut the hair of their children in such a fashion as to make their heads resemble the little yellow flower, the emblem of peace. This yellow flower is called ba- shta' (haircut).[78]

1.9 Finding of the Four Colors (Hlu-ah-wah-tah)[79]

And the people said to the *sho'-ka wa-ba-xi* (the leading *sho'-ka*),[80] "O, younger brother, it is not possible for the little ones to live upon the surface of the water. Go, therefore, and bring to us four bugs that dwell in the water that we may appeal to them for help." The *sho'-ka* went forth and returned to the people with the white leech. To this water bug the people spoke, saying: "O, grandfather, it is not possible for the little ones to dwell upon the surface of the water." Whereupon the leech sped forth, rippling the surface of the water by his swift movements. The leech could give no help to the people, but he said to them: "Behold the ripples upon the surface of the water. Make of me part of your bodies, then the little ones shall live to be old and have wrinkles like the ripples of the water."

Again the *sho'-ka* went forth and returned with the bug resembling a black bean (the whirligig). The black bug could not help the people but he promised to make the little ones live to be old and have wrinkles like the ripples on the surface of the water.

The *sho'-ka* went forth the third time and returned with the dark leech. The people appealed to him, but he could only promise to make the little ones to reach old age and to have wrinkles like the ripples on the surface of the waters.

For the fourth time the *sho'-ka* went forth and returned with the spiderlike bug (the water strider). The people appealed to him, but he could only promise to make the little ones live long, become old, and have wrinkles like the ripples upon the surface of the waters.

Then, in their distress, the people turned to the Hon'-ga *wa-non* (the elder Hon'-ga[81]) in silent appeal. The Hon'-ga *wa-non* spoke to the *sho'-ka wa-ba-xi*, saying: "Go again and make further search for help." At that very moment the people were startled by a voice that arose toward the rising sun. Again they heard the voice as though approaching. For the third time came [they heard] the call, yet nearer, and the people turned to the *sho'-ka* and with one voice said to him: "Lead us forth; we will send that person to the land of spirits, it matters not whose son he is." The voice called again, and a man stood before the people. They seized him to slay him, when the man spoke, saying: "Spare me, O, Tsi'-zhu, and I shall be to you a *hon'-ga* (a sacred person). When you go toward the setting sun against our enemies I shall give to you that which will bring you success, four different-colored clays with which to paint your faces." That person was Hon'-ga Zhin'-ga (Crawfish). The Tsi'-zhu set him free that he might live and be to them a Hon'-ga.[82]

Still the people were in distress, as it was not possible for the little ones to dwell on the surface of the water. So they said to the *sho'-ka wa-ba-xi*: "Go again and make search for help." The *sho'-ka* went forth, always willing to obey the demands of the people. In the midst of an arrow-wood thicket he came upon the great elk and, walking side by side with him, brought him to the people who, looking up to him, said: "O, grandfather, it is not possible for the little ones to dwell on the surface of the water!" The elk made reply: "It is well you have come to me. I shall help you. I am *o'-pon ton-ga* (the great elk)."[83] In a loud voice, the great elk called to the wind of the east, of the south, of the west, and of the north and then threw himself upon the water. As he arose, the waters had reached in depth to the middle of his sides. Again he threw himself upon the water, and it receded in depth to his belly. A third time he threw himself upon the water, and it receded in depth to his knee joints. The fourth time he threw himself upon the water, it receded until land appeared and there was no water left except in the depressions of the earth.

The people now set foot upon the land, but there were other things for the elk to do in behalf of the little ones. He shook his great body, and in response the black crawfish appeared from the soft earth and stood before the people, holding in his claws a bit of the dark soil of the earth; then the great elk said to the people: "Behold, the dark soil of the earth. When you go forth to fast you shall put this upon your faces and you shall shed tears while this sign is upon you. And while you fast you shall remain awake, else the length of your lives will be shortened." Again the great elk shook himself, and the red crawfish appeared before the people, holding in his claws a bit of red clay; then the elk spoke, saying: "Behold, the red clay of the earth. This also you shall put upon your faces, but when doing so you shall not shed tears, for it shall be a sign of your determination to overcome your enemies, who dwell toward the setting of the sun." The elk shook himself again, and the blue crawfish appeared from beneath the soil, having between his great claws a bit of blue clay. Then the elk spoke, saying: "Behold, the blue clay of the earth. This also you shall put upon your faces when you go forth to fast, and [you] shall shed tears when it is upon you, for it shall be a sign of your appeal for strength to overcome your enemies, who dwell toward the setting sun." Once more the elk shook himself, and from beneath the soil the yellow crawfish appeared, having between his great claws a bit of yellow clay. Then the great elk spoke to the people, saying: "O, Tsi'-zhu, you shall put this yellow clay upon your faces when you go against your enemies, who dwell toward the setting sun, and you shall not fail to overcome your enemies. Behold the right side of my body, O, Tsi'-zhu, it is the low-lying lands of the earth. Upon these lands you shall find the animals that will supply you with food. Behold my buttocks. They are the rolling hills of the earth, in the midst of which you shall find the animals that will serve you as food. Behold the base of my neck that represents the hilltops of the earth. Among the hilltops of the earth you shall find the animals that will serve you as food. Behold the curve of my neck that represents the gaps of the ridges of the earth. Among the gaps of the ridges you shall find the animals that will serve you as food. Behold the lower tines of my antlers. They represent the branches of the rivers. Along the branches of the rivers you shall find animals that will serve you as food. Behold the flat branches of my antlers. They represent the low-lying lands along the rivers. Within these lands you shall find the animals that will serve you as food. Behold the smaller branches of my antlers. They represent the small creeks of the earth. Among the creeks of the earth you shall find the animals that will serve you as food. Behold the hairs of my head. They represent the forests of the earth. In the forests you shall find the animals that will serve you as food. Then, O, Tsi'-zhu, there shall be days, peaceful and serene, wherein you shall find the animals that will serve you as food."

1.10 What to Dream Of (Saucy Calf)[84]

In the olden times, far beyond memory, it was the habit of the young men to walk through the village in groups of three or more, painted in gala style and dressed in all their finery. Each man carried upon his arm a *i'-tsin* (war club), which had no significance beyond that of a mere ornament designed to set off the fine clothes and accompanying decorations, for the thought of war was not in the minds of these young men.

One day, as the sun passed midheaven and was on its downward course, a man came out of his house and stood at the left of the door thoughtfully watching the groups of young men who strode through the village, conscious only of their pleasing appearance. Their stature, the manner in which they carried their war clubs, [and] the firmness of their footsteps all suggested strength. Their proud bearing stirred the admiration of the observing man, but the thought of the uselessness of it all came upon him as murmured to himself, "O'-ga-xe in-ge" ("There is in it no profit"[85]).

The sun went down, leaving the land in shadowy gloom, but the man stood, unmindful of the time, being held by the thought that in some way the latent strength of the "newly grown men" should be awakened and directed to a useful purpose. Suddenly a consciousness of the stillness of the village broke upon him, and he became aware that half of the night had already passed, and wondering if the thoughts that had so disturbed his mind might not themselves be idle, he turned to go into his house with the hope that sleep might drive them away. But, alas, stronger than ever they crowded upon him, so that instead of entering he dropped to the ground at the left of the door and sat leaning against the side of his dwelling, when at last sleep overcame him. When he awoke the sun was shining in his face, and he said to himself: "Day has come, and all the thoughts that took so strong hold on my mind have come to nothing, so I will think no more of them." He entered his dwelling and ate his morning meal in silence. Soon a feeling of unrest came upon him, and he went to the hills, where he wandered all the day long. The sun went down, and the shadow of night covered the land as the man approached his village. When he came to the little ridge formed by the ashes thrown along the outskirts he paused as though undecided about his movements. He dropped to the ground and lay reclining against the ridge all the night long in restless sleep. The chill of the morning awakened him; he sat up and saw the dawn rising. Reaching his hand to the ground, he took from it a bit of the soil, which he moistened and rubbed on his head and forehead as though in the act of mourning, for he was sore distressed in mind. Then he arose [and] left the village that he might go where he could be quite alone and cry to Wa-kon'-da for some sign as to the meaning of the thoughts that had taken possession of his mind in so mysterious a manner. For six days he wandered without eating or drinking, always crying to the mysterious and invisible known to him and to his people as "Wa-kon'-da." On the morning of the seventh day the man tottered to his feet, for his strength was nearly gone. He said to himself: "For six days I have kept and cried, and nothing has come of it. I will go to my home before I die, for I feel as though death is near."

He started for home, but he was obliged to stop frequently, for he was weak from hunger and thirst. He came to a brook and broke from a yellow willow tree a branch to use as a staff. All day he traveled, until the sun went down. As the gloom of dusk came he found himself where two foot-worn paths joined and became one, leading to the village. With a sigh of exhaustion he fell to the ground, saying: "Death must be near; I can go no farther. I will lie here. If in the night I die, my brothers will find me when the morrow comes."

It was not long before the man's eyes began to close with the sleep of exhaustion, [and then] he heard sounds like the voices of men speaking in low tones. Strengthened by the hope that his brothers had come to seek him, the man lifted his head and looked around but could see no one. Once more his eyes began to close, for his weary body craved rest; again he was aroused by the sound of rustling grass as though disturbed by approaching feet. He raised his head, believing that his brothers had indeed come in search of him, but the sound died away, and he could hear nothing save his labored breathing. When he was nearly unconscious he heard footsteps coming toward him, and he felt sure that his brothers had indeed come, but as he looked to see, the sound of the footsteps ceased. Again he lay down and was about to fall asleep, when he was aroused by the heavy thud of a foot close to him. He looked up as quickly as he could but saw nothing, nor could he hear any sound. Then he said to himself, "In some way I have displeased Wa-kon'-da, and in this way he is making me feel his anger. I will listen no more to these strange sounds."

The man covered his head with his robe, and as he was falling into a quiet sleep, his feet were suddenly kicked violently aside as by a heavy foot, and a strange voice spoke:

Stranger. "Arise! In your vigil and your cries you have fixed your thoughts longingly upon all the peoples of the earth.[86] Turn your face this way, and look upon me."

The man. "My grandfather, I turn my face, and I look upon you."

Stranger. "In what aspect do you see me?"

The man. "My grandfather, I see you standing before me having in your arms seven pipes, each one adorned with human hair."[87]

Stranger. "In your vigils and your cries you have fixed your thoughts longingly upon all the peoples of the earth. These pipes shall be yours. In your journey toward the setting of the sun you shall use these to make your enemies fall."[88]

(The man, in fear, turned his face away, and again the voice spoke.)

Stranger. "Turn your face this way, and look upon me."

The man. "My grandfather, I turn my face, and I look upon you."

Stranger. "In what aspect do you see me?"

The man. "I see you standing before me, and clasped firmly under your left arm I see a number of sacred birds, each of which is folded in mysterious wrappings."[89]

Stranger. "In your vigils and in your cries you have fixed your thoughts longingly upon all the peoples of the earth. These sacred birds shall be yours. In your journey toward the setting of the sun you shall use them to overcome your enemies."

(The man, in fear, turned his face away, and again the voice spoke.)

Stranger. "Turn your face this way, and look upon me."

The man. "My grandfather, I turn my face, and I look upon you."

Stranger. "In what aspect do you see me?"

The man. "My grandfather, I see you standing before me as though in the midst of the sky, your naked body, in every part, tinged with the crimson color of the dawn."

Stranger. "In your vigils and cries you have fixed your thoughts longingly upon all the peoples of the earth. The crimson color that you have seen upon my body shall be yours.[90] In your journey toward the setting of the sun you shall use it to make your enemies fall."

(The man turned his face away in fear, and again the voice spoke.)

Stranger. "Turn your face this way, and look upon me."

The man. "My grandfather, I turn my face, and I look upon you."

Stranger "In what aspect do you see me?"

The man. "My grandfather, I see you standing before me; clinging to your body are animals of all kinds, their faces turned toward me."

Stranger. "In your vigils and in your cries you have fixed your thoughts longingly upon all of the peoples of the earth. The animals you have seen shall be yours.[91] In your journey toward the setting of the sun you shall use them to make your enemies to fall. Turn your face this way, and look upon me."

The man. "My grandfather, I turn my face, I look upon you."

Stranger. "In what aspect do you see me?"

The man. "My grandfather, I see you standing before me as an aged man with wrinkled brow and bent shoulders; a white downy feather adorns your head, and pressed against your breast is a little pipe, from the stem of which smoke issues with a hissing sound."

Stranger. "In your vigils and your cries you have fixed your thoughts longingly upon all the peoples of the earth. The little pipe you have seen shall be yours. In your journey toward the setting of the sun you shall use it to make your enemies fall. You shall live to see your brows furrowed with wrinkles and your shoulders bent with age.[92] Turn your face this way, and look upon me."

The man. "My grandfather, I see you standing before me. At your side stands a little house [a sweat house]."

Stranger. "In your vigils and your cries you have fixed your thoughts longingly upon all the peoples of the earth. The little house you have seen shall be yours.[93] In your journey toward the setting of the sun you shall use it to make your enemies fall. Turn you face this way and look upon me."

The man. "My grandfather, I turn my face and look upon you."

Stranger. "In what aspect do you me?"

The man. "My grandfather, I see you standing before me, and firmly grasped in your right hand I see a war club."

Stranger. "In your vigils and in your cries you have set your thoughts longingly upon the peoples of the earth. The war club you have seen shall be yours.[94] In your journey toward the setting of the sun you shall use it to make your enemies fall."

The man. "My grandfather, I look upon you."

Stranger. "In what aspect do you see me?"

The man. "My grandfather, I see you standing before me. In your right hand is firmly grasped a *wa-xthe'-xthe* [a war standard]."

Stranger. "In your vigils and in your cries you have fixed your thoughts longingly upon all the peoples of the earth. The standard you see shall be yours.[95] In your journey toward the setting of the sun you shall use it to make your enemies fall."

1.11 Instructions to the Mother (Charles Wah-hre-she)[96]

[As part of the child-naming rite, the priest in charge of the rite gives the following special instructions to the new mother. The mother brought with her into the ceremony a new robe that would be used for the baby.]

Wi-tsi-ni-e, my daughter-in-law, I see you have brought with a you a robe that you have dressed and decorated for the comfort of your little one. It is a sacred robe that should be put to use with proper ceremony. This ceremony you will observe for a period of four days, during which you will paint red the parting of your hair. It will be a sign that you appeal for a long and fruitful life for yourself and child to the force of day whose path lies over the middle of the earth.

You have reddened the head and the forelegs of the robe, which typify that part of the earth whence rises the force of day [the sun] to take his westward journey. Red is the color of the day when it is young, the time when you will rise and go forth to prepare food for the little one whose tender life is wholly dependent upon your efforts. A narrow line runs from the head of the robe along the middle of the back to the tail. This line typifies the path of the force of day who ever travels from east to west. Midway of the path is a round spot, which represents the force of day when it has reached the middle of heaven. Here he marks the time when you will turn your thoughts from other things to the feeding of the little one so that the nourishing of its life may be continuous. The force of day continues his journey and in time reaches the edge of the earth, behind which he finally disappears. The hind legs and the tail of the robe are reddened to typify the glow that warns us of the ending of the day when your thoughts will again turn to the care of the little one. When you put these symbolic marks upon this sacred robe your thoughts reach out in appeal to Wa-kon'-da for yourself and child.

As the shadow of night spreads over the land you will take your little one in your arms, draw this robe over you, then rest in sleep. The robe that you draw over yourself and child typifies the heaven, whence comes all life, and the act is an appeal to heaven for protection.

The procuring of food for the little one should always be done with a feeling of gratitude toward the mysterious power that brings forth life in all forms. There is a plant that is dedicated to use as a sacred food in the bringing up of the little ones, known as *tse'-wa-the (Nelumbo lutea)*.[97] You will at times go to the lake to gather the roots of this plant for use in feeding your little one. When about to go to the lake you will paint red the parting of your hair, as a sign of your gratitude to the power of day who passes over your head and over the plant you go to seek, shedding his life-giving power upon you as he goes upon his journey.

When you come to the edge of the lake you will look about for a staff to support you as you work in the water. You will choose the willow for your staff, for it is a tree that clings persistently to life. By this act you will make an appeal to the great life-giving power for a long and fruitful life for yourself and the little one. With the willow staff in your hands you will step into the water and take up from the soft earth beneath a root of the sacred plant, the *tse'-wa-the*. You will find clinging to the root some of the soft earth from which the plant draws nourishment and strength. Take this bit of soil and touch your forehead and body with it, an act that will be as a sign that you appeal to the earth wherein there is life-giving power. When you have performed this act return the root to the earth beneath the water with the wish that the plant shall forever be plentiful. Then gather enough of the roots to satisfy the little one and yourself.

The maize is another sacred life-giving plant. You raise this plant from year to year. When you prepare the ground for planting the seed you will take one grain and put it in a hill, [and] you will press down upon the soil with your foot and say: "My father-in-law bade me do this, as an expression of my faith that the sky and the earth will yield to me not only one ear of maize but one animal as well, or even one herd of animals." In the next hill you will put two grains, in the next three, the next four, the next five, the next six, and in the seventh seven, always repeating the words at each planting.

1.12 Instructions to the Wife of a Priest (Saucy Calf)[98]

[During a break in the initiation ceremony for a new clan priest, the wife of the initiate was brought in, and the presiding priest gave her the following instructions as to her new role as a priest's wife.]

My granddaughter, the *wa-xo'-be* [bundle] is now yours, to take care of until there comes a time when it will be passed on to someone else. There may come a time when a warrior will wish to use this particular *wa-xo'-be* in a war expedition. If ever that happens, the warrior will come to your house in an appeal to you, not only for its use but also for your good wishes for success during the time that he is gone on the expedition. When you hear that a warrior is about to come to you, then you shall prepare yourself to receive him ceremonially. Should you happen to have a robe of black[-bear] bearskin you will be fortunate, for the black bear is a symbol of strength and courage. This robe you will spread upon the ground at your accustomed place in the house, [making it] ready for you to sit upon while you wait for the coming of the warrior. Dress yourself in any garment that you think will be most becoming to you, but do not fail to remember to paint the parting of your hair red. The red line symbolizes the path of the force of day and also represents the path of life. When you have put upon your head this symbol, then you will take your seat upon the bearskin robe and put this *wa-xo'-be* in your lap. Upon the departure of the warrior from the house with the *wa-xo'-be*, you will remove the symbol from your head and say while doing so: "My grandfather bade me to say, when I do this act, I remove this symbol from my head and wipe my hands upon the bodies of the enemy."

In time, you will hear that the warrior has started on his journey. Then you are to remember him. On the following morning, as the sun begins to rise, paint the parting of your head red, put a narrow blue line upright on your right cheek, one horizontally on your forehead, and one on your left cheek like that on the right. This is the symbolic painting by which you send to the warrior sympathy and courage and your wish for his success. You must remove these symbols from your head and face before the sun reaches the zenith and, while you do so, say: "My grandfather bade me to say, when I do this, I remove these symbols from my head and face and wipe my hands upon the body of the chief of the enemy." On the next day, as the sun rises, you will again paint yourself in the same manner, but add a red line to each of the blue ones on your face. Before the sun reaches the zenith you must remove the symbols, and as you do so repeat the words I have just given you. On the third morning you will repeat this ceremony, this time adding a blue line to the red and blue lines and later remove them as you did the others. On the fourth morning you must perform the same ceremony, adding to the three lines on your face a red line and later remove them in the same manner as before.

Before the sun rises on the fifth morning you must arise and go out of your house and take from the earth a bit of soil and put it on your head. This is the rite of vigil and the sending of courage. You must give all your thoughts to the warrior who has gone against the enemy carrying your *wa-xo'-be*. In this way you will give him aid. When the shadow of evening comes, making indistinguishable the faces of men, then remove from your head the soil of the earth. In doing so remember to repeat these words: "My grandfather bade me to say, when doing this, I remove from my head the soil of the earth and wipe my hands upon the body of the chief of our enemies that he may come to his death at the hands of our warriors." You will repeat this rite for a period of four days, when your duty to your *wa-xo'-be* and to the warrior will be fulfilled.[99]

1.13 Instructions in the Painting of the Sacred Robes (Hlu-ah-wah-tah)[100]

[The wife of the candidate together with other female relatives and friends are brought into the ceremony. Each woman has her fees in a bundle, and each is handed a digging stick and a woven bag, symbolic of her work.]

Ho! My daughter-in-law, I shall now tell you of the rite of *ki'-non* [ritual of painting]. The first part of the *ki'-non* rite, which you may wish to observe in order to successfully bring up your little ones to maturity, is this: if it so happens that the animal brought to your house is a result of the first chase, and the animal is a mature female buffalo and you think the skin suitable for a covering for your little ones, you shall dress the skin, making it pleasing to look upon and soft and pleasant to the touch. You shall then say: my father-in-law has sanctioned the act I am about to perform and has said that it shall not be without a purpose. You shall take red clay that has been gathered from a cliff and with it redden the sides and the legs parts of the robe, as also the full length of the back from the head to the tail. Again you shall say: my father-in-law has sanctioned this act and has said that it shall not be without a purpose, for in thus consecrating this robe I shall successfully bring to maturity my little ones for whom it is made.

The next act in order is: that if the animal brought home to your house happens to be a mature male buffalo you shall dress the skin, making it pleasing to look upon and soft and pleasant to touch. You shall say: my father-in-law has sanctioned the act I am about to perform and has said that it shall not be without a purpose. You shall then redden the sides of the robe, as also the full length of the back, and shall say: this act it not without a purpose, for it is sanctioned. My father-in-law has said that by performing this act I shall successfully bring my little ones to maturity. This act shall not be without a purpose, for it is sanctioned. My father-in-law has said that by thus consecrating this robe I shall make my little one difficult to be overcome by death.

The next act in order is: that if the animal brought home to your house happens to be an immature female buffalo and you think the skin suitable for a covering for your little ones, then you shall dress the skin, make it pleasing to look upon, making it soft and pleasant to the touch. You shall redden only the leg parts of the robe. Then you shall say: my father-in-law has sanctioned this act and has said that it shall not be without a purpose, that by thus consecrating this little robe I shall successfully bring to maturity my little ones, that by this act I shall make my little ones difficult to be overcome by death.

The fourth act is: that if the animal brought home to your house happens to be an immature male buffalo, you shall take particular pains in dressing the skin, make it pleasing to look upon and soft and pleasant to the touch; then you shall redden the leg parts and the entire length of the back. When you have finished this, you shall say: my father-in-law has sanctioned this act and has said that it shall not be without a purpose, that by thus consecrating this robe I shall successfully bring to maturity my little ones, and I shall by this act make my little ones difficult to be overcome by death.

Hau! This is all.

1.14 Counting the *O'don* (Shun-kah-mo-lah)[101]

[In certain rituals a man who has won all thirteen different *o'don*, or war honors, is asked to act as a *wa'-don-be*. At the appropriate point in the ritual the man takes his place standing in the middle of the house of mystery. He has with him a bundle of seven willow sticks and a bundle of six willow sticks. He first takes the bundle of seven, symbolizing the Hon-ga (Earth) division. Taking one stick at a time he recites his *o'don* and drops the stick on the ground, although he says that he places it on the *wa-xo'-be*. He then takes the bundle of six sticks, symbolic of the Tsi'-zhu (Sky) division, and does the same.]

I rise to count my *o'don*. It is at your request, O, Water people, Land people, and Man of Mystery, that I rise to recount my *o'don*. You well know that the *o'don* that have been awarded me are not altogether clear of doubt (a conventional plea of modesty), but it is your wish that I recount them on this occasion, and I cannot but give consent to your request.

The Seven *O'don*

(1) This (willow sapling) represents the *o'don* known as "striking the enemy within the camp limits." A Pawnee warrior was slain within the camp limits on Salt Creek. Do-don'-i-non-hin [a personal name] was the first to strike the warrior, and being next to him in the attack, I gave the enemy the second stroke, which entitles me to a like *o'don*. O, thou *wa-xo'-be* that lies before me, I place this upon thee.

(2) This (willow sapling) represents the *o'don* called "*wa'-thu-xpe*" (meaning is uncertain).[102] I won it in a fight by a great war party, composed of both the great divisions of the tribe. The sacred charcoal was still upon my body and face when I performed this act, and there exists no doubt of my title to count this *o'don*. O, thou *wa-xo'-be* that lies before me, I place this upon thee.

(3) This (willow sapling) represents the *o'don* known as "triumph of a *do-don'-honga* of a great war party." Ni'-ka-ga-xthi [a personal name] came to me in his bereavement and, weeping, asked me to go forth to slay an enemy because of his loss. I went forth and came back in triumph. O, thou *wa-xo'-be* that lies before me, I place this upon thee.

(4) This (willow sapling) represents the *o'don* called "victory." I won the *o'don* when, as the officer carrying one of the standards of a war party, I struck an enemy. O, thou *wa-xo'-be* that lies before me, I place this upon thee.

(5) This (willow sapling) represents the *o'don* called "striking of an enemy in an attack by a great war party." I won this *o'don* when, under the leadership of Mi-ka'-zhin-ga [a personal name], a war party attacked and slew a number of the enemy. O, thou *wa-xo'-be* that lies before me, I place this upon thee.

(6) This (willow sapling) represents the *o'don* called "the killing of an enemy in the open country." I won this *o'don* by striking a single enemy attacked at break of day by a war party of which I was a member. O, thou *wa-xo'-be* that lies before me, I place this upon thee.

(7) This (willow sapling) represents the *o'don* called "taking a head in an attack by a war party composed of warriors of only one of the great divisions." I won this in an attack made by a war party led by Wa-kon'-da-u-ki-e [a personal name]. O, thou *wa-xo'-be* that lies before me, I place this upon thee.

The Six *O'don*

This (willow sapling) represents the *o'don* awarded to a member of a clan war party. I won this *o'don* in an attack made upon the enemy by a war party led by Ku'zhi-wa-tse [a personal name]. O, thou *wa-xo'-be* that lies before me, I place this upon thee.

(2) This (willow sapling) represents the *o'don* awarded to a successful leader of a war party carrying only one *wa-xo'-be*. I won this *o'don* as leader of a war party carrying a single *wa-xo'-be*. O, thou *wa-xo'-be* that lies before me, I place this upon thee.

(3) This (willow sapling) represents the *o'don* called "striking of an enemy in an attack of a war party carrying only one *wa-xo'-be*." I won this *o'don* in an attack made by a war party led by Gthe-mon'-zhin-ga [a personal name]. O, thou *wa-xo'-be* that lies before me, I place this upon thee.

(4) This (willow sapling) represents the *o'don* called "the hitting of an enemy in an attack in the open country." I won this *o'don* in an attack made by a war party led by Tse-do'-a-mo-in [a personal name]. O, thou *wa-xo'-be* that lies before me, I place this upon thee.

(5) This (willow sapling) represents the *o'don* awarded to the successful *do-don'-hon'-ga* of a war party of only one of the two great divisions. I won the *o'don* as the successful *don-don'-hon'-ga* of a war party. O, thou *wa-xo'-be* that lies before me, I place this upon thee.

(6) This (willow sapling) represents the *o'don* called "taking the head of an enemy in an attack made by a war party carrying only one *wa-xo'-be*." I won this *o'don* in an attack made by a war party carrying but one *wa-xo'-be*. O, thou *wa-xo'-be* that lies before me, I place this upon thee.

Part Two

Folk Stories

2.1 Tradition of the Omaha Departure from the Osage (Pah-nee-wah-with-tah)[1]

The Osage say of the Omaha "They went away in an angry mood and never returned because they were slighted in the distribution of sinew."

When the Osage people moved westward from the eastern country, they came to the Mississippi river. The country was new to them, and those of the people who were adventurous went long distances to see what they could find of game. Two men who were leaders of several bands went and were gone for some time. It seems that the two leaders in their expedition found a great forest where the signs of bear and deer were plentiful, and both agreed to bring their followers to this forest to hunt for a time without the knowledge of the tribe, which they did.[2] After they returned, they secretly went away [again] with their following and were gone a long time. After a number of days they returned with a large quantity of bear and deer meat and hides. This was against the long-established rules of hunting, so when finally the secret hunting by these two men and their followers became generally known in the tribe, the people were greatly displeased but made no open protest.

Now in those days the hunting season for the bear and the deer was opened with an elaborate ceremony called *ta-a-ki-tia-ci* ("chasing the deer upon [?]").[3] Even when the tribe happened to be separated into two or three groups, each group would observe the ceremonial opening of the hunting season. This ceremony was adopted for the purpose of giving to the hunters of the tribe an equal chance of securing game. To the ceremony all the *non'-hon-zhin-ga* [clan priests] were invited.

When all the *non'-hon-zhin-ga* had assembled, a bundle of arrow shafts, together with feathers, arrowheads, and sinew, was placed before the Deer clan [priest], and at the proper time he sent to the representative of each clan a shaft with feathers, an arrowhead, and sinew. This served as a notice that the season was opened and that on the following day every hunter was at liberty to go and hunt.

Now, when the deer hunting season came around following the misconduct of the two leaders, the *non'-hon-zhin-ga* were assembled—all were invited, the two guilty leaders included—and when each man had taken his accustomed place the ceremonial arrow shafts were laid before the leader of the Deer clan. The unwonted silence and solemnity of the *non'-hon-zhi-ga* and the gravity with which the leader of the Deer clan[4] conducted the distribution of the arrow shafts on this particular occasion foreboded an evening of an unusual and serious character. Usually the master of ceremony sent [off] each arrow shaft with some pleasant and encouraging remark, but at this time he silently handed each shaft to the *sho'-ka* and indicated with his hand where he should take it. The leader of the Deer clan withheld the shafts that should have been sent to the two leaders who violated the hunting rule. When the *sho'-ka* took his seat, which was an indication that he had fulfilled his duty, the two men looked questioningly at the master of ceremony and then at the *non'-hon-zhin-ga*, but no responding glance came from either.

None of the members offered an explanation; nor was any asked for by the two men. The act amounted to an expulsion from the tribe and a denial of the privileges granted to every member. After a moment silence the two men arose and looking neither to the right nor to the left went out of the house, and not long after that they and their followers went away and were never heard of again.

In recent years when the Osage became acquainted with the Omaha and the Ponca, they came to the belief that the people of these tribes were the descendants of those who went away in an angry mood because, in the distribution of sinew, they were slighted.[5]

At about the same time that the Omaha and Ponca left the Osage, another group of clans went away and never were heard of or seen again, but these went away with the consent of the tribe. It seems that their leaders explored the new country and found, far down the great river, a land in which persimmons, paw-paw, and other fruits grew in abundance. In asking permission of the tribe to absent themselves for a time they gave as their reason their desire to cure the persimmons in a sufficient quantity to last till the next season, as it was the custom to do. In this way another group left, never to return.

Once in a while a story would arise and spread among our people that some white man had seen this group far down the big river, but we have not yet learned it to be true.[6]

2.2 Making the Buffalo Come (Charles Wah-hre-she)[7]

Many years ago there came a famine among the Osages. The corn, beans, and squashes were eaten up, and the crops failed. The buffalo disappeared from hunting grounds. Food could not be found anywhere. It was known that a certain young man had supernatural powers. The people, in their distress, thought to appeal to him through the children that had been made *o'-xta*[8] [favored], and so one morning they called together all the children of that [status]. When it was explained to the children what was wanted of them, and they understood, they chose a girl as messenger to approach the young man, for one possessing extraordinary powers and [who] is a *wa-kon'-da-gi*[9] must be approached in a ceremonial manner. A little pipe was filled with tobacco and put into the hands of the girl. She came to the wigwam of the young man, and entering the door she stood before him, offering him the pipe. She told him that all of the *zhin-ga' o'-xta* [little favored ones] in their distress from the lack of food had sent her to appeal to him to make the buffalo come. "Are you sure that all the children sent you with this message? Is there no one who held back and will not appeal to me?" the young man asked. "All with one voice appeal to you," the girl replied. "Then," said the young man, "I shall try."

The young man went away and was gone for seven days. In all this time he went through the rite of *non'-zhin-zhon* [vigil] and in some mysterious manner found himself in the spirit land of the buffalo. In appeal to the buffalo spirits he said, "My people are in sore distress for want of food, and they sent me to appeal to you for succor." "Are you sure that all the people sent you?" asked the buffalo spirits. "All sent me," the young man replied. "We will give relief to your people," the buffalo spirits said, "but in the chase we ask that they refrain from shooting seven buffalo. These we will mark on the forehead with the downy feather of the eagle so that they may be sure not to kill the ones thus marked." With this message the young man hurried back to his people. He begged them to have pity on him and to be very careful to keep from killing any of the seven buffalo that were marked with the white feather. Then he told them to move to a large hill, which he pointed out. "This side of that larger hill you will find enough buffalo to keep you," he said to them. "Chase only the herds this side of the hill and do not go beyond."

The people moved, and then on this side of the hill they saw buffalo on the prairies as far as their eyes could see. There was much rejoicing, and the people hurriedly prepared for the chase. They killed a large number of buffalo. When the hunters entered the camp on their return, the hides were examined, and it was found that none of the marked buffalo had been killed. But at the next chase it was found that one had been killed, and the young man came to the people who had gathered about the sacred buffalo, and he told them he would never again consent to go to the buffalo spirits if the people were ever again in sore distress as they had been. He said that he had [given?] to them, that he had the power to make the buffalo come, and he had hoped that the people would carry out his wishes, but they had failed to do so. He further said to them, "Had you fulfilled all you promised to do and all your obligations I would have always been ready to help you when in distress, but now by your own act you have made it impossible for me to do anything for you. Hereafter you will never find the herds as plentiful as you have found them. They will gradually disappear and never come back to you. They will finally be gone."

2.3 Deer-Hunting Stories[10]

Some Osages were sitting together on an evening telling improbable stories of deer hunting and remarkable shots. One said; "As I was hunting in the woods I scared up a buck but could not get good aim at it because of the brush through which it ran. It came to an open space just over the brow of a low hill. I fired, but [it] was too late. However, the ball struck the limb of a tree on the same hill and glanced downward striking the deer in the spine and killing it. I did not know this till I came to it while moving in the direction it took." Another one said: "I was hunting in an open prairie, and I startled a deer out of the tall grass. I took aim and fired. The ball struck the deer in the back of the head going through and killing another deer ahead that arose out of the grass. I killed two deer with one ball." Others made up stories of like character over which there was much mirth. One who had been silently enjoying the stories spoke up at last and said: "I have enjoyed your stories, and I believe them because the one which I am about to tell you is as true as any we have listened to.

"My uncle had killed three deer, and, as he had been hunting on foot, he came home for horses to bring in the deer that he had killed. I was the only boy and did all the errands such as bringing in the horses, watering them, and driving them to the pastures. And so when my uncle came in all out of breath, he hurried me, and I started on a run for the horses. I ran along a ridge that had a slight embankment over[laden] with heavy grass. On coming to this ridge I saw five deer coming directly toward this ridge. I knew that they would run right along the ridge as I was doing, and, as I desired to have the fun of frightening them, I hid under this embankment, peering through the tall grass along the edge. They came so close to me that I could almost reach out and touch the one nearest me, and then I sprang up with a yell. But instead of leaping away in fright and scattering in every direction as I expected they would, every one of them dropped dead, and so we had eight deer instead of three."

2.4 The Vision of a War Leader
(Charles Wah-hre-she)[11]

A story often told, even to this day, narrates the experience of a man who had been chosen to be leader of a war party and who, during his fasting [rite of vigil], witnessed a night scene that he regarded to be a response to his supplications. . . .

During the first night of the period of fasting, which is always spoken of as the time when the supreme test of courage comes to the faster, the man heard cries of strange animals in a fierce combat and was shaken by the thud of their feet as they struggled in the darkness. Sometimes, in their conflict, they came close to where he sat holding the stem of his little pipe pointed upward as an offering, but with a stout heart he maintained his position, until he heard the sounds of their cries and the snapping of the twigs finally die away in the distance. He had scarcely recovered his composure when he heard the whistle of a man, the response by another, their footsteps as they approached each other, and their voices when they met and spoke in low tones. He heard them coming toward him and passing by him, speaking to each other now in loud whispers and again in muffled tones. They continued to act in this manner through the night up to the break of the day, when they ceased to trouble the faster. The man, as he determined to do at the start, [had] gathered together his courage and kept his place unmoved throughout the night. When the sky in the east was reddening, he took a bit of soil of the earth, put it upon his brow, and started to wander about and to wail.

After the first night the man was not disturbed again by animals or spirits. But on the sixth night of his fasting, as he settled down for his rest at the foot of a tree, his back leaning against the trunk, his feet put together and planted upon the ground, while he still held his little pipe, something swept across his face so swiftly that he felt the air disturbed by the force. He began to wonder what it might be, when it swept across his face again, going in the opposite direction. Believing that the thing, whatever it was, would return, he lowered his head so that if it should pass again he could make out what it was by the aid of the dim light of the skyline. The thing or things did return, and with his experienced eyes he recognized the forms of two birds. They sped swiftly by, one chasing the other. At times the pursuit was so close that the two birds appeared as one. As the birds passed he noticed that the large one was in flight and the smaller one hotly pursuing. Again they passed, but this time the smaller bird was in flight. He heard their cries in the distance, as one overtook the other and they fought. He recognized one as the cry of an owl, the other as that of a hawk. It was not long before the birds returned and sped by the sitting man. The whole night long the two birds fought and alternately put the other to flight, while the man marveled at the strength of their wings, for they did not at any time stop to rest.

As the morning star appeared in the east, the faster heard again the sound of the approaching combatants, like the blowing of the wind through the forest. They came near, then with marvelous quickness the hawk darted under the man's bent knee, while the owl sped on, clattering his mandibles in rage. The hawk spoke to the man and said: "Protect me against my enemy; it need be for a little time only, until the break of day. The darkness of the night puts me at a disadvantage, for my strength is in the broad light of the day. Give me protection till the pale light of dawn appears in yonder sky, then in your sight I shall vanquish my enemy, and I will reward you by giving you that dauntless courage with which I attack my foes."

The owl returned, alighted upon the ground near the man, and demanded in an angry tone, "Give over to me that person that I may put him to death. I also can give reward. I attack my foes in the darkness of night in their sleep and vanquish them. You shall have the same power that I have to see in the night. This I offer to you as a reward. Push over to me that person."

The man moved not, for the power to attack a foe when he was deep in slumber did not appeal to him as the right sort of courage and made the man's sympathy incline toward the hawk, but he spoke not, and neither did he move.

Soon a pale streak of light appeared along the eastern horizon, [and] then the hawk spoke to the man saying: "You have rendered me a service. Now, as a reward, take from my left (the man was a Tsi'-zhu) wing the shortest feather there, and when you are about to attack your foe attach it to your left shoulder, so you will do to him what I am about to do to yonder person. I go to attack."

The hawk, without effort, rose in the air, and when he had reached a certain height, he paused. At that moment the courage of the owl seemed to depart from him, and with much flapping of his wings he took to flight. Like an arrow released from a strong bow, the hawk shot downward in attack and struck the fleeing owl in the head, severing it from the body. With an exultant cry the hawk soared around a few times in the light of the rising sun, alighted on a tree nearby, and spoke to the man: "Fail not to remember me when you attack the foe."

The faster arose to go to his home, murmuring to himself, "Thus the power of day overcomes the power of night." It was on the seventh day of his fast when Wa-kon'-da, stirred to pity by the sufferings of the man, had offered him the choice of vanquishing his enemies in night attacks or in attacks made in the broad light of day, and he had chosen the latter, as that, to him, required true courage.

The man was successful, not only as leader in this expedition for which he had been chosen but in all the subsequent expeditions of which he was leader, for whenever he was chosen as leader the young men needed no urging to join his war party.

2.5 Death of an Old Warrior[12]

A long time ago a young man married two sisters.[13] They were the daughters of an old man who by his valorous deeds had won for himself a prominent place in the tribe [in] his younger days. The young man was a good hunter and kept his family well supplied with meat and skins. When the season came around for hunting the black bear,[14] the young man and his two wives prepared to go to a country where they knew bears were plentiful.

While the preparations for the journey were going on, the old warrior told his daughters and his son-in-law that he wanted to go with them so that he could once more enjoy the taste of black bear's fat before he took his journey to the spirit land. "We are always glad to have you with us" the three said, almost in one voice, and so the old man eagerly gathered his little belongings together and got himself in readiness for the long travel.

The time came to move, and the young hunter, with his two wives and his father-in-law, started for the bear country, which was far away from their home. All four walked because the few horses they had were burdened with the provisions and camping outfit.

One morning after the party had been gone two or three days, the young man and his wives quarreled over some trivial matter, and, coming to blows, they acted in a very disgraceful manner that greatly displeased and mortified the old warrior. For a long time the old man sat in silence, and then he spoke to the three saying: "I was happy in the prospect of feasting once more on bear's fat before I died, but now you have, by your outrageous conduct, made me very unhappy. And now, since I can never get over this, I must take myself home and let you go on your way with your shameful behavior." Then all three joined in an earnest protest against the old man's leaving, declaring that the quarrel was over and would not be repeated. "You are too feeble, you will never reach home," they said, but the old man would not listen to their entreaties and went on tying his clothing in a bundle convenient to carry.

It happened that while the four were talking a brother of the two women came with his family to join them, and an explanation was made to him by his sisters of the trouble, and he also tried to persuade his father not to leave, saying, "You know, Father, this kind of thing is apt to take place at any time, in any family, and now that the trouble is over there is no reason why you should not go on with us and have a good time once more." "This kind of thing has never happened in my family, and I never approve of such conduct," the old man replied, and he arose to go.

Seeing that nothing could persuade the old man to remain, the son spoke to his wife and said, "You go on with your sisters-in-law, and I will take Father home. As soon as I get him back to the village I will return and overtake you." He then followed the old man.

A month had passed when the young hunter with his family and that of his brother-in-law returned to the village with plenty of bear meat and skins. They were gladly received by their relations, and greetings were exchanged with inquiries [made] after friends and kindred who were not present. Suddenly a little child, a granddaughter of the old warrior, said. "I want to see my father and my grandfather." The people fell to silence and looked inquiringly at one another. Then, almost in a whisper, the two sisters and the sister-in-law said, "They never came home?"

A searching party made up of most of the young men and warriors of the village went out, following the outgoing trail of the hunter. They came to a hill, the top of which arose higher than any of those around. Close to the edge of a wooded ravine, at the base of the hill, they came upon the body of a man; it was that of the son of the aged warrior. His breast was pierced with many arrows. Tightly grasped in his right hand was a broken lance, which he had wrenched from the hands of one of his assailants.

From the hoofprints of the horses where they had charged again and again, the warriors saw that the young man had fought his way, step by step toward the ravine. Arrows lay scattered upon the ground where the struggle had been the fiercest. Midway up the hill lay a bloody shield, which told that the young warrior gave as well as received wounds as he fought. The hoofprints of the charging horses led to the very top of the hill. There lay the body of another man; it was that of the aged warrior. His breast was pierced with many arrows, and the ground around was torn with the hoofs of horse, showing that the struggle there had been the greatest. The young warrior had fought there until his father fell, and he had shot away all his arrows in defense of the old man.

While the warriors stood around in silence, picturing in their minds the struggle that had taken place there, an old man stepped toward the body and spoke, saying, "Here is a wish fulfilled. How often this man has said to me, I wish no other death than that of a warrior. Like a true warrior he has died bravely. I shall sing of his name so that the warriors now living and those yet to come will hear of him and his son."

2.6 Origin of the Hair Bundle (Me-ke-wah-ti-an-kah)[15]

The Osage tribe lived along the Missouri river[16] and had planned on a buffalo hunt; among them were two young men who decided not to go, [saying they] would rather remain at home and care for their aged parents. However, after the tribe had gone the two young men moved their camp, going a long distance away, where they found game plentiful. At this place they built a wigwam, making their parents comfortable, keeping the home well supplied with food, [they] both being skilled in hunting. These young men belonged to the Mi-k'in' clan.[17]

One day the younger of the two spoke to the father, saying: "I think I can find a stray buffalo, so I am going out on my horse; if I do not come home for some time don't feel uneasy, because I will be safe." Riding away he saw a stray buffalo and after chasing it killed it. While in the act of butchering it he was attacked by a war party and taken captive. The horse of the young captive broke the lariat and went back to camp. For many days the war party traveled westward until they reached the camp of their own village. Here the young man, who had been made captive, was bound hands and feet to prevent his escape.

In the home of the war leader, the mother, who had a long scar across her face, would touch the captive with the hot meat she had cooked. This she did at each meal; she also permitted all her people to [do this] with the young man and [to] treat him cruelly in many ways.

As this young captive stood bound to a post some crows flew about him in the air. One stopped near him and said to him, "Keep up your courage; you shall yet live and see your parents." During the afternoon a great storm arose, driving all the people into their houses [and] continuing for two days; the people were obliged to remain in their homes. From being tied up the young man became very stiff, but in stretching himself, he found the thongs with which he was bound yielded to the pressure and without much effort slipped from his hand and ankles. It was his chance for escape, so he hurried to a corn field, where he found the ripening corn and was very glad for he was quite hungry from such abuse. Plucking some of the ears, he hid himself but not for long, for he heard the warriors making search for him. Waiting until the warriors had passed over the hills, the captive, knowing the customs of his own people, thought it would be wise to seek protection in the home of the chief.[18] As he entered the village he saw a big tent, neatly set up, and taller than the others; this he took for the home of the chief and hastened to it and sat down in the doorway.

Now it happened that the daughter of the chief, seeing the young captive, asked her father to buy him that she might have a brother. [Although] the captor [had said] would not part with the young man, not even for horses or other goods, after entreaties on the part of the maiden, the father said, "We will keep him; he is in the house of refuge, and no one can take him." Eating and drinking of what had been placed before him, he was assigned the place usually given the son of a family; the mother assisted by the daughter cut and made moccasins and leggings for him. Then the chief called some young men and told them to hasten to the homes of the subordinate chiefs and some of the warriors and summon them to come, for he had something to say. When all had arrived the chief told of the young captive who had taken refuge in his home and [said] that he was now as one of his own sons according to the wish of his daughter and that he wished them all to protect him as such. Addressing the young man by signs, [the chief] told [him] that he must not attempt to escape but try to be content in his new home. To this he consented.

Returning to his camp, the captor, with his followers, learned that the young captive had fled to a chief's home. Hurriedly they went there but found that he no longer belonged to them and that anyone who offered him any harm would be punished as if he had abused the son of the chief. Carefully the young man was guarded until hostility toward him was gone.

Being quite skilled in the hunting of the buffalo and small game, he refused to have his adopted father go . . . , telling him he could do it for him. Just as other young women helped their brothers so the chief's daughter got the pack horses for her adopted brother.

For two years this young man remained in the family of his adoption, in the strange tribe. One day while alone with him the young maiden said, "Are your father and mother living?" "Yes," said the young man. "Have you brothers and sisters?" To this he said, "I have one brother." "Would you not like to see them?" The young man said he was contented in his new home but that he would be happy to see his relations by blood.

Upon the return of her parents the maiden said: "My father, my elder brother has parents and a brother living. He would be very happy to see them once more, and it would make me glad to have him go and see them." The father, desiring to please his daughter, let the young man go. The chief sent proper escorts with the young man so that no harm would befall him. [After] traveling a number of days, the young man recognized landmarks, telling his guards that he was in his people's country. Becoming excited, they could not be persuaded to continue with the young man but returned to their own homes.

On an afternoon as he traveled alone he recognized an Osage in the act of butchering a buffalo. So intent was this man he paid no attention to the intruder. Having laid aside his bow and quiver, he was not prepared to protect himself and for a while stood frightened. Waiting till he was himself again, the young man said, "I am he who was lost over two years ago," giving his name. "Are my parents and brother living?" With some hesitancy the man spoke saying: "The people whose names you mention are living, but you are dead; it is your spirit that has come back to disturb my peace."

Hearing the young man's story, the Osage was satisfied and, packing the meat on his horse, led the way to the camp of the young man's family. There was much rejoicing at his return, and he was welcomed heartily by all except his brother. The young man gave of his horses to both his father and his brother, although the latter showed no signs of rejoicing at his return.

Resuming his old methods, the young man began to once more hunt for his parents and care for them. During the long evenings, he talked much with his father, asking many questions concerning the rites of his people, chiefly on those matters pertaining to war and the ceremonial organization of a war party. Having learned from his father the first thing to be done in organizing a war party, the young man did not make known to the *non'-hon-zhin-ga* his heart's desire.[19] He appointed himself as *do-don'-hon'-ga* without any men and alone went [through the] *non'-zhin-zhon* [rite of vigil], remaining six days. On the seventh day he returned [and] gathered together a number of men and told them of his purpose to go against the people who had taken him captive and so cruelly treated him. Among those he most desired [to capture] was the old woman with the scar on her face who had so abused him when he was [a] captive. The warriors were glad to help him but refused to capture the old woman.

On the day for the march the young man sent for the *wa-xo'-be* in the possession of his brother but was refused on the ground[s] [that he was a ghost] and not his brother and [that] if taken by him [it] would be lost. This did not alter the young man's desire to go on the war party, for he was able to compose his own songs and *wi'-gi-e* during the march, [and] his warriors were willing to go with him even if he had no *wa-xo'-be*.[20] As they went to capture the enemy, the young man never failed to make mention of the fact that they must capture the old woman with the scar. This was his revenge for abuses.

The location of the village was the very place where now stands Charley War-hre-she's farm.[21] In obedience to the leader, the warriors approached in the night and made an attack where the captors dwelt. Among those whom they took as captives were a young girl and the old woman [with the scar?]. In the haste of the capture no attention was given to what they took, but as the young man gazed forward, [he] saw a man on horseback coming toward him, [and] he recognized the rider as the one who was his adopted father. Immediately he gave [the] order for them to release the horses they had taken. He let the pursuers know that he was the adopted son of the man and did not intend to take his horses. This act was very gratifying to the old man, the chief, and he waved a sign of appreciation.

When the pursuing warriors stopped the chase, the Osage halted. The young girl that had been captured they scalped, and [they] made a *wa-xo'-be* of the hair, which is known as the *pa-hiu-ghon-ge wa-xo'-be*. Having accomplished a victory, the young man returned home and was met by his brother, who ran to meet the leader and offered to sing the songs of victory. Remembering that the *wa-xo'-be* had been refused him by his brother, he scornfully declined the offer of his brother, saying that he had his own songs and could make [a] proper ceremonial entry into the village. With the permission of the *non'-hon-zhi-ga* [clan priests], the young leader made the scalp *wa-xo'-be*.[22]

2.7 Origin of the Whistle Bundle[23]

There were four brothers who took care of and protected their aged parents. Two of the brothers were married. One day, when the people of the tribe were about to go on a buffalo hunt, these four brothers held a consultation and agreed to stay at home and continue to look out for their parents. After the hunting party had gone the brothers took their parents and moved to a part [of the country] that they knew to be full of black bears. Here they pitched their camp in the woods. These brothers [went on] a hunt, [and when] they returned [they] found their parents had been slain by a war party and the wigwams burned.

The three older brothers decided to follow the trail of the enemy and take revenge for the death of their parents. The younger brother had gone some distance away and refused to join the brothers. Upon being asked why he refused, he said he would join them if they made him the leader.[24] This was done. All were satisfied with the arrangements, so they started with the new leader in pursuit of the enemy. Not only did the younger brother act as leader but he did all the scout work, and, in company with his dog, found the trail fresher the farther he went. Each evening the young scout reported to his brothers. On one day he hurriedly came and reported that he had found the camp of the enemy. Much to the surprise of the brothers, a pack of gray wolves was with the young man. All started for the attack. Stealthily they approached the camp, the man giving war cries and the wolves [giving] howls, and the charge was made. This caused a panic in the camp, and the enemy fled, but the wolves were too swift for them; they caught the men, sometimes by threes, [and then] the brothers clubbed them to death. Thus the four brothers avenged the death of the parents. In commemoration of the victory the brothers made the whistle *wa-xo'-be*.[25]

2.8 Origin of the Mourning Dance (Black Dog)[26]

It has long been the Osage custom for mourners to take upon themselves for a certain period of time the fasting rite [rite of vigil]. Many years ago a prominent man, upon the death of a relative, took upon himself the fasting rite. In order to be entirely alone in his fast he had wandered far away from home, when he suddenly heard the voice of the relative for whom he was mourning, asking him to slay a man in order that he might have company while on his way to the spirit land. At once the mourner hastened home, organized a small war party, and went forth against a hostile tribe. He found the enemy [and] attacked them, killing a number of the warriors. He brought back a scalp and fastened it to a pole, which he planted at the head of the grave of his relative. By this act the mourner believer that he had sent the spirit of the slain man to overtake and accompany on its journey the spirit of the relative for whom he mourned. Other members of the tribe followed the example of the man, but they ceremonially organized their war party, using the ceremonies of the *wa-sha'-be a-thin* [war] rite,[27] and thus it became the custom among the Osage to secure a spirit to accompany that of a dead member to the spirit land.[28]

2.9 The Lost Warrior (Saucy Calf)[29]

An Osage warrior who was sent out to scout became lost and could not find the war party. For many days he wandered about; [he] was nearly starved, when he came to a Pawnee village. At that time the Pawnees and Osages were bitter enemies and were at war. The warrior knew that death was certain if he should enter the village in the daytime and openly—so he waited until it was dark and the noises of the people ceased. He entered an earth lodge and sat down near the fire, which had died down. In the middle of the lodge a man lay with his back to the fire, and his wife lay beside him. Close to the fire lay a pipe and a tobacco bag. The warrior took up the bag and silently filled the pipe and sat smoking. The wife of the sleeping man lifted her head when she smelled the tobacco smoke and looked at the stranger. She quietly awakened her husband and said to him: "There is a man setting by the fire smoking your pipe. He is not of our tribe, and you had better rise and speak to him." The husband rose and stirred up the fire into a blaze and then addressed the warrior both by signs and speech. "Who are you and where did you come from?" The warrior answered: "I am an Osage. I was with a war party but by accident became separated from the people. I wandered about many days and suddenly found your village this morning, and I stole in the dark fearing to enter while it was yet day. Starvation has driven me to throw myself upon your mercy."

"Are there others with you or are you alone?" asked the Pawnee.

"I am alone," replied the Osage. "Where my people have gone I do not know. I left them and have not seen them these many days."

It was by merest chance that the Osage entered the lodge of the principal chief. He himself was a powerful man, but he knew that precaution was necessary to prevent the killing of the stranger. The smoking of the pipe was through no design by the Osage, and to him there was in it no special significance, but to the Pawnee it was a sacred act that bound him to protect the stranger with his life.

The chief spoke hastily to his wife, who, wrapping her robe about her, hastened out of the door.

Soon four powerful men appeared at the inner doorway. Two of these advanced and took places near the fireplace opposite the stranger, while the other two stood as though on guard at either side of the door.

The chief, addressing the four men by terms of relationship, said to them: "You see an Osage, one of our bitterest enemies, has entered by house, and he has smoked my pipe. By this act he has placed me in the position [of having] to protect him at all hazard, and I shall do it. I have sent for you that I might ask your assistance."

"What are you," asked one of the newcomers of the stranger, "and are you alone or have you come with others?"

"I came alone," replied the Osage. "I was with a war party of many men but became separated from them by accident. This happened many days ago, and only this day I came upon your village. Starvation has driven me into your village and into this chief's house, and now my life is in your hands."

The Pawnee looked toward the door and spoke hurriedly to one of the men standing there and pointing in different directions as he spoke. When he had finished, the man at the door went out.

In the meantime, the wife of the chief had returned and was busy preparing food for the Osage. First she placed before him a wooden bowl filled with pemmican and by signs told him to eat quickly, as did the chief and the three men. By the time the Osage had finished the pemmican the woman [was setting] before him a bowl of corn, and the protection of the stranger was assured.

The Osage stayed with the Pawnee two years, hunting for his host, and then he was sent home—conducted by ten men. When they came within a day's journey of the Osage camp they let the Osage go home alone.

2.10 Captive of the Pawnee[30]

A long time ago two young men friends were out hunting together. One of the young men had been presented with a *wa-xo'-be*, and he was feeling happy because he had about collected all the necessary articles for the initiation.[31] Having secured all the meat and pelts that they could carry, the two young hunters agreed to move toward home. In discussing the route to be taken, one of the young hunters said: "Let us not take the usual route but take another course. I have had a bad dream, and the scene of my dream was along the old hunting trail." "Dreams never come true," replied the other, "and I do not believe there is anything to fear. I want to take the old hunting trail because food camping places are within easy distances and there is better grazing for horses than the way you want to go. But there is nothing against our separating, each taking the route most suitable to himself. I shall take the old trail."

Early in the morning the two young men packed their horses, broke camp, and moved homeward. The dreamer, with his family, went one way, and his friend took the old hunting trail. Toward dusk the man pitched his camp at one of the customary camping places,[32] and a brother-in-law, who was a widower, drove the horses out to a good grazing place. When the brother-in-law returned and entered the tent he said: "*Ta-hon* (brother-in-law),[33] when I was coming back from tending the horses I saw some men stealing along the brow of the hill, and they skulked into the bushes when they saw me." "Oh, don't be scared," replied the man. "What you saw was a flock of turkeys going to roost." Soon after, the little boy who had been sent to the creek to get water also came in and said: "Father, as I was coming back I saw some men, and they ran and hid in the bushes when they saw me." "My son," said the man, "you and your uncle can't tell the difference between turkeys and men. You both get scared at a lot of harmless turkeys."

Nothing more was said about the matter during the meal or after, and when the older people tired of the conversation and storytelling all went to bed without any thought of fear.[34] Toward morning the brother-in-law, who had but recently lost his wife [and] was mourning for her, arose and went out to wail. He went out some distance from the tent, and as he stopped to begin to wail he saw in the twilight the shadowy forms of a band of warriors stealthily approaching. He made no outcry but began to wail in a loud voice, and instead of using the usual endearing terms in his cry, he said: "Warriors are about to attack us. Arise and make your escape." But the people in the tent failed to understand him, and with loud war cries the warriors rushed upon the camp. The little boy happened to be the first to rush out of the tent, and the fleeing uncle met him and, taking him under his arm, made his escape. Both the father and mother were killed, and the little daughter was carried away captive.

Years after, when peace had been made between the Osages and the Pawnees, and the two tribes met on one of their annual summer buffalo hunts, some of the Osage chiefs were invited to a feast by one of the Pawnee chiefs. When the feast was over and the Osage were going out, a woman stopped them and began to talk to them in Osage. She told them this story and inquired about her uncle and her little brother, speaking of both by name. It happened that both [her] uncle and nephew [?] had remained at home when the tribe went on the hunt, and the woman was disappointed not to see them. She was asked if she would not like to come back to her people, but she said that she could not do it, as she had a large family of children and she could not very well leave them. The woman was content to remain with her captors.

———

2.11 The Boy Driven from Home[35]

There was a man who had a son, the only boy he had. The lad was very bright and active, but the father and mother neglected him and never showed him any affection. But the boy had a brother-in-law, his sister's husband, who became fondly attached to him. He made for the lad tops, throwing sticks, [and] ball and ball sticks as the seasons for the games came around. One day the man made a fine bow and some pointed and blunt arrows for the lad, to his delight. The man, with a good deal of patience, taught the boy the use of the bow and arrows, and he soon became skillful with the bow.[36] For a long time the boy amused himself with hunting and shooting birds and other small game, but there came a time when he wearied of this and became ambitious to hunt large game like the big men. The brother-in-law then taught him to ride and to manage the horse and how to shoot with the bow and arrow when riding at full speed. In this he soon became practiced and proficient, and he longed to try his skill on the buffalo, and he desired to do this with his father's favorite horse, which he had been strictly forbidden to ride.

One day the runners came in and reported the finding of a large herd of buffalo. The men went to the chase, and about sundown they came home with a great supply of meat and hides. Now for two or three days after a chase like this and [after] the scattering of a great herd, the calves that had been separated from their mothers would run about in search for them. It is then that the little boys ambitious to shoot big game would go out singly or in numbers to shoot calves. It was on the day following this great chase that the boy of this story stole out of his wigwam with bridle and lariat and his bow and arrows and went to where his father's herd of horses were put to graze. He had no difficulty in catching the favorite one and, hastily mounting, he was soon galloping over the prairies toward the field of the chase of the preceding day. When nearing the field, he saw in the distance ahead a small dark object bobbing up and down on the smooth prairie and coming straight toward him. It was a calf that had lost its mother. With heart beating in excitement, the boy watched the little black animal as it swiftly approached, for it was coming straight toward the horse and rider, mistaking them for its mother. The calf had come within the distance of a bow shot when it saw its mistake, and then it took flight in the opposite direction. The boy let loose the reins, [and] the horse needed no urging—it sped forward and gained upon the calf at every leap. The little hunter drew an arrow from his quiver and held it in readiness as his horse brought him closer and closer to the game. Being well trained in the art of riding the boy needed not the reins to guide the horse, but in one important particular he had never received any instructions, and that was to glance ahead as he rode to see that there is no danger in the way to the horse's feet. The lack of training in this one respect made it possible for him to fall into the accident that was the starting point of his life's career. The horse was now side by side with the calf: the boy put the arrow to the bow and string [and] leaned forward, and with a quick motion of the arms, he pulled and then let go the arrow. It struck in the right spot and the calf fell to the ground in death. The boy seized the reins to stop the horse—just ahead of him there stood a tuft of grass, which to the trained hunter is always a sign of danger, for beneath it there would be either the hole of a badger or a prairie dog. The horse's right foot went squarely into this tuft of grass, into the prairie dog's hole. Horse and rider rolled over the ground in a confused mass; the boy arose unhurt, but with some difficulty the horse got to its feet, and it could not move, for its leg was broken.

The lad removed the bridle and lariat from the horse, and sad with fear and misgivings he started for the camp. It was dusk when he got home. He cautiously looked into the door of the wigwam and saw that his mother was sitting there all alone. He went to her and told her of the accident in tones of penitence and pleading, but instead of [giving him] the motherly sympathy he expected from her she reproached him with harsh words. While they were yet speaking, the father came in, and the mother broke forth afresh in her tirade against the boy as she told the story of the loss. The father listened with some patience at first, but as the woman went on with her scolding he lost control of his temper, and, seizing the boy by the arms, he threw him violently to the door, telling him in angry words to go away and never to come back.[37] The boy picked up his quiver and went out of the door crying, while his mother sat muttering words of reproach against him.

The boy went away; he did not know where he was going, but he went straight ahead crying continually as he walked over the prairies. One day, after he had been gone for a number of days, he fell asleep, for he was overcome with thirst, hunger, and exhaustion. He did not know how long he had lain where he dropped when suddenly he was startled and awakened by the loud neighing of a horse close by. He arose to a sitting position when the horse spoke to him: "Your grandfathers have been moved to pity by your constant cry," it said, "and they have sent me to bring you to them, so, get on my back, and I will carry you to them." The boy managed with some difficulty to mount, and the horse carried him some distance to a great herd of horses of many different colors. When the boy dismounted, the horses gathered around him in great excitement, neighing loudly and whinnying and rubbing their heads against him as though in tender affection. This went on for some little time, when suddenly the horses tossed up their heads with loud snorts as though in alarm at some approaching danger [and] then galloped swiftly away and disappeared beyond the hills in the distance. The boy looked around to find the cause of alarm, and he saw a man mounted on a spirited horse chasing two buffalo at full speed. Just as the man shot one of them, the lad threw himself in a patch of tall grass and hid himself. The man saw the boy, but he rushed on in pursuit of the other buffalo. When the thud of hoofs died away in the distance, the boy raised his head above the tall grass to see if he had been discovered, and to his astonishment he beheld two young women bending over the buffalo that had fallen, hard at work removing the skin. While the lad was still peeping through the tops of the tall grass at the young women, the hunter suddenly appeared and stood with them. He took his knife from his belt and then saying something, [he] pointed with it toward the patch of grass where the lad crouched in hiding. The man bent to his work, and the two women came to the hiding place of the boy. By signs they told him to rise and to follow them. The hunter gently grasped the boy's hand and by signs asked him whence he came and to what tribe he belonged. The boy replied by signs, pointing eastward to the Osage country and making the sign for the shaved head and the roach, and the man understood. The boy also told that his father and mother had beaten him and that he had run away to go and die in some strange country. "You shall not die," the hunter said. "You shall come to my home and be my son, and you shall grow up to be a man of some importance." The boy nodded assent, and the father and the daughters took the little stranger to their wigwam.

The man was one of the great chiefs of his tribe, and although he had confidence in his power over the people, he thought, for the safety of the lad, to announce to them without delay his determination to make the boy his son. This he did, and from the very time of his entrance into the camp the lad's life and person were safe from harm. The chief had two young daughters but no sons, and so it was that when he went to the chase the daughters brought the horses to carry in the meat and skins. The young man not only relieved his sisters of this unpleasant task but made himself useful in helping his father in the work of butchering. He took care of the horses, watered them regularly, and saddled them when the camp was moved, and the people soon learned to regard him as one of the tribe, and in speaking of him they would say "the chief's son" instead of "the little Osage."

When the lad had grown up and become a man, the chief sickened and became a helpless invalid, and so he could not go to the chase and keep his wigwam supplied with meat. It was then that the young man spoke and said: "Do not be troubled, Father. I will go to the chase and secure meat and skins, and my sisters can bring for me the packhorses as they had been doing for you before I came. I will take your place and keep our house supplied."

The young man became skillful in shooting the game and not only that—he [also] knew how to find the fattest cows and kept his father's house supplied with the best of meat. One day when the hunters surrounded and chased a great herd, the young man killed four fat cows, and as he had no one to help him butcher, the sun was fast going down before he had finished. He told his sisters that they would have to sleep out that night as it would be impossible for him to finish butchering before it got dark. It was then that the two young women went aside and spoke to each other in low tones. "This young man is not our brother by blood," they said, "and it would not be wrong for us to marry him. If we do not marry him some strange woman will, and then we will have no one to take care of us. And so let us marry him and do it now."

The young women proposed, the young man accepted, and the three became husband and wives without further ceremony. When they got home in the morning the young women themselves announced to their relatives the marriage, and they were received with the greatest happiness.[38]

Up to this time the young man had no horses of his own. [After] he married he felt troubled that he had no property of his own and spoke to his wives about it. They tried to make him contented with those he had been using, but he said that they were not his and that he must have his own.

He suddenly disappeared one day and was gone for a long time. The people came to the belief that he had gone home to his own tribe and the relatives of the young wives felt insulted at the supposed desertion, but the two sisters were sure of the affection of their young husband, and they waited patiently for his return. One bright morning, when the young man had been gone so long that he was almost forgotten, the two sisters who were at work in their wigwam [and] heard a great noise toward the opposite side of the camp. The sounds seemed to be moving toward their side of the camp, and so both the women laid down their work and hurried out to see what all the shouting was for. They saw coming toward their wigwam a big herd of horses of all colors followed by a crowd of cheering people. One rider was driving the horses, and as he drew near the two sisters recognized their husband. One of the women seized a kettle and ran to the creek for water, while the other hurried into the wigwam to start the fire, and soon the two were setting side by side with their husband as he ate of the food they had prepared and set before him. The people were glad to see the return of the chief's son, but they were curious to know from what tribe he captured so fine a herd of horses. The old father was also curious and troubled, for he suspected that his son had seized the property of some tribe friendly to his own people and that some act of reprisal would follow the seizure, which would bring about hostilities between the two tribes. But the old chief, with the rest of the people who had gathered at his wigwam, waited patiently for the explanation that would come sometime from the young man.

When the young man had finished his talk with his wives, and he had partaken of the food they placed before him, he spoke to his father and to the visitors and said: "You, perhaps, suspect that I have stolen the horses I have brought home from some tribe, but it is not so. It may be that my father remembers having seen a large herd of wild horses on the day that he and his daughters found me. I was standing close to that herd when my father came by chasing buffalo, and the horses, taking alarm, fled over the prairies. It is from this same herd that these horses have come. Examine them closely and you will find no saddle marks on any of them. I found a way of capturing and taming them, and I have done so. No one can dispute my right of ownership in them. They rightfully belong to myself and my wives, and nobody has been robbed."

Not very long after this the old chief died, and the young man became chief in his stead by inheritance and proved himself to be a good leader of the tribe.[39] He was hospitable and generous to all.

One day, when the people were out on their annual summer buffalo hunt, they were suddenly and unexpectedly joined by the Osage tribe with whom they had been on unfriendly terms for many years. Overtures of peace and friendship were made and accepted between the two tribes, and the people exchanged hospitalities and made presents to one another, and all former hatred was forgotten.[40] The young chief did not take part in all this, but he went to the Osage camp and went from wigwam to wigwam in search of his father and mother. A man asked him who he was looking for, and the young man answered in Osage, "I am looking for so-and-so (giving his father's name)." "He and his wife are both dead," the man said, "but a daughter is living, and yonder is her wigwam."

The young man went to the wigwam pointed out and entered the door. He was cordially greeted and signed to a place by the fireside. "Make haste," the man of the house said to his wife. "He looks as though he might be a man of some importance. Let us set food before him." Before the woman moved, the young man said in Osage, "You do not know me but I know you both very well and I have come to see you. This is my sister and you are my brother-in-law. My father turned me out of doors because I killed his horse, and now I am a member of another tribe." The sister covered her face with both hands and wept, for she remembered how cruelly he had been treated by [their] parents and had long given her little brother up as dead.

The three ate together, and when they had finished, the young chief asked his sister and her husband to come to his wigwam the next morning. Early in the morning, the two went to the chief's house, and when they had feasted the young man took his sister and her husband to see his fine herd of horses and told them to select ten and accept them as a gift, for he had learned that they were very poor.[41]

2.12 The Woman War Leader (Tho'-xi Zhin-ga)[42]

One summer, back in the olden times, the Osage Indians were moving westward on their annual buffalo hunt. Among the many wigwams there was one that had but a single occupant, the widow of a warrior who had died when the people were preparing to take their journey. Following an ancient tribal custom the widow mourned, ceremonially, for her husband. As a sign of mourning, she put moistened earth upon her forehead at the beginning of day, before the sun arose, fasted until dusk, [and] then washed her face and ate a little food.[43] All through the day she wept as she worked in and about her wigwam or when on the march. She could not go to the hills to be alone as it was the custom to do when in mourning, for she had no friend or relative upon whom she could depend to care for her house and her horses. Occasionally, as it happened to be convenient, a man or a lad would water her horses for her or drive them to her wigwam and help her to saddle and pack them when the whole camp was to move.

Day after day the widow mourned, shedding tears without ceasing. Then, on a certain day, there were sounds of rejoicing throughout the camp, for runners had returned and reported the finding of signs of buffalo. The widow did not permit this to interrupt her mourning, and she continued the outward expressions of her sorrow, while she mentally appealed to the Unknown [Wa-kon'-da] to give her some sign of his approval of what she desired to do for the spirit of her husband.

In a few days more there was still greater excitement, for a runner returned and reported the finding of a large herd of buffalo not a great distance from the camp. A council was held by the chiefs and their advisors, who decided to have the chase that day lest the herd stampede should the wind change and blow in the direction of the camp. The herald [crier] was sent throughout the camp to proclaim the order for the chase, and soon the hunters and the boys [who were] to follow them with the packhorses were astir. In the midst of all this movement a man prominent in the affairs of the tribe came out of his wigwam and, standing near the door, spoke in a loud and commanding voice.

"Remember the widow in mourning, ye valorous men," he said. "She has no man to go to the chase for her. I call upon —— and —— to ride her two running horses to the chase and upon —— to follow them with packhorses. Let pity move you to do this for her."

The young men called upon by the man came quickly to the widow's house, mounted her horses, and soon joined the other hunters, who were moving toward the herd on an easy lope.

Toward sundown, the two hunters and the young man with the packhorses returned to the widow's house with all the horses laden with meat and hides. Then the same man who had called upon the three young men to go to the chase for the widow again came out of his wigwam and, standing near the door, called to four young women by name to come to the help of the widow in the work of curing her meat and the dressing of the hides. These young women promptly appeared at the widow's house and began their work. All night long they worked, jerking the meat [and] stretching the hides upon the ground with pegs and fleshing them, and toward morning they completed their task.

The man who called upon these young people to come to the aid of the widow was one who had served as captain in a number of successful war expeditions, and in calling for help for the widow, he employed a term used by captains in giving their commands. Both the young men and the young women understood this, and therefore they were prompt in responding to the call. These young people served the widow throughout the entire hunt. During all this time, the widow continued her mourning for her husband.

The buffalo hunt was over, and the people returned to their permanent village. Early one morning the widow stood at the door of her wigwam and called in a loud voice the names of two young men. These young men promptly responded to her call, and when they had taken the seats assigned to them in the wigwam, the widow informed them that she was going on the warpath to secure companions for her husband on his journey to the land of spirits and that she desired the two young men to act as captains[44] for her. The older of the two young men accepted the office without any objections, but the younger man hesitated because, he said, neither he nor the older man had ever been on the warpath and he was afraid to take [on] such responsibility. [Without] making [a] decision, he went out of the house, and standing near the door, he called in a loud voice to men who had been successful captains and appealed to them to take command of the widow's men, but none of them responded. Then he entered the house, took his seat, and told the widow he would accept the office no matter what happened to him.

Applicants to join the war party came but slowly because the captains chosen by the widow had never been on the warpath, and no woman was ever known to have led a war party. Twelve applicants came and were accepted. None of these had ever been on the warpath, but neither the leader nor the captains offered to reject any of them on this account.

Early the following morning, the warriors and the captains, mounted on their best horses, assembled at the leader's house. The leader had saddled and packed her own horses with provisions she had prepared for ten men, for she had expected no more than that number, for a journey of thirty days. The privates, at the command of the captains, took charge of the packhorse, [and] then the leader mounted her favorite horse and led forth her men. The sides of the avenue that extended westward through the village were thronged with people eager to see the novel sight. The dignified bearing of the leader, her captains, and her men commanded the respect of all the spectators, although there was a general feeling among the experienced warriors that the leader was not wise in the choice of her captains. Steadily the leader and her men marched between the two lines through the village and on to the westward hills, while the throng watched until the little company passed out of sight.[45]

As in a war party led by a man the woman observed the rite of *non'-zhin-zhon* . . . [rite of vigil] during the entire journey out. When on the march, she rode apart from her warriors, and in the evening she kept her vigil at some distance from the camp, always appealing to the invisible power for success. When the warriors had prepared their evening meal, the leader was ceremonially conducted to the camp and water was placed before her to wash from her forehead the sign of fasting, [and] then food was offered to her so that she might refresh herself before going to rest for the night away from camp.

On the morning of the eighteenth day of the journey, as the gray dawn stretched itself along the eastern horizon, the warriors saddled their horses and that of their leader for the march. They mounted and were about to start when, behind them, along the trail, a gray wolf uttered a series of mournful cries. The younger of the captains addressed the leader, saying: "*Do-don'-hon'-ga*, come a little nearer and let me speak quietly with you. The gray wolf whose cries we have just heard tells me that not far from us is a camp that is given to you." Then, at that very moment, there arose before them the cry of another gray wolf as though in response to the other one. The older of the captains then spoke, saying "The wolf whose cry we have just heard before us tells me that the camp is but a little distance from us and that we must prepare to attack."

Then, as though to confirm the words of the young captains, a scout returned and, addressing the leader, said: "*Do-don'-hon'-ga*, there is a camp at the foot of this hill, and we must hasten to make the attack."

At the command of the captains the men dismounted and hastily painted their faces with sacred charcoal.[46] Then both captains shouted the order: "My valorous men, it is done. Charge!" Down the steep hill the fourteen riders rushed with the speed of an attack hawk, the symbol of the courage of the warrior. The war cries and the thud of the hoofs of the horses smote the still air and struck the campers with sudden terror. As the fourteen warriors swooped through the camp, women and weaponless men fled toward the woods and the hills. Many were struck down by the shoulders of the horses, some were knocked down with war clubs, and other fell pierced by arrows and lances.

The sun arose and revealed to the leader her warriors returning in triumph. The trophies, the scalps of eight of the enemy, that they had taken were fastened to the tops of slender poles of willow sapling. These the warriors presented to their leader, who imagined that the spirits of the enemies slain were hastening to overtake that of her husband to accompany him to the land of spirits. Forty horses were the spoils they turned over to her,[47] and the two captains proudly reported to her that none of her men were hurt.

Then, addressing her men, she said to them: "My valorous men, you have acquitted yourselves valiantly and have brought to fulfillment all my purposes. Long will the fear of you remain in the breasts of the enemies living and in the breasts of the spirits of those you have slain. Having struck the enemy, we will now hasten homeward and enter our village as warriors returning triumphant."

On a certain morning, as the sun arose, there was a sudden stir throughout the Osage village. Men, women, and children ran toward the hills, shouting, "The war party is returning!" Mounted on her own horse, the leader slowly rode down the slope of the hill in advance of her men. The scalps, stretched upon hoops and fastened to the tops of slender poles, fluttered in the breeze, the bearer of them [riding] a few paces behind the leader. The two captains, riding side by side, were the next in line in the procession. Then followed the privates, each one leading some of the captured horses.

Looking neither to the left nor to the right, the leader and her men marched between the two lines formed by the people. As the leader approached the village with her men, she addressed them, saying,

> My valorous men, you have acquitted yourselves valiantly.
> You enter your village in triumph.
> Here lies the edge of the village,
> Here, the ground worn bare by the feet of the people.
> You now approach the back of the house from which you started out.
> You now come to the front of the dwelling.
> You have come to the door of the house and pause.
> You enter the house and stand within.
> You have come forth from the darkness of death and now stand in the light of life.

The bearer of the scalps, who had taken his place near the fireplace as the warriors entered the house, thrust the tops of the poles through the smoke hole and then withdrew them, and in this manner the war expedition was brought to a close.

At the command of the leader, the two captains, on the same day, conducted the distribution of the spoils. The three young men and the four young women who had served her throughout the buffalo hunt were not forgotten by the leader in the distribution, for she regarded the work performed by them as the beginning of the expedition and a part of it. The two captains reserved four of the best horses for the leader as her share of the spoils and then proceeded to distribute the rest of them without regard to their quality.

The widow continued to live alone. Then one day, about a year from the time of her war expedition, two elderly men visited her at her house. Each one addressed her in the most formal manner [and] made known to her the wish of a certain man to make her his wife. The two messengers were men highly respected in the tribe, and she received them with much courtesy. The man whom they represented was also a man of considerable importance, and she respected and honored him.

For some little time the woman sat in silence and in deep thought, [and] then she broke into sobs that she could not control, finding relief from them only in loud wailing. When she had dried her tears and composed herself, she gave her reply to the messengers. "I shall accept your good words," she said to them, "and the offer of the good man who sent you to me. It is not for my husband that I wept, for I have ceased to mourn for him, but it is for myself that I have shed these tears because I have no father, mother, uncle, aunt, or brothers upon whom I could call for counsel in this important matter. There are no blood relatives to give me away, to offer me their good wishes, and to send me away with an affection true and strong. I have to decide for myself, an act which is unbecoming to a self-respecting woman. Bring to me, tomorrow, whatever things the good man has to offer, and I will perform all the acts necessary for the completion of the ceremony."

Pleased with their success, the two old men returned to the one who sent them and made their report to him. On the following morning the relatives of the good man formed a procession headed by the two messengers and approached the house of the widow. Some carried kettles of cooked food, some articles of value such as deerskin leggings, jackets, robes, bows and quivers of arrows, [and] women's skirts and jackets, and many of them led fine horses. The relatives of the man contributed the best of their horses. All these goods were sent according to custom as gifts for the relatives of the woman sought in marriage.

The sides of the path along which the procession approached the widow's house were thronged with the people of the village, who had turned out to see and admire the gifts being taken to the widow. On arriving at the house those of the procession leading the horses hitched them to racks arranged around the dwelling. Those carrying the smaller gifts entered the house and placed them down near the fireplace. The widow, who sat alone in her wigwam, greeted each one as she assigned him or her to a seat. In a formal little talk she thanked them for the gifts they had brought and then dismissed them.

The widow called to her house a *wa-je'-pa-in* [crier][48] . . . and sent him to invite the three young men and the four young women who had served her at the time of the buffalo hunt and also the two captains and the twelve men of her war party to partake of the feast provided by the relatives of the man seeking to marry her. The invitation included the families of the invited guests. The guests came, and the widow explained to them why she had invited them to the feast provided by the relatives of the man offering to marry her. As she had no relatives to enjoy it, therefore she had asked them instead, for they had acted the part of kinsmen. When the guests had feasted, she asked them to distribute among themselves the gifts brought to her, as her relatives would have done if she had had any.

At the request of the widow some of the women, when the feast and the distribution of the goods was over, assisted her in preparing to go to her husband. They retrimmed her riding saddle and put it on her favorite horse; they also put upon the horse the ornamented buffalo-hair lariat by which it was to be led. With the aid of two women, the widow put on her best dress and robe, and then [they] helped her to mount her horse. The young man who had taken care of the widow's horses then took his place at the head of the horse, taking in his hands the lariat to lead it. The two captains took their places at either side of the horse. Each of the four horses that were her share of the spoils captured by her men was led by a man who had been with the war party. The other guests each led a horse, for the widow had many. When the widow had mounted her horse, the *wa-je'-pa-in* [crier] gave a call as a signal that the procession was about to start. Then the relatives of the good man who had gathered at his house ran a race to meet the procession. The five winners were entitled to the horse the widow rode and the four captured horses. All the people of the village followed the procession to the house to see the ceremony of marriage. When the widow dismounted, the sisters of the good man conducted her into the house and gave her a seat beside their brother, who was seated in the place of honor. A wooden bowl with a little boiled corn and a single spoon in it was set before the couple; each took a mouthful out of the same spoon, and the two became man and wife.

The horses and the goods brought by the widow to her husband to be distributed among his relatives outnumbered those brought to her by them, for the guests had contributed to her pile in order that her liberality might not be overshadowed by the good man's relatives.

The woman lived to see children and grandchildren and was respected and honored by all the people.

2.13 The Youngest Wife[49]

Many years ago, when the buffalo were still plentiful, the Osage Indians were on their way to the hunting grounds. There was a young man in the tribe who married and lived with two sisters. It happened that the husband came upon the younger of the sisters when a man was speaking to her. Then, in a fit of jealousy, the husband whipped the young woman in a brutal manner. The young wife returned to her house, gathered up a few of her belongings, and started for home. No attempt was made by any of her friends to stop her, for they thought she would soon return to camp, fearing to make the journey alone. But Wa-zha'-xa-in, for that was the name of the young woman, was not a timid person, and she did not even look back as she made her way over the hills.

The journey was long and wearisome, but after many days Wa-zha'-xa-in entered the old camping place the people called home. It was in the early part of the day when the young woman reached the village site, and although weary and footsore from her many days' travel she at once set to work to build herself a house, for, the houses of the people being portable, [they] were all taken along when they went away, and none remained in the village.

On passing through the deserted village on her way to the nearby woods, the young woman was delighted to find a small ax with a broken handle near a fireplace. This little ax she used in cutting the poles for the frame of her house. With considerable difficulty the young woman dragged the poles close to the site of her uncle's wigwam,[50] for she had a strong affection for the old man, and she began the building of her little dwelling.

With a heavy pole that she had sharpened at the lower end for the purpose, Wa-zha'-xa-in drove six holes in the ground, in a straight row, about an arm's length apart. These were for the support of the frame poles of one side of the house. Then for the poles for the opposite side she drove an equal number of holes. For the frame poles of each end of the house she drove four holes. Having completed this part of the work, she planted the poles firmly in the holes, and, bending the tops of those that stood opposite each other so that they overlapped, she bound them securely together with strips of the inner bark of linden saplings. The tops of the poles at each end of the structure she also bent over and fastened to the other intersecting poles in a similar manner. The ridgepole and the other horizontal poles for steadying the whole frame she also fastened with strips of bark. When the builder had completed the work of constructing the frame of her house, she thatched the sides all around with the stalks of the blue-joint grass that grew around the place in abundance. From the cache of her uncle's family she took hides for the roof of her house [and] also corn and other provisions [as well as] cooking utensils.

One more thing was necessary to the completion of her home—the fireplace. It was simple to construct, being only a shallow excavation in the ground within which to kindle the fire. Yet, to the ancient people, and to those who followed their teaching, the fireplace had a profound and sacred meaning; it brought them into close touch with Wa-kon'-da, whose abiding place is in the sky and in the earth. It was the place prepared for fire, one of Wa-kon'-da's great gifts to man. Around the fireplace, for ages past, the family had gathered to share their sorrows and their joys, and it figured prominently in the ancient rites of the people as an emblem of the unity of the family. Around it had sat the ancient men as they thoughtfully sought for Wa-kon'-da among the stars, in the space beneath them, in the earth, and in the waters. The sanctity of the fireplace was the theme of the conversations of the older people that often took place in the presence of the young woman, but she never fully understood their words, being yet young and inattentive to matters requiring serious thought. Now, in her solitude and loneliness, as she contemplated the construction of her own fireplace, the words of the old people that had chanced to abide with her memory crowded through her mind and revealed their import and meaning. With a feeling of reverence, she knelt and hollowed the ground to make her fireplace. Then she felt that she had at last completed her little home.

The sun had gone down, and it was dark when Wa-zha'-xa-in finished her fireplace, but she kindled a fire with the fire sticks she found in the cache and soon had her little house aglow with a ruddy light. She prepared her evening meal, and while she ate, her mind busied itself with plans for her future welfare.

The young woman finished her meal, fed the fire with fresh wood, and then shifted her position so that she sat with her back to the fire to think, a habit of women when they desired to meditate quietly. Outside there was a low rumbling of continual thunder and occasional flashes of lightning but no violent wind to disturb the woman. She had hardly begun to think when she heard voices and footsteps approaching her house. The voices were those of two men; the rustling sounds of their footsteps came within the door, and there was a dull rattling as though of poorly dressed buffalo robes. "This is the house. Let us sit here at the door," one of the voices said. Wa-zha'-xa-in turned her face toward the door to see who her visitors were, but they were invisible. After a short pause one of the men, addressing the young woman, said: "We have come, *ci´-ge* [youngest daughter], to talk to you, to tell you that we are pleased that you have left your husband and your sister. They have been unkind to you, and it is well that you have left them. Do not return to them when the people come home from the hunt or you will live an unhappy life."

"You have built for yourself a little house, clean and comfortable, and the fire that you have kindled in it burns brightly. Fire is one of the great gifts of Wa-kon´-da to man; therefore, treat it with reverence, and he will bless you. Always keep clean the fireplace, for it is sacred. Around it the family gathers for comfort, and the little one are strengthened by the warmth of the fire. A thoughtful man honors a woman who keeps clean her fireplace, for it betokens her reverence for things sacred, her kindliness and her hospitality."

"You have a little daughter, who needs a mother's care and guidance. She would be better led by you in the paths of virtue than by her father and your sister. They love not children and have not the qualities that would win their love and obedience. Therefore, make it your first duty to secure possession of her and bring her to your little home. Having done this, give some thought to the man who has offered himself to you. He respects you and is earnest in his desire to make you his wife. Lay aside your sense of modesty, go to him, and tell him you accept his offer. Bring him to your home and you will both be blessed with many children, and you will be honored by your people."

"You will have many horses, servants, that will carry for you your burdens. Be kind and gentle to them, for although they speak not they know human kindness. Teach them to know you through your kindness, and they will not run away from you when you approach them."

"Many will be your cares, *ci´-ge* [younger daughter], but always be mindful of the fire and the fireplace; they are sacred."

"We now rise to go, but we will visit you from time to time to let you know of our pleasure when there come to pass important events favorable to you."

Wa-zha´-xa-in sat listening to the voices of the men and the sounds of their footsteps as they went away. When she could hear them no more there came over her a sense of loneliness and a longing to hear their voices again. Then there came before her a vision of eight little children standing in a line, hand in hand. She recognized the child standing at the head of the line as her daughter, but although the others, who alternated in sex, were strangers to her, she felt that they, in some way, belonged to her. The vision faded away, but it left with her a feeling of joy, for she looked upon it as a revelation of her future life.

In the afternoon of a certain day, as Wa-zha´-xa-in sat in her little house sewing, she heard outside the voices of many people, the sounds of the work of unpacking of horses and the setting up of wigwams. The people had come home, and a strong desire came upon her to run out to greet her uncle and the rest of her relatives, but she overcame her emotions and sat quietly sewing. After some little time, her door was suddenly darkened and a man entered. It was her uncle who spoke to her in words of kindness: "Is it you my niece, and are you well?" "I am well, my uncle," she replied as she offered him her hand. He grasped her hand gently and then said, "It is well for us all that I come home and find you alive, for I had resolved to slay your husband if you had never returned." The young woman wept quietly for a time, and when she had dried her tears she said: "My uncle, I want my little daughter." "You shall have her before the sun sets," he replied and arose and went out. Then the friends of the young woman came to greet her; some wept over her, and some laughed in joy as they embraced her.

Wa-zha'-xa-in's sister had set up her wigwam, and she and her husband were sitting within when the uncle came. Without a moment's pause, he spoke and said, "I do not speak to you husband but only to you my niece. You have both been unkind to your sister so that she has had to leave you. She will not return to you; therefore I have come for her daughter, as it is best that she should be in her mother's care. I shall expect no opposition from either of you." The old man then spoke to the child, saying: "Come with me to your mother; she waits to see you." The child needed no second bidding; she hastily gathered up her playthings and followed the man, while the father and his wife sat in silence.

In the evening Wa-zha'-xa-in sat in her little house with her child in her lap, enjoying the light of her fire. She remembered the words of her two invisible friends and wondered if they would come again. Then it occurred to her that without any thought of them, she had secured possession of her daughter as they had advised her to do. Then there came upon her the memory of their advice concerning her lover, and she resolved to obey them. She sat thinking for a long time as her child slept, and then she noticed that the village had become quiet in sleep. She laid the child down, covered it up with a robe, and silently went out. She made her way directly to the house of her lover, for she knew that like the others it had been pitched in its old site. Standing close to the side of the door, she called him by name, in a low tone. There was a movement within, and in a moment her lover stood at her side. She said to him: "I have come to accept your offer. Come with me to my own house." "Wait here a little while, and I will be with you," he replied. The man went back into the house. Soon he came out again with a bundle under his arm. She quietly took this from him and bade him to follow.

The next morning Wa-zha'-xa-in went to her uncle's house and, after some hesitation, said to him: "My uncle, I have found for myself a man. He is Ga-hi'-ge-wa-tse-xi." The uncle looked into the face of his niece, smiled pleasantly, and then said: "You have done well, my niece; he is a good man, and I am sure he will be kind to you. I have no fine horses, but I will give you two good pack-horses. Now we must let your other relatives know of this very soon, before evil reports are started throughout the village." The uncle[51] sent a *wa-je'-pa-in* [crier] to tell all his relatives that he had consented to the marriage of his niece to Ga-hi'-ge-wa-tse-xi, who was now at her house. It was not long before the men and women relatives of Wa-zha'-xa-in came toward her house, bringing gifts of clothing, household goods, and horses for the couple. The women relatives set to work and built an extension to her little house so that there [would] be two fireplaces instead of one. Around both fireplaces they spread robes for the comfort of guests and visitors.

Ga-hi'-ge-wa-tse-xi sent word to his relatives about his marriage, and they also hastened to make known their approval of the marriage. They brought gifts of provisions, clothing, and horses for Wa-zha'-xa-in. Thirty horses were brought in all by the relatives of both the young couple, and the smaller gifts filled many parfleche cases. The people of the village also showed their plea-sure in many little ways, mostly by inviting the couple to dinners.

It was late in the evening when Wa-zha'-xa-in sat by her own fireplace, the one she had made herself, watching the flames of the fire as they leaped mer-rily upward. Visitors had ceased to come, her husband had gone out to drive his horses to a meadow he had chosen for them, and her little daughter lay asleep in her arms. She wondered why her husband should be so late coming home, and as she listened for him, she heard footsteps approaching, but they were those of two men. They came into her door but no one was visible; she could only hear the sounds the persons made as they moved to sit down and their voices when they spoke to each other. She remembered the voices of her invisible friends. After they had taken their seats at the door one of them spoke to her, and her face brightened with pleasure. "We have come again, *ci-ge*, to tell you that we are happy to find that all is well with you. You have your little daughter, you have a husband, a comfortable home, and many horses. Your relatives and your friends have been good to you, and you have everything to make you happy. Your life will be fruitful and your cares will increase. But in all your joys, do not forget the fireplace; remember that it is sacred. The fire will be your constant companion; it will help you to give cheer and comfort to those dependent upon you. Remember, also, that a thoughtful man honors a woman who keeps clean her fireplace, for it betokens her reverence for things sacred, her kindliness and her hospitality. We rise now, *ci-ge*, to go away for a time, but we will come again at the next happening."

A year passed, and Wa-zha'-xa-in gave birth to a boy. The womenfolk of both wife and husband promptly visited the mother and child. They looked into the face of the little one and some said, "He looks like his father," and others, "He looks more like his mother than his father." A woman not a relative of either the mother or the father came and visited the child. She brought with her a little cradle board. At its head was a frame like a bow, elaborately carved, and to it were attached little balls hanging on strings; there were also small bunches of deer's hooves fastened to the frame. Upon the little board were symbolic carvings that expressed the wish of the woman who brought it as a sort of a gift to the child. These carvings were a cross carved about the middle of the board where the back of the child would rest, the new moon at the head of the board, and within the new moon a star. The four winds [the cross], the new moon, and the star were symbols of long life, and the woman carved the pictures of these on the cradle board as an expression of her wish for a long life for the child. The mother and the father were pleased, not so much for the gift as for the wish that it expressed, and they gave to the woman one of their horses.

One night Wa-zha'-xa-in sat in her house mending by the firelight the moccasins of her husband and her little daughter. The children were asleep, and the father had gone out to care for the horses. The woman had finished her work, had tied the moccasins together in a bundle, and was putting her awl and her sinew into her workbag when she heard the voices of two men at the door. They entered, but she could not see them and thought it strange; then she remembered her two invisible friends. From the sounds they made she knew they had taken seats near the door as they had been doing. One of the men spoke, saying: "We have come again, *ci-ge*, this time to tell you of our pleasure that you have a son. You shall be the mother of many children and grandchildren. Long shall be your life, and you shall be honored by all your people. Remember to keep your fireplace clean; it is sacred. It has no lips, but it speaks; it tells all who behold it that you have a reverence for things sacred, that you have a kindly spirit and delight in making others happy. We now rise to leave, but we will come again."

After this Wa-zha'-xa-in gave birth to a child each year for six years, so that in all she had eight children, four girls and four boys. At the birth of each child the invisible friends of the mother visited her to express their pleasure. The eighth child was the last, and the visitors came no more.[52] As years passed, the children matured. The parents arranged marriages for them, and they in turn had children. Wa-zha'-xa-in's husband then became eligible for the title of *ni'-ka don'-he*, honorable man.[53] According to tribal custom, at every marriage ceremony four old men were chosen, on account of their success in married life, to give advice to the bride and groom. At such ceremonies Wa-zha'-xa-in's husband was always the first to be chosen for this office, and when giving advice to the bride he never failed to extol the virtues of his aged life companion.

Wa-zha'-xa-in and her husband lived to be bent and gray with age, but they were always happy. Their children and their grandchildren delighted to gather about them to hear of their early life.[54] Others also loved to listen to the story that showed a dutiful obedience of the wife to the ancient religious teachings and [the] loving acquiescence of the husband.

Wa-zha'-xa-in's sister and her husband were childless. Their married life was unhappy, for one loved not the other and quarrels between them were habitual. They had never cultivated the qualities that win friendship; therefore, they were always friendless, and so, in their old age, they lived alone.[55]

2.14 The Unfaithful Wife (Pah-nee-wah-with-tah)[56]

A good many years ago a young man fell in love with a married woman. Although she had long been married and had children, she was young in appearance and pleasing to look upon. The woman was equally in love with the man, and the two carried on their secret love meetings for a long time until they could endure no longer the restraints of the duties of the woman to her husband and children. And so one day, at one of their secret meetings, they conceived a plan by which they could live continuously together. It was not long after this that the tribe prepared to go on the annual summer buffalo hunt, the time being way back in the buffalo hunting days.

On the morning that the people were busy packing their horses for the first day's journey, the woman very suddenly took sick and told her husband and children that she was going to die and begged them not to bury her in the ground but to put her body up in a tree as she had an abhorrence for burial in the ground.[57] The husband respected her wish and so, when she died, after the usual funeral ceremonies, he chose a tree with spreading branches and placed the body beyond the reach of wild beasts. Then, as the people took their journey westward, the husband began his mourning, secluding himself from all human association through the day and coming into camp only at night. It was the custom in those days for a man to mourn the death of his wife or any dear relative for the period of from one to four years, and in that time he denied himself the pleasures of human association and the ordinary comforts of life, thus going through a long period of mental and physical suffering.

At about the time that the people talked about going on the hunt, the lover told his friends that he would go to the north on a visit among the Omahas, who at that time were on friendly terms with the Osages. And so upon the day the people began to take their westward journey, the man went away and was not thought of, except by his near relatives.

All day long the lover watched, from his hiding place, the movements of the people until all had disappeared in the distance among the westward hills. Then when dusk came and all was quiet, he hastened to the tree in which the woman was put by her husband and helped her down. For about a month the two lived together in the deserted camp, the length of time in which the man could have made the journey to the Omaha country and back had he really gone there. It was then about the time for the people to have had their hunt and to be on the return homeward, and the two started out to meet them, the woman having disguised herself as an Omaha man. She had her hair cut closely and [had it] roached, which was the style in those days of both the Osage and Omaha men of wearing the hair, and she cut her deerskin moccasins and leggings of the common and well-known fashion of the Omahas.

The disguise of the woman was complete, even to the dialect, and so when the two came to the camp of their own people they without question believed the man when he told them that he had brought with him an Omaha friend. The prominent families vied with each other in their attempts to please the stranger; they feasted him and loaded him with valuable presents so that his daily life was practically among the best of the people.

Quite frequently, the stranger on returning to his wigwam with leftover[s] from the feasts[58] would send the choicest pieces of meat to the two daughters of the man mourning the death of his wife. He would explain in doing so that when at home that was his custom, that his sympathies were with the motherless and he like to feed them when he could do so. This act made much impression upon the families who lived near, and they also sent food to the motherless girls.

It happened one day that when the older of the two girls went to the wigwam of the stranger to return a bowl in which food was sent to her and her sister, she lingered to watch unobserved the stranger who was so kind to her. The stranger was busy dressing his hair and painting his face so that the girl unembarrassed made her observations. The man's robe had fallen to one side and his buckskin leggings had worked down so as to expose a part of his bare leg. She noticed a deep scar on the leg, very much like one she had often seen upon her mother when she was living. This set the girl to thinking very seriously, and when her father returned at night from his days fasting and mourning, she told him of what she had seen, and he only said that there were many incidents where two persons met the same kind of accident and were scarred in a similar manner. The girl, under some pretext, went again to the house of the stranger and saw him when he had washed the paint off his face. In that face she recognized, without the least doubt, the features of her mother, and when her father came home at dusk, with sunken cheek and voice husky with constant wailing, she said to him: "Father, mourn no more. My mother is not dead as you suppose. She is the person who is being entertained by the best people in the belief that she was an important person of another tribe." It was then that the father put aside his mourning to watch and to satisfy his own mind that the stranger was really his wife and that she was practicing the perfidy not only upon himself but also upon all the kind people. Before long he learned that it was really true, and he was seized with an unresistible desire [to take] revenge upon both herself and her lover. He watched their every movement with a hatred that drove from his mind all other feeling. He saw them go together one morning toward the brook, and he hid himself in a bush. When they came near, he confronted them. He desired to shoot the woman first but fearing that the man might escape he took aim and shot him first. The woman started to run, but he quickly reloaded his gun and shot her down. He stripped the woman of her disguise and then called the people, and when they came he spoke not a word but pointed to the two dead bodies and the people knew.[59]

2.15 Mourning Dance for Yellow Ears (Saucy Calf)[60]

In former times the Osages used to mourn for their dead horses in the same manner as they did for their dead relatives. A story is told of the mourning for a horse by the people who owned it. They gave in its honor the *wa-sha'-be a-thin wa-tsi* [war-mourning dance],[61] the same as they would have done for a brother, sister, or other relative. The event was so notable a one in the history of the Osage tribe that it served as a mark for reckoning time. In counting the years since the happening of any event worthy of remembering, the historians would say; "That happened about so many years after the weeping over Non-ta'-ci (Yellow Ears)." This is the story:

An elderly man who had a beautiful young wife suspected for a long time [that she was] having secret relations with a young man, but he could never come up on the two together to confirm his suspicion, although he watched with the greatest care. But one day he caught them in the woods enfolded in each other's arms, and it was then that he determined to punish the young man. He refrained from making a personal assault upon the young lover, which he had a right to do by the well-established usages of the tribe, but he set to work and quietly asked of his friends where the young man was in the habit of grazing his horses. Upon finding out, the offended husband saddled his riding horse and started out in the direction of the place he was told the young offender kept his horses. He found them and drove one, a handsome white horse with yellow ears, into a miry place and stabbed it to death. It happened that a friend of the young lover was out to water his horses and by chance came upon the dead animal, and he hastened home to tell his friends of what had happened. When the two sisters of the young lover heard of the death of the white horse with yellow ears they cut their hair, rent their short jackets, bandaged their feet and put away their moccasins as was the custom in mourning, and gave vent to their feelings by wailing and the wringing and clapping of hands. The horse was a favorite one not only because of its beauty but also for its gentleness, its willingness to carry, and its usefulness as a runner. It was the habit of every member of the family to pet the horse and caress it just as they would a child, so the punishment was meted out to every member of the family by the injured husband as well as to the real offender.

For six months the two sisters mourned, putting moistened earth upon their foreheads and wailing every morning before sunrise, "Non-ta' ci-hi wa-xpa-thin un tha gi the tha a a" ["Yellow Ears—I make myself pitiful"].[62] When the usual length of time for mourning was over, the two sisters, the principal mourners, announced to the people that they would give the *wa-sha'-be a-thin wa-tsi* [mourning dance] in honor of their beloved horse. The time they appointed for the ceremony was midsummer. In those days the Osages never stayed continuously in any one place through the year but were ever on the move, following the herds of buffalo or moving from place to place where deer and other game might be plentiful. And so it happened that when midsummer came, the time appointed by the mourning sisters for the great funeral war dance [mourning dance], the people were out on the summer buffalo hunt. The morning of the day set for the dance came, bright and clear. The sacred pipe had been sent to the brave warrior, now to act as principal mourner and to lead the war party that was to go out, after the dance, to kill an enemy for the deceased. He had accepted the pipe and bag of tobacco, stripped himself of all clothing except the breechcloth, and had gone out to fast and wail in appeal to the supernatural for strength and success. The two men chosen to lead the dance had arrived and taken their places, each carrying a *wa-xthe'-xthe*, or standard.[63] The *xthe'-ts'a-ge* [commanders] who were to act as a council of war and who were to give the order at the dance and when on the warpath had also come and taken their places, and everything was ready for the dance to begin, when runners hastened into the camp to report the finding of a large herd of buffalo within a short distance. With all the excitement usual on such an occasion, the hunters brought in their running horse and started out for the chase, leaving the two *wa-sha'-be-a-thin* and the *xthe'-ts'a-ge* standing ready to dance.

The chase was a success, and the hunters came home with their horses burdened heavily with great quantities of fresh buffalo meat. The *wa-sha'-be-a-thin* (standard bearers) and the *xthe'-ts'a-ge* were sitting waiting in their places, and all night long they sat there waiting. In the morning the people again assembled and took up the dance just where they had left off to go to the chase.

The *wa-sha'-be a-thin wa-tsi*, or standard-bearer dance, was over, and the war party, made up of the *do-don'-hon'-ga* (leader), the *xthe'-ts'a-ge* (war council), and *tse'-xe-k'in* (kettle carriers, or privates) started out against one of the tribes at war with the Osages. They traveled for many days until they found the enemy, fought them, defeated them, and returned with many scalps. And it was thus that the people sent Non-ta'-ci for whom they mourned and fought to the land of the spirits, and the chief mourners washed their faces, satisfied with the respect and honor showed them by the tribe, and ceased their weeping for their dead.

2.16 The Two Young Men Who Mourned Their Living Father (Andrew Jackson)[64]

There were two young brothers who, in speaking of the various tribal customs and ceremonies, used to say to one another, "Someday we will do something that no other man has ever done."

When the two boys grew up to be young men, the older brother said to the younger one, "Younger Brother, I have reached the age when a man should marry, set up a house for himself, and raise children. I wish you would remind our father of his duty toward me and tell him that he should follow the custom of our people and secure a wife for me."

For some time the younger brother gave no serious thought to this request, till one evening as he was idling away the time about the village he happened to remember it, and [so] he hastened home to his father. The old man was sitting alone by the fireplace, and the son took a seat close by his side. The young man spoke, saying: "Father, at the request of my brother, I speak to you. My brother has reached the time of life when men marry, set up a home, and raise children. The custom of our people prohibits his making his own choice; it is for you to select for him a wife, and this he asks you to do."

While the young man was still speaking, the elder brother came in and sat down by the fire. The old man sat in silence for some time as though in serious thought and then he spoke, saying. "My son, your father is dead, and being dead, it is not possible for him to select a wife for your brother."

The two young men listened to this reply in as serious a manner as it was made, although both knew that he was making a jest at his own as well as at their expense. [It was] an allusion to his inability on account of his great age to have further children. As an official jester[65] he spared no one, not even himself or his children. Then the younger brother spoke and said, "Elder Brother, our father has just died, and being dead, it is not possible for him to secure a wife for you. Instead of marrying we must mourn."

The young men stripped themselves of their jackets, leggings, and moccasins as men do when they go to mourn, and they put moistened earth upon their foreheads as a sign of deep mourning. Side by side the young men went though the village, wailing as though in real grief and using the [?] terms for their father, and the people of the village said, in true sympathy, "The old man is dead." Many hastened to the house of the old man but found him sitting quietly smoking his pipe.

The young men went though the village, then on to the hills where they went through a fast of seven days and seven [six?] nights, which is the longest time set for mourners to fast. When the young brother had completed the seven days' fast, they did not return to the village but, having had their weapons brought to them, started out as on the warpath. This was not taken very seriously by the people, and no further thought was given to the incident.

Several months had passed when one high morning a column of smoke was seen to rise in the distance among the prairies. It was a signal given by a war party returning successful. The *non'-hon-zhin-ga* [priests] ran to meet the warriors, although they did not quite know what war party it might be. They found the warriors to be the sons of the old jester, and seeing that they had actually secured the scalp of an enemy, the *non'-hon-zhin-ga* brought them into the village with all the ceremonial forms and songs that belong to a war party returning victorious.

To the ancient *non'-hon-zhin-ga* songs the young men entered the wigwam where sat the old man in his accustomed place by the fireside, and between his legs the sons planted the slender pole to the top of which dangled the scalp of an enemy they had slain. In this manner the young men had secured a spirit to accompany that of their father to the spirit land while the old man was yet living.

The old man promptly secured wives for his two sons, [they] having shown themselves worthy of wives.

2.17 The *Wa-kon'-da-gi,* or Medicine Men[66]

The *wa-kon'-da-gi,* or medicine men, were much feared by the people, and great care was taken not to offend them in any way. If any person should, by chance, gain the ill will of a *wa-kon'-da-gi,* he, by the use of his supernatural power, can make that person himself suffer or some near relative dear to him, or he may destroy a horse belonging to him. The *wa-kon'-da-gi* had the power to help the people or to make them suffer, and many stories are told of the demonstration of their magical powers.

War parties go out depending on the *wa-xo'-be*, or the sacred hawk, for success, believing it to have supernatural powers, but there have been times when it failed to act. In such an event, the *wa-kon'-da-gi*, or medicine man, is appealed to, if there happens to be one in the party. When the war party after many days [of] travel fails to find the enemy, and the men become weary and discouraged, the *wa-kon'-da-gi* is appealed to. The *wa-kon'-da-gi*, with much incantation, prepares for the test of his powers. When he has smoked his pipe and sung his songs, he cuts a circle in the ground with his knife, removes the sod from the ground in the circle, and then mellows the earth in the hallowed spot. This being done, he takes from his medicine bag a piece of buffalo tallow, rolls it into a ball about the size of a walnut, and places it in the center of the sacred ground. All this preparation is made at sundown and at a place removed from the camp, and when [it is] finished the men are forbidden to approach the sacred spot or go near it through the night. The next morning when the sun begins to rise, the *wa-kon'-da-gi* selects a single man to go and see the prepared earth and the bit of tallow placed in the center. The man, without disturbing the ground or the piece of tallow, makes his examination and then returns to the camp to report. Addressing the leader of the war party, he would say:

"*Do-don'-hon'-ga*, I have seen the footprints of horses and mules in the mellowed earth and the marks of human teeth in the ball of tallow." Then, with much gladness, the whole party would go to examine the hallowed earth and the bit of tallow and find the report of the man to be true. The footprints discovered in the mellowed earth are taken to be those of mules and horses to be captured by the war party and the marks of human teeth found in the ball of tallow to be those of the man to be killed. When such signs appear on the place prepared by the *wa-kon'-da-gi* they will never fail to come true. It is supposed that the spirit of the man to be slain by the war party comes to the bit of tallow to give the sign of death as do the spirits of the horses and mules of their capture.

A story of the display of supernatural power by a *wa-kon'-da-gi* is often told. At one time a number of Osages were out on the warpath. They were out a great many days and had traveled far without seeing any signs of the enemy. Food became scarce, and the men were faint from the need of it. Hunters were repeatedly sent out to find deer or buffalo, but they came back weary and footsore without having seen any signs of game. One day, as some of the hunters came back to report that they could find no game, Ca'-be-ki-e, a young *wa-kon'-da-gi*, arose and said to all the men of the war party: "I see that none of you are hunters at all. I could take a gun and shoot a deer from where I am standing now." At this one of the men handed him a gun. Ca'-be-ki-e took the gun [and] leveled it at a bunch of grass beyond the head of a small ravine nearby. When he fired a large buck rolled over and died. At the same moment a doe sprang up, and before it had gone very far Ca'-be-ki-e fired again and killed it. This man was one of the greatest of the *wa-kon'-da-gi*.

A story is told of a *wa-kon'-da-gi* who was called upon to doctor a sick child. He doctored it, and when it was getting well, he said it needed the care of some responsible person, and he would get one. He untied his moccasin string of the right foot and turned it into a snake, which he put under the child's pillow. He cured the child and received a large fee.

2.18 Strange Medicine Man[67]

Pa-thi Wa-kon'-da-gi was a medicine man and belonged to society of medicine men.[68] These medicine men shot each other with pebbles, beetles, fish bones, rattlesnake fangs, and other things of a magical nature. The Osage medicine society has now become lost, Louis Pryor's[69] father being the last [medicine man].

Pa-thi Wa-kon'-da-gi lived when men like To-wah-e-he,[70] Pah-nee-wah-with-tah,[71] Ne-kah-wah-she-tun-kah,[72] and Mo-she-to-moie,[73] who today are old men, were boys.[74] They remember him and the awe in which he was held by all the people, old and young. Many tales are told of the mysterious things that he did in a magical way.

Pa-thi Wa-kon'-da-gi was a young man of about twenty or twenty-five when he began to be known as a medicine man of a most unusual power. None of the men who speak of him say anything about his parents, and from this fact it may be presumed that they had no position of importance in the tribe.

The first time that he became known as a medicine man was when he returned from another tribe where he [had] . . . lived for a number of years with his young wife with whom he had eloped. This young woman was the wife of another man; [s]he fell in love with him, and . . . the two ran away. After a few days Pa-thi Wa-kon'-da-gi wanted to return with the young woman to the tribe, but she refused to go home with him, fearing that she might be killed by her former husband,[75] and so they agreed to go [to] another tribe with whom the Osages were on friendly terms. These people lived a long distance from the home of the Osages, and so the journey of the young couple was full of danger and hardships. They suffered much for want of food, as the young man had not prepared himself for a long journey, thinking that he would return to his home in a few days. He had only his knife and so could not go hunting. One day, when their moccasins were completely worn out, they saw a herd of elk resting along the edge of a bank. The young man had been suffer[ing] much from distress on account of his wife, who began to show signs of weakness from want of food and exhaustion. Pa-thi Wa-kon'-da-gi to this time had not thought of the magical powers he had but recently acquired, and now when he saw the elk and realized how helpless he was to secure one, which he could easily do if he had his bow and arrows, the thought of his . . . dream and the determination to try the power it gave him came upon him.

The young man stripped himself of his moccasins, leggings, and robe and stealthily approached the herd, while his wife sat and watched with eager expectation. When he came within arrow shot of the herd, the young man point[ed] at a large elk with his knife and uttered a magic cry. The knife shot from his hand like an arrow and struck the elk behind the shoulder; it leaped forward, staggered, and then fell. His dream stood the test, and he now knew that he had the powers of a medicine man. He tried, after that, his powers in many ways with success.

The wife happily helped her mate to dress the meat, having first built a fire and satisfied her hunger with some choice bits broiled. They drew the skin from the legs of the animal and out of each pair made moccasins, and they jerked as much of the meat as they could carry and then proceeded on their journey.

After many days they reached the village of the tribe to whom they were going for protection and were welcomed with every kindness. They went to the house of a man whose name was familiar to all the older people of the Osage tribe, and he received them in the relationship terms of son and daughter. And so in this family of prominence the young fugitives were cared for and protected. The young man in return for the hospitality took care of the horses, while the young wife helped in the cooking, dressing of meat, and the bringing in of wood.

One night the young man heard drumming and singing not far away from the house. After listening for some time the young man said to his host: "Father, I want to go and see the dance." "Do not go there, my son," replied the old man. "I fear that some harm might come to you. Those people who you hear singing and dancing do not respect each other's lives and seek by magic to destroy each other. They particularly like to try their magical powers on strangers, and they have been known to take the lives of even their own kin for slight offenses, so I would not like to have you seen at their gatherings."

Notwithstanding this, when the host left the house, the young man stole away and went to see the *xobe watsi*,[76] or mystery dance. He sat in a dark place within the door and watched, but by their magical sense the dance[rs?] became aware of the presence of the stranger and began surreptitiously to shoot at him with their pebbles, [their] beetles, and [the] other harmful objects

[they] used in their magical art. The young man felt them pierce his body and knew the individuals from whom they came. When he had received a number of these shots, the young man returned them with double the violence [with which] they came to him so that the persons receiving the return shots fell to the ground and lay writhing with pain. Then the medicine men knew that they were dealing with a person whose magical powers were not to be trifled with. They invited the young man to take part in the dance, and he returned every shot with greater violence [than] with which they were sent, and the shots that he made himself were almost deadly. When he had become weary of the exhibition of his lesser magical powers, he suddenly stooped down and drew from his moccasins the strings, throwing one at the left of the door and the other at the right, where each became a *she-ki*, or rattlesnake, coiled and ready to strike anyone who came near. Each member of the society became motionless with fear, and when anyone made the slightest move the snakes rattled their tails and raised their heads as though to strike. The young man held his hosts in fear until they begged him to take back the snakes. After this he became a prominent and respected member of the society, and he was looked upon with awe by all the tribe.

What his name was before he left his people is not known, but when he returned he was called and known by the name of Pa-thi Wa-kon'-da-gi, which may be freely translated as Medicine-man-of-another-tribe.

The story of the dream by which Pa-thi Wa-kon'-da-gi got his magical powers is as follows:

When a young man, not long before he left the tribe with his stolen wife, he went to *non'-zhin-zhon* [rite of vigil] upon one of the large hills that lay to the north of the town of Bartlesville [Oklahoma]. Becoming weary of his fast and disappointed at the lack of results, he sat in the shade of a stunted oak and amused himself by throwing stones into a hole in the trunk of the tree. It took many stones to fill the hollow of the tree up to [top of] the hole into which he threw them. He did not suspect at the time that this act was a part of the magical plan. The sun had nearly set when he had filled the hollow of the tree with stones, and thinking to wash the *non'-zhin-zhon* sign [soil] from his face according to the requirements of the rite, he started down the hill toward the creek. He came to a slight depression in the side of the hill into which he fell and lost consciousness of all things natural and awoke to the supernatural. Before him appeared an animal, which he called *ki-tha-ha-pa* ("head at both ends").[77] At each end of his body the animal had a head, and his scaly back was curved. He closed his eyes tightly and blood oozed out of the tightly closed lids; the muscles of the body contracted making the scales rise, and between them blood appeared and trickled. When this was done a great wind arose tearing the grass and breaking the tops of the tree. The then strange animal spoke to the young man, giving him power over wind and rain and other mysterious powers. The young man decorated his shield as well as his robe with a picture of this mysterious animal.

Pa-thi Wa-kon'-da-gi shunned the society of other young men, but there was one with whom he liked to talk about his mysterious dreams and of the strange animals he saw in his fast dreams and the magical powers he received from them.

It is said that at one time when the tribe was returning from an annual summer hunt Pa-thi Wa-kon'-da-gi asked his friend to go with him to the hill where he had had his dreams to see the strange animals, for there were more besides the one he saw in his first dream. The young man did not dare to refuse to go with him, although he had no desire to see them or to have anything to do with them. On the side of the hill in the depression into [which Pa-thi Wa-kon'-da-gi] fell where he had his first dream there was a hole in the ground about the size of a spider's hole. He told the young man to stand near this hole and to watch it while he himself went on the other side to make the animals come out. "Don't run away when you see them, they will not hurt you," Pa-thi Wa-kon'-da-gi said to him. The young man, though excited with fear, did as he was bidden and stood watching the hole in the ground. After some time he felt gusts of wind coming out of the hole and heard sounds as of heavy breathing, which became louder and louder, and the wind, which increased, tore the hole open, and there came a roar of thunder and wind, and he saw the treetops carried away by force of the wind. Stricken with terror, the young man ran away and never stopped until he got home.

2.19 The Death of Village Maker[78]

Many stories are told of Village Maker and Not Stingy, medicine men who lived about the time of Strange Medicine Man. These two men were both noted for their magical powers and were feared by the people. Village Maker loved power and delighted in exercising it on all occasions and for that reason held the fear and hatred of the people, while Not Stingy, desiring to have the respect and love of the people, never used his power to the injury of anyone. He was mild mannered and kindly in disposition and was slow to take offense at insult or effrontery. The following story is told of the killing of Village Maker by Not Stingy. . . .[79]

Not Stingy had two wives, both of whom were good and pleasing in appearance. Village Maker, knowing that Not Stingy had magical power, sought to bring about, in various offensive ways, a contest with him but never succeeded. At one time, in the spring of the year, Village Maker went to the house [of] Not Stingy while he was away and by force took one of his wives and kept her. Not Stingy felt keenly the insult but never attempted to revenge it or to recover the possession of his wife. In the fall of the year, when Not Stingy was away from home, Village Maker took the other wife and kept her, which forced Not Stingy to abandon his home and to go and live with his sisters.

Village Maker was persistent in his efforts to get into magical combat with Not Stingy, and so when some traders came with rum Village Maker secured some. He then sent for Not Stingy to come and drink with him. Not Stingy, like the other great men, had a fondness for rum, so much so that he had not the strength to resist the temptation of his enemy. At the feast that preceded the drinking both men were most courteous to each other and were extravagant in their compliments to each other. When the rum was served, which Village Maker did himself, he gave his guest a very liberal quantity with the usual compliments that go with the offer of drink. Not Stingy was not outdone by his host in the matter of courtesy, and being a man of scrupulous honesty he was sincere in his expressions of good wish[es] for his host.

Village Maker for a second time served the rum, after which the two became less guarded in their speech. When Village Maker was well under the influence of the drink, he said to his guest: "Not Stingy, you are a peace-loving man, are you not?" "Yes," replied Not Stingy. "The good will of the people is more to me than anything else." "You resent no insult, though you keenly feel the indignity," continued Village Maker insinuatingly. "I bear no malice," Not Stingy mildly replied, "not even to one who has wantonly wronged me." "That," said Village Maker in an aggravating manner, "to my mind is not wholly due to a forgiving spirit but largely due to lack of courage to maintain your dignity and self-respect. To speak plainly, I think you more of a woman than a man." "It takes a great deal of courage," replied Not Stingy, "to control oneself when greatly wronged and to avoid disgraceful encounters. A man may not resent an insult and yet have no fear of those who have brutal instincts." At this Village Maker became angry and made a motion as though to shoot (magically) Not Stingy who said: "Do not do so, for if you do I will make you to know something of which you are really ignorant." Notwithstanding this, Village Maker shot his companion, who immediately threw out the magical arrow from his body. Not Stingy reached down to the edge of the fireplace and touched the ashes with the tips of his fingers and then his lips and tongue, and then reaching [to the] back of him, he pulled from between the frame of the wigwam and the covering an undressed deerskin and threw it violently to the ground. In an instant the raw skin became alive and stood as an angry buck with bristling hair. It looked fiercely at Village Maker for a moment and then shook itself with great force, making its bristling hairs fly all around the wigwam. Village Maker's eyes, nostrils, and mouth became filled with the flying hairs and the more he tried to throw up the hairs he swallowed, the more they irritated him. His two wives, whom he took away from Not Stingy and who were present, also became choked with the hairs that filled the house. For a whole season the three suffered from the effects of the hairs, and one by one they died.

2.20 Big Bear and Runs-to-meet-men[80]

Big Bear was a Con'-dse'-u-gthin [Upland Forest band] and a respected medicine man of that village. He was successful in the treatment of diseases, and the people preferred his services to that of other medicine-men. It happened that Runs-to-meet-men, a noted medicine man of the I-u-dse'-ta [Little-Osage band], was visiting friends in the Upland Forest village, when in an emergency he was called to treat a person who was suddenly taken sick, and although everybody knew that if Big Bear had been home he would have been preferred, he [Big Bear] took it as a slight and became offended. When he had heard of it, he went out and, standing in front of the door of his house, began to address the people of the village. "For many years," he said, "I have been doctoring your children, and in all that time none of you have ever expressed dissatisfaction of my treatment in any way. Today a stranger comes, and you run to him with a trifling ailment and are loud in your praises of his success in curing it. From now on do not come to me when your children moan in distress and with pain. I will doctor no more; go to your newly found medicine man."

Big Bear went into his wigwam, and taking his bundle and rattle from their accustomed place, he began singing his dream songs and giving magical cries. Then Runs-to-meet-men, who had heard the speech of Big Bear and his songs and his cries, suddenly fell sick, and he said to his anxious friends who were about him, "I am going to die. Big Bear has shot me and nothing can save me. Before I die I make this request of you; when my breath leaves me, put my body in a whole buffalo robe, binding it tightly together, and throw me in the river where the water is deepest and leave me."

In accordance with his dying request [his] friends threw his body into the river and then sent a runner to tell his relatives that he had suddenly died. Late in the evening when the runner was approaching the outskirts of the Little Osage village, he saw a man sitting in the path with a white dog. The man said, "Why are you running into the village in such haste?" "Runs-to meet-men is dead," replied the runner, "and I am hastening to tell his relatives." The man said, quietly, "I am Runs-to-meet-men, who died suddenly in the Upland Forest village and was thrown into the river. I have come back to life and am now on my way home. You may go no further for if you do you will throw my people into sorrow all for nothing."

The runner returned home, and when Big Bear heard the news he gathered together the medicine men of the village, and with rattles in his hands, he sat singing with them in the expectation of being shot at by Runs-to-meet-men. Suddenly he seized a brass kettle and put it over his head and then fell forward, dead. Runs-to-meet-men had shot at him, the "arrow"[81] going through the bottom of the kettle into Big Bear's head and killing him. This man never came back to life.

2.21 The Cruel Medicine Man and the Orphan[82]

I-tsin'-ke was a wicked, despotic man. By his supernatural powers he held the people in fear of him and treated them cruelly. At the surround of the buffalo, no man who had killed one would dare to butcher it before I-tsin'-ke came and claimed the tongue and other choice pieces. Any man who by some mischance offended I-tsin'-ke would die in some mysterious manner. So great was his supernatural power that his control over the people was absolute.

There was, however, a person who had not a bit a fear for I-tsin'-ke, and that was Wa-hon-i-zhin-ge, the orphan. Although Wa-hon-i-zhin-ge knew from the actions and the talk of the people of their abject fear of I-tsin'-ke, he had no occasion to oppose him, having never met him face-to-face or been troubled by him.

The herd was a large one, but as the hunters approached it they were not at all happy, for they knew that I-tsin'-ke was present and that all the choice pieces would be seized by him to feed his numerous wives. When the hunters had arrived within running distance of the herd, the signal for the attack was given, and all rushed forward with their utmost speed. Soon the hills and the valleys were alive with fleeing buffalo and pursuing men. Being strong and active, Wa-hon-i-zhin-ge was among the first to reach the fleeing herd, [allowing him] to select the fattest buffalo. When Wa-hon-i-zhin-ge had shot down his choice, his grandfather came running up, he having watched the young man from the start, but he was horror stricken when he found that his grandson had already turned the animal on its back and had begun to butcher it. Another man had also been watching Wa-hon-i-zhin-ge, and that was I-tsin'-ke for he knew that the young man was strong and swift of foot and would likely kill a fat animal, so he followed him up. When the grandfather saw I-tsin'-ke coming, he, with renewed effort, hastened toward his grandson to warn him. "Hurry," he said to the young man, in an undertone. "He has come. Cut out the tongue and give it to him." But the young man pretended not to hear and worked the harder to finish his work.

I-tsin'-ke had come, but he stood speechless with anger and astonishment at Wa-hon-i-zhin-ge's impertinence. At last he spoke in a voice loud with anger: "Who killed this buffalo, and why do you butcher it without fear of me?"

"I killed the buffalo," replied Wa-hon-i-zhin-ge calmly, "and being the killer it belongs to me by all the rules of hunting. Therefore I butcher it without fear of anybody."

"You should fear me as all do," shouted I-tsin'-ke, and trembling with anger, [he asked], "Who are you that you should defy me thus?"

"I am Wa-hon-i-zhin-ge, and I fear no man." And Wa-hon-i-zhin-ge [said] as calmly as before, "You can make other men tremble with fear of you, but you cannot do that with me."

"Cut out the tongue and give it over to me," demanded I-tsin'-ke with a violent gesture. "It belongs to me."

"I will not give you the tongue," replied Wa-hon-i-zhin-ge. "It belongs to me and not to you as you say."

"I'll kill you!" cried I-tsin'-ke, and [he] made a motion to draw an arrow, when Wa-hon-i-zhin-ge stepped quickly up to him and stamped the ground with his right foot, and lightning shot up from the earth around I-tsin'-ke, stunning him.

"Do no more," said I-tsin'-ke when he had recovered from the shock. "I meant no harm and was only jesting. Let us put away all angry feeling and be friends instead of enemies."

"We will not be friends," exclaimed Wa-hon-i-zhin-ge, showing anger for the first time. "You have treated my people cruelly, and I'm going to make you suffer as much as you made them suffer. As soon as I get back to camp, I'm going to take your best wife away from you."

I-tsin'-ke, though defeated for the time, went away believing that Wa-hon-i-zhin-ge would not go so far as to carry out his threat, but when he got home and entered his wigwam he found that his youngest and best-looking wife among his twenty-four wives had gone. Shaking with anger and rage, he hastened to the door of Wa-hon-i-zhin-ge's wigwam and, standing at the door, shouted angrily, "Wa-hon-i-zhin-ge, release and send back to me my wife, or come out and fight me."

The young woman was sitting in the middle of the wigwam with Wa-hon-i-zhin-ge, brushing his hair, and when she heard her husband's angry call she trembled violently with fear. "Do not be afraid," said Wa-hon-i-zhin-ge, without moving. "He will do you no harm. Look in the very middle of my head; you will find there two small bugs, one red and the other black. Take them and put them in the palm of my right hand."

The woman found the bugs and put them in the palm of Wa-hon-i-zhin-ge's right hand. He blew them with his breath through the door at I-tsin'-ke, and the moment they touched him they turned one into a tiger and the other into a lion.[83] They both attacked I-tsin'-ke, tore him into shreds, and devoured him.

When the people saw this, there was great rejoicing among them. All the *wa-je'-pa-in* (criers) ran about the camp calling out the news. Then the people flocked to Wa-hon-i-zhin-ge's wigwam to thank him, [and] they brought him many valuable gifts and finally made him their chief.

2.22 Wah-ti-an-kah (Bacon Rind)[84]

When Wah-ti-an-kah was a young man, a large body of Osage warriors marched against a certain enemy tribe. The young man served as a scout in the expedition. The Osage defeated the enemy and made their way home with captives and spoils. During the homeward march, Wah-ti-an-kah went aside to take the rite of vigil. He fasted eight days and on the morning of the ninth,[85] as he arose from his night's rest, a man suddenly appeared before him and said: "I come as a messenger from a person toward the east." Wah-ti-an-kah looked eastward and saw a man whom he recognized as the sun, [and] then he fell to the ground unconscious. When he revived he discovered that his eyes, ears, mouth, and nostrils were infested with maggots. He had died and come back to life. He arose and found that he was in his full strength and vigor. He hastened to a brook, stood amid its rushing waters and cleansed himself, then went home.

For a long time Wah-ti-an-kah could make no meaning of his vision. Then one day, as he sat with his family, he suddenly became silent and motionless. After a time he spoke and sent for some of the prominent men of the tribe. He told them that a large war party was approaching the camp. The men aroused their warriors to action. They met the enemy, slew many of the bravest, and completely routed the rest. The people, in their wonder at the strange manner in which Wah-ti-an-kah gave the warning, fell to calling him Wa-kon'-da.

When Wah-ti-an-kah became conscious of the infirmities of old age he called together his children, grandchildren, and great-grandchildren. When all had enjoyed the feast he had provided, he spoke, saying: "I wish to say a word to you before I depart for the spirit land. Be content with the things it pleases Wa-kon'-da to place within your reach. Do not take the rite of vigil and suffer hunger and thirst with the hope that you will see Wa-kon'-da. He is invisible. I have tried to see him, [but] I have failed. No living man has seen him, no living man ever will. Wa-kon'-da is invisible, but we know that he is in all places, in the sky and in all things that move therein; he is in the earth, in its still waters, its springs, lakes, and rivers, in its dark forests, and in its grasses. He is everywhere. Our people call me Wa-kon'-da, but it is wrong to apply that name to a man. A few times I gave to the people timely warning of approaching danger, and without thinking they called me Wa-kon'-da."

2.23 Dreamers (Shun-kah-mo-lah)[86]

In the early days there were men [and women] whose dreams came true. There came a time when an Osage lost his horse. After searching for the horse for some time the owner found the tracks of the horse. He called together some of his friends to go with him to follow the trail. Being a boy ready for some adventure, I volunteered to join the party. We followed the trail for two days. On the second morning, after the three men had gone through the dawn ceremony of wailing (I made the fourth one of the party), one of them said to the owner of the horse, "I think we had better discontinue the pursuit [the horse had been stolen by some men of another tribe]. I had a dream in which I saw the horse return in the spring when the new grass starts up to the camp in which we live, and so it is wise that we stop here and return to our people." The man was known by us as one whose dreams come true, and so without questioning the wisdom of discontinuing the pursuit, we started for home. There was plenty of game, so all the winter we remained in this camp, and then one morning, when the new grass began to come up and the trees to bud, the owner of the lost horse went out to look for his remaining herds, and approaching [them] he saw in the distance a horse feeding alone. He went to it, and there he found his lost horse. He hastened to his wigwam with it and called to his friends to come and see the horse that was lost and returned. Besides the friends there came a great crowd because the people knew of the theft of the horse, of the party that went in pursuit of the thieves, and [of] their return because of the dream. This event added much to the reputation of the dreamer among the people.

At another time the two great divisions of the tribe were having the *wa-sha'-be*[87] [war] dance at the village of the Con'-dse'-u-gthin [Upland Forest band]. At that time I was living among my own people, the Pa-ciu'-gethin [Big Hills band],[88] and had heard of this dance. I wanted to join one of the two war parties going out, for there was another war party gotten up, a *wa-xo'-be u-kon-da* [clan war party],[89] but this last, which I hurried [?] to join, had gone, so I came to meet the larger war party. We were gone a good many days, when we came upon an [enemy] war party. We attacked it, and I killed two warriors. I struck one of them before anyone did, and as I had properly decorated myself with the sacred charcoal there was no question about my right to count the *o'-don*. After the killing of the two hunters we returned toward home, singing as we marched abreast on our horses the victory songs. We marched all night and took a little rest toward morning along a small stream. Some of the men, as the dawn appeared, arose to go though the customary wailing, when one [of our men] saw a man going up the stream on the other side. Before the wailers had time to pick up their weapons, I was well on my way toward the man, who was making his flight; I splashed across the stream and soon overtook the man and struck him with my bow, at the same time calling out my name and claiming the *o'-don*. He was a man of the Wichita and was unarmed and completely at our mercy. Out of pity we released him and spared him. I was awarded the *o'-don* nevertheless, and I have been counting it at the *wa'-don-be* ceremonies[90] as *mon-zhon'-dsi-ga-xthi*,[91] because after the killing of the first two men the character of our journey turned from that of a war expedition to one of ordinary travel as on a hunting trip. The name of such an *o'-don* is different from that of one won on a regular war excursion.

The manner of the smaller war party that went ahead of us was a little insolent because they marched out of camp through the ceremonial grounds of the larger war party composed of men from both sides of the tribe and did not offer to join. This little party had a *wa-xo'-be*, and so their excursion was called *wa-xo'-be u-kon-da* [isolated bundle or clan war party] as a distinction from ours, which was a *do-don'-hin-ton-ga* [a large or tribal war party].

When we came home we heard that this small war party had returned successful. They also had killed two men. This war party had [been] gone for some time when the leader, for some cause, resigned and the man next in rank was chosen leader. They were camped near a stream, and while the men were roasting buffalo meat toward the middle of the day, the new leader stood aside wailing. Suddenly he stopped the wailing and approached his men, to whom he said, "In my dreams as I stood wailing, I saw two on horseback approaching this spot, and now I wish that two men be sent to yonder rise to watch for them." Two men were sent to the slight rise in the distance to watch, and as the sun was nearly in the middle of the sky, they arose and hurried toward camp, giving the signal that the two horsemen were also at hand. The warriors hastened to prepare for the attack. They waited till they came close to camp and then made the attack. Both men were killed, and the leader of the small war party was looked upon as a true dreamer.

2.24 The Woman Dreamer[92]

Ten select men went on the warpath. They were gone seven days when they found two men of the enemy, who were on foot. They threw their blankets and leggings on the ground and left a servant to care for them. The two men led the warriors into an ambush, which was surrounded by a ravine. Late in the afternoon a fight started. At dark a warrior returned to the servant and said to him: "Select two robes for yourself among these and two pairs of moccasins, [and] hurry home and tell the people all the ten warriors are slain; I care to live no longer." Then the warrior hurried away in the growing darkness. The servant could not believe that two men could exterminate ten warriors. While he was still struggling with the doubt, he heard the thud of many feet passing by in the dark [and] also a voice he recognized to be that of the leader, saying, "I have done that which I vowed I would do; now we hasten toward home, my valiant men." The servant rushed forward crying out, "Wait for me, I'm coming." A cold and whirling wind swept around him as he heard the sounds of the hurrying feet dying away in the distance. Then he knew that all the men had been killed, and it was their ghosts that were hurrying homeward, conscious only of the blows they had dealt in their desperate struggle and not of the bodies they were leaving.

In the village that the ten men had left but a few days before, a woman, in the middle of the night, long before the usual hour for weeping (approach of day) went out and wailed, her sobs and cries betokening great grief. The cry ceased not until the sun appeared against the horizon.

The chief called some of his men and said to them, "I will ask one of you to go and find out what woman that was who wept from the middle of the night till sunrise, and why she was so grief stricken. It is unusual for one to cry before the break of day." A man hastened away and returned to repeat: "It was Wa-zhi'-xa-win, the dreamer, who had spent half the night in lamentations." "Go to her," said the chief, "and ask her why she wept so." [He returned to the woman and asked why she wept.] The woman replied, "Bring to me a pipe filled with tobacco and light it for me, and I will find out for you the cause of my grief." When the pipe was brought to the woman and lighted, she took four whiffs, then said: "Spare me the pain of telling that which will bring sorrow to all the people; bear with patience your eagerness to know till tomorrow when the sun rises. On the brow of yonder hill a man will appear; hasten to him, and he will tell you."

All eyes eagerly turned toward the hill the next morning as the sun was rising, and there the figure of a man appeared upon its brow. Man, woman, and child ran to meet the man; they surrounded him, and in a voice broken with grief, [he] said: "They all fought bravely and died." They all wept so that their combined voices pierced the sky.

Years before, this woman, Wa-zhi'-xa-win gave timely warning to the people by one of her dreams and saved them from disaster, at which time the chief said: "Let no man or woman dreamer speak of dreams so long as Wa-zhi'-xa-win lives, She is the only dreamer."

2.25 Spirit Woman (Hlu-ah-wah-tah)[93]

Many years ago a war party that had gone out for nearly a year was returning unsuccessful. The region through which they were passing was a mountainous one. Just about sunrise, the warriors, by order of the leader, broke camp and were about to march when the leader addressed one of the kettle carriers[94] and said to him, "Go after some water. I am thirsty." [The] kettle carrier replied, "*Do-don'-hon'-ga*, by your order we are about to march; the spring where we found water is a long way off, and if I go after water the march will be delayed. Can not you wait until we come to a stream on our march?" The leader ordered his men to put down their burdens and wait while the kettle carrier went for water. Then the kettle carrier, seizing a vessel, hastened to the spring that was located on the side of a mountain off in the distance. As the man approached the spring, he saw not far away from it a beautiful woman sitting on the grass dressing her hair, which was the only covering she had for her body. The woman appeared not to look at him, and without taking further notice of her he hurried on, dipped the vessel in the spring, and started back to his waiting leader. He passed by the woman on his way and had not gone very far when suddenly he became conscious of an irresistible desire to return to the woman and speak to her, although suspicion lurked in his mind that she was not a real woman. The habit of promptly fulfilling the orders of his leader also drew his mind away from the woman, but her influence was greater, and so he was drawn toward her against his inclination. He returned to her and passed a short time with her and then hastened back to camp with the water for his thirsty leader. The leader seized the vessel and drank and then passed it to the officer next in rank. Then the kettle carrier whispered hastily to the leader. After a minute's thought he said to his men: "My thirst is not yet quenched. Drink the water in the vessel, while I go to the spring and drink some more. Wait here until I come back."

The leader was gone for some little time, and when he came back he ordered his men to march with the greatest speed possible. This they did, keeping up the pace until sunset and darkness came, when they were obliged to camp for the night. Nothing unusual happened through the night, and after an undisturbed rest the men marched again before sunrise and traveled at the same pace that they did the day before. They traveled in the same way on the third day and on the fourth, as though fleeing from an imminent danger.

On the morning of the fifth day, as the sun was rising, the leader ordered his men to resume the march but to travel at a moderate pace, as he believed that the danger which necessitated their flight was passed. He was yet speaking when a kettle carrier spoke to the leader and said, "*Don-don-hon'-ga*, there sits a woman not far from here." "Bring her to me," the leader said. The leader spoke kindly to the woman, advising her to go home, but she refused to do so. For a long time the leader spoke to her, but neither arguments nor threats could break her determination to follow the men. Thus, prompted by the fear of personal harm by supernatural means for the wrong that he had done the woman, he ordered his men to treat her with respect, and he not only took care of her himself but refrained from a further violation of her chastity.

The leader and his men resumed their journey and in time reached home with the spirit woman. She made her home with the leader, who treated her as a member of his family and accorded her all the honors due from a father to a daughter, and she conducted herself in the manner of a chaste woman.

There came a time when a young man of the Wa-zha'-zhe division was taken with an uncontrollable desire to make the spirit woman his wife, and he made love to her. She accepted his courtship and in time became fondly attached to him. Then when each knew that one could not live without the other they agreed to marry according to the custom of the people. The parents and the relatives of the young man sent many valuable presents to the warrior, who was now looked upon by all the people as the father and protector of the woman. The father and mother accepted the presents and shared them with their relatives. Then, after a time, the adopted relatives of the young woman dressed her up in the finest clothes they could find, and they had her taken to the young man with presents that greatly outnumbered those that were made by the relatives of the young lover. Then they, the young woman and the young man, sat together in the midst of their relatives and ate together, and all knew that the two were married.[95]

Many children were born to the couple, and the mother and all the children were known to possess the power of restoring the minds of young people and hunters when spirits make them lose their senses.

2.26 The Flute Ghost Story (Ben Wheeler)[96]

A long time ago there was an old man and his wife who had an only son, a newly grown young man. The old couple made everything of the son, and they let him have all the things that were in their power to give him. There was also another old man and a woman who had an only son, a young man about the same age as the other. The two young men became fast friends and one was never seen without the other, they being so fondly attached to each other. It happened that one sickened and died, and the other grieved and sorrowed for his friend as though for a near relative. Soon after the death of the young man, the people began to prepare to go on the annual summer hunt. The young man in mourning, when his parents busied themselves in preparation for the long journey, spoke to them and said, "Father and Mother, you are preparing to go with the people on their hunt, and you expect to share in all the joys of the hunt as you have always done. I am sorry to tell you that you will have to go without me this time. While this grief that touches my very spirit is upon me I cannot go where every day there will be effusions of joy all around me. I must stay here and [?] alone. The father and mother of my friend will also remain, and I will take care of them till the people return. Go, then, as you are preparing to do, and feast once more upon buffalo meat. It is my wish that you go and it must be so."

Upon a certain day the people saddled and packed their horses and began their journey toward the buffalo country, and the parents of the young mourner followed them, in respect to the wish of their son.

The young man carried his few belongings to the wigwam of the aged parents of his friend to live with them till the return of the people. Then the young man took upon himself the rite of *non'-zhin-zhon* [rite of vigil]. For seven days he fasted, putting moistened earth upon his forehead and going far away from home. He remained away all day long and came back to his home when the sun went down. On the morning of the eighth day, the young man spoke to the aged couple and said to them "I have completed my *non'-zhin-zhon*. I have gone through the full seven days, yet there are other things for me to fulfill, and for those I ask that a small wigwam may be set up for me where I may be alone." The old woman set to work and built a small wigwam where the young man moved his things. There he stayed all day long, and when night came, the aged couple would hear him go out toward the deserted village, [and] then they would hear the sounds of a flute going around the village. This went on for four nights, and then on the fifth night the old couple heard the sounds of two flutes instead of one, one at one end of the village and the other at the other end, one following the other. This went on for another four nights, the young man always returning to his little wigwam just at dawn and remaining alone all day long. The young man repeatedly cautioned the old couple against disturbing him; he asked them not to look in upon him or even to give any thought to what he was doing.

On the evening of the ninth night the aged couple again heard the young man go out toward the deserted village with its skeletons of wigwams, for the people had left the frameworks of the wigwams standing. This time the couple heard the sounds of the two flutes united and playing in unison. All night long the two flutes played around the village and always in unison. Just at break of day, the old people heard the young man come back to his wigwam, and then they heard also the voices of two young men in earnest conversation. For four nights this went on. After that the old couple heard the flutes no more, but there was always the sound of the voices of two young men in the little wigwam. The young warrior asked that food for two be prepared by the old woman, which she did, hand[ing] [it] in to the little wigwam without coming or looking in. In that way the two young men lived together.

One day two men came back to the village upon some errand and reported that the people were returning with a great supply of buffalo meat. The hunt was a success, and all the people were happy. There had been no deaths or accidents, and there was no sorrow.

The two men were preparing to go back to meet the people when the young man spoke to them and said, "I want to ask a favor of you two men. I want to ask you two men to each take a bag and go from wigwam to wigwam when you get back to the people and ask for a bit of the skin of any animal that they have secured. Let one man begin at one end of the camp and the other at the other end. Then when you have completed the work, you will bring me the bags."

The two men did as the young man asked them, and in a few days they came back with the two bags with bits of skins secured by the hunters. These two bags the young man carried to the grave of his friend, and then he set to work to remove the stone coverings. He removed the body and then filled the grave with the skins from the two bags and set them on fire. When the skins of the animals were consumed by the fire, the dead young man opened his eyes and came to life.

The two friends returned to the wigwam and found the aged couple and the two men who brought the bags of skins.

2.27 The Young Warrior and His Dead Wife[97]

Many years ago a man died, and in his honor the *wa-sha'-be s-thin wa-tsi*, or standard dance [mourning/war dance], was given by the tribe. This ceremony was performed at the request of the parents or other relatives of the dead person and for the purpose of organizing a war party to go against some enemy of the tribe to secure a spirit to accompany the dead to the spirit land.

After the ceremony, the war party went out and was gone for many months. Among the warriors of this war party was a young man who had but recently been married. He had departed from the old custom of waiting for his parents to choose him [a wife] and buy [her] and had taken the woman of his own choice to his home and lived with her.[98] The two loved each other and lived happily together up to the time the young man joined the war party and went away.

The war party was successful in finding the enemy and in a battle killed some of them and took scalps. After this they started for home, and in a few days, the young man, becoming anxious to see his wife, left the war party and made for home all by himself. When within four or five days' journey from home he came upon a deserted camp, which he recognized as that of his own people. They had been on their annual summer hunt and had gone home. [As he was] looking over the site, he suddenly saw a woman approaching him. Seeing that it was his wife, he ran to meet her and embraced her. She told him that the people had been on the hunt and that they were on their way home; they had broken camp the day before, and she waited for him, knowing that he was on his way home and would pass through the old camp site.

While the young man was speaking to his wife, he suddenly said, "On yonder hill I see a newly made grave; someone must have died when the people were camped here." For some little time the woman did not reply, and then she said, "Yes, a boy died, and they buried him up there. Should not we hasten homeward?" Without further talk, the young man led the way, and with hastened footsteps they made their way toward home, following the winding trail that lay reddened with dead grass.

On a dark evening, after a few days' journey, the young man and his wife entered the camp and quietly sought the wigwam of his sister where they had made their home. When they found it the young man hurried in, but the woman remained outside.

The greeting that the young man received from his sisters was one of sorrow and tears, but he could not suspect that the feeling they expressed was for his own sufferings when he was away in a strange land. When the sisters had dried their tears, the young man said, "Sisters, I have brought a woman home with me; she [has] remained outside. Go and bring her in." The two sisters looked at each other in silent surprise, and then one of them said, "What woman is it, Brother? We do not understand." The young man with like surprise answered, "Who else could it be but your sister-in-law, my own wife, whom I found waiting for me on my way home? Go bring her in." "It is impossible," the two women replied, their voices broken with sobs. "Our sister-in-law died only a few days ago, and we laid her away among the hill near one of the old camping places, how can she [have] come back?" Upon hearing this, the young man fell backward, his eyes turned upward and his body became rigid, and he was dead.

2.28 Return of the Dead (Charles Wah-hre-she)[99]

A long time ago some of the Osages went out on the warpath. After wandering about for many months the warriors found the enemy and fought them. Before the battle had gone very far, the Osages found that they were outnumbered and that the chances of winning the fight were against them. A consultation was held by the leaders in which they agreed to retreat in as orderly a manner as was possible. In the retreat a young man was wounded, and his friends carried him along until he died, and then they hid his body in a bush to save [prevent] its mutilation. The warriors made good their retreat with but this one loss, and when the fight was over they took up their march homeward.

In a day or two the dead warrior came back to life and began nursing his wound, which healed rapidly. It was not long before he was [able] to take up his march toward home, which he did. On his way he came across eight stray horses, all of which he succeeded in catching and taking with him. One morning, after a journey of many days, he came upon a small stream that he knew to be in his own country. This he followed for some distance when to his joy he came to a deserted camp, which he recognized as that of his own people. He looked around and saw in the trees some things deposited there that could not be carried.[100] Then he went in search of the site of his own wigwam, for he knew its place in the camp arrangement.[101] He had no trouble in finding it, but to his great grief he saw strewn around it the locks of his widowed mother. "Who could she have mourned for but my wife?" he said to himself. He looked around and on the brow of a low hill not far away he beheld a newly made grave. "There they have buried her," he murmured, "there I will go and die, for what else is there for me to live [for]?" He made his way up the hill and opened the grave, and there sat his wife as though still living. He entered the grave and sat by the side of his wife, taking her hand in his, and waited. The hot sun beat upon his head, but he was unmindful of it all. Night came and still he sat unmoved. Thus he sat for two long days without eating or drinking.

When the sun was rising, on the morning of the third day of his watch, the young man saw, in the distance, a figure approaching him. He kept close watch of it, and as it drew near he recognized it to be that of a woman. He made no movement whatever, and the woman came on, turning neither to the left nor to the right. Her head was covered so that the young man could not make out who she was, although he tried very hard to do so. She came on and on, paying not the slightest heed to him, until she came to the very foot of the grave; then, without any warning whatever, she suddenly turned to nothing. At the very moment the woman disappeared in that mysterious manner, the young man felt his hand tightly grasped by that of his wife; he turned to look into her face, [and] her eyes opened and her lips moved:

"Your sufferings have moved them to pity," she said, "and so they have let me come back to be with you yet a little while longer. They also wish to come back and can do so if you will help them. Four days and four nights you must keep awake and help them. I will help you to bring them back, so come now, and let us go to yonder little stream and build the wigwam in which to receive them."

Hand in hand the two went down to the little stream and began to work. While the wife set to work cutting the poles for the framework of the wigwam, the young man went to the trees where he saw bundles deposited among the branches, and, bringing them down, [he] examined them. There were buffalo robes for use as rugs to sit upon and rush mats such as were used for the covering of wigwams. They had been put in the trees by some of the people who could not very well carry them on the long journey. These things the young man gathered into one great bundle, which he swung upon his back and carried to the place where his wife was building the wigwam. Already she had partly finished the framework, and when he came with the rush mat covering she put him to work fastening them on, while she herself went inside to lay down the buffalo robes for the comfort of her guests.

The wigwam was finished and the two fires[102] built just as the sun was setting, and the two took seats at the accustomed place of the host and hostess at a ceremonial feast and waited. The fires burned cheerily in the gloom of the wigwam, and it was not long before the young man heard the approach of many footsteps. The door opened and closed, and the wife assigned seats to the guests as they came, but while the young man could hear their footsteps and see the soft buffalo robes under their [weight] he could not see any part of the persons. Those who came and were already seated began to carry on conversation about things of common occurrence in daily life, but in all there was nothing to indicate that there was anything serious in the purpose of the gathering.

Suddenly there arose from the place of the principal guest a man's voice. It made a short and formal address to the hostess expressing the thanks of the guests for her hospitality, [and] then it announced the arrival of the time to begin the ceremonies. The sounds of a big drum filled the room, and the dance began. All night long the dance went on without ceasing, and all the time the young man strove to see the strange and invisible dancers. It was past midnight when the young man began to see plainly the toes of the dancers, and then when the light of the dawn began to penetrate the gloom of the wigwam he could plainly see their feet up to their ankles, but to his disappointment the dance stopped and the guests began to take leave of the hostess and to walk out, visible only up to their ankles. When all had gone the wife spoke to her husband, congratulating him upon his being able to keep awake all through the first night and begging him to use his utmost strength to keep awake all the rest of the four days and nights.

The day passed without either of the two falling asleep, and dusk came. The wife hurriedly built the fires and then took her seat beside her husband at the place of the host and hostess. Then the guests began to come, the wife greeting and assigning them to their places. The young man could see the people up to their knees as they passed him to take their places. When all had come, and the voice at the principal guest's place had made its speech, the big drum began to sound again and the dance of the second night began. As the night advanced the young man could see the thighs of the dancers grow more and more visible. Then, when dawn appeared, the dancers took their leave and went out in file, visible up to their hips.

Again, when the dancers had all gone, the wife spoke affectionately to her husband, expressing gladness at his success in keeping awake the second night of the dance. All the day long the two kept each other awake, and when the shadows of the evening came the wife again kindled the two fires in readiness to receive her nightly guests. When the fire began to burn, cheerily she took her place by the side of her husband as on the night before and waited with him. They came and were greeted as before, and when they passed to take their seats they were visible to the young man up to their hips. The principal guest made his little address of thanks, the drum struck up, and the dance of the third night began. Around and around the wigwam the dancers stepped, keeping strict time to the beat of the drum and visible to the young man only up to the hips. Gradually the dancers began to be visible to the young man up to the middle of their waists, and then when the pale light of the approaching dawn began to penetrate the wigwam, the guests took their leave and marched out in a procession, visible to the young man up to the armpits. The third night of the dance was successfully passed, and with tender words the wife expressed her gladness and the hope that her husband might keep up his strength to pass the fourth and the last night with equal success.

The day was passed in work about the house by the two and in keeping each other awake. When the sun crept behind the hills and the shadows began to deepen, the wife again kindled the two fires, and soon the gloom of the wigwam was driven away by the light of their red flames. Then the guests began to come in, and as they passed to take their seats they were visible to the young man up to their armpits. It was their last night; it was to be his last effort to see them, each from the crown of his head to the soles of his feet. He would do his utmost to keep awake so that these spirit people might come back and live again on earth. The principal guest had made his speech of thanks, and the big drum began to boom. Then the dancers arose, each one visible to the young man up to the armpits. The dance went on and on way into the night, and gradually the people began to be visible up to the tops of their shoulders, their throats began to appear, then their chins and their mouths, and then their noses. Dawn was coming and also the full vision of these spirit people. The wife grasped tightly the arm of her husband to keep him awake. He put forth every effort to keep awake: he must see them in full, he must bring them back to life. The dancers brought down their feet with greater vigor, the young man could see their eyes, soon he would see their eyebrows, then their foreheads—but they seemed to be moving away from him, and the sound of the drum became a mere mumble in the distance, and then he fell limp upon his wife's lap.

When the young man awoke he saw that the sun had risen high and that the visitors had gone, never to return. "Ah," said the young wife, who still held her husband in her arms, "if only your strength had held out they could all have come back as I have done. Now we will never see them again." "We did all that human strength could do," the young man replied. "We could do no more. Now that it is all over, let us prepare to move on and to find our friends who are still living."

The young man up to this time had forgotten about his horses [and] now hastened to go after them, while his wife hurried to tear down the wigwam and to replace the things that she and her husband had borrowed for the comfort of their guests. The horses were brought in and packed, and soon the couple were on their way westward to find their people, following the trail that was now nearly obliterated by the rains.

For many days the two traveled, until one day the husband saw off in the distance the chasing of a herd of buffaloes by many riders. "Those are our people," the young man said to his wife, "and they are out on the chase. Pitch the wigwam by yonder little stream while I go to let them know that we have come back to them again. I will bring home some meat, so keep a fire burning."

Having thus spoken, the young man urged his horse to a long and steady lope, and when he had ridden over several hills he came suddenly upon a man who was working hard at the butchering of a large fat cow. The man stood up and looked steadily for a few moments at the newcomer and then dropped to the ground in a dead faint. He did not come to for some little time, and then he slowly raised himself to a sitting position, pale and with a confused expression. Still trembling, the man looked again upon the face of the young man, and with a voice scarcely audible he said, "We left you dead upon the battle field; I carried you myself. Why do you now return to disturb me?"

"You think you see my spirit," the young man replied, "but you see me in my real flesh and blood. I came back to life, and not only that, I have come back with my wife."

"Impossible," exclaimed the man. "Your wife died many days ago and was buried. How could she come back with you?"

"It is true that my wife died and was buried," the young man said, "but it is equally true that she has come back to life as I have done and has come back with me. Look yonder, where the smoke rises from the trees near the little stream; there she has pitched her wigwam and there is where I want you to go with me so that you may see that what I tell you is true. And so, make haste. Put all that meat on my horse, and we will go."

Without another word the man threw the hide on the back of the horse and then all of the meat that he had already dressed, and the two strode side by side toward the trees where the smoke of a wigwam arose to the sky. The sun was still high when they came to the camp, and there stood the woman near her door waiting for the return of her husband. The older man timidly approached the woman and took her hand and then fell to the ground unconscious. When the man came out of his swoon, he saw that the woman had placed before him some of the meat that she had cooked. She gave him a bowl of cold water to drink and then bade him to eat. He ate in silence while his mind busied itself with the question as to whether all that was happening to him was real or as to whether his senses were deceiving him.

The man had eaten the simple meal prepared for him by the woman, and then the husband spoke:

"My friend, you are now about to go back to the camp, and I want to send a message by you to my mother. Tell her that I want her to bring together all of the prominent men, the chiefs and the braves, and to tell them that my wife and I have come back and will soon be among our people again. This she will do tonight, and tomorrow I want her to come after us. You will favor me by showing her the way."

It was dark when the man got back to the camp, but straightway he went to the wigwam of the young man's mother and told her of the return of her son with his wife, giving her the story, and with all haste she sent for the official messenger of her clan and sent him to call the chiefs and the braves to her wigwam, as well as to [call] all of her near relatives, to hear of the return of her son and daughter-in-law from the land of spirits. Not only did the chiefs, the braves, and relatives come, but all the people came to hear. The man repeated the story he told to the widow without the slightest change, and all listened with the closest attention. When he had finished one man arose and said, "We all know that when a man is about to die the spirits hover about him; he sees them, he speaks to them, and he tells his relatives and friends about them, and then he dies. It is so with this man. He is about to die, the spirits hover about him, he sees them, and now he tells us about them, and soon his relatives will be carrying him to the hills to bury him. It is, therefore, folly to listen to him any longer, for you all know that the man he speaks of was killed in battle, and we all know that the woman died and was buried after we had started on this hunt."

"I believe what this man has told me," the widow said, "and early tomorrow morning, I am going with him to bring home my son and his wife, and then you will all know the truth."

The chiefs and the braves arose and left the wigwam, and all the people who had gathered around outside to hear the news moved slowly away to their home, expressing among themselves the belief that the messenger whose story they had just heard was near to death and that was why he had been having frequent communications with spirits.

Very early in the morning the widow started out accompanied by her son [and the?] messenger. The sun was up high when they arrived at the camp of her son. The young man and his wife had packed all their belongings and saddled their horses in readiness to move when the mother came. Upon taking the hand of her daughter-in-law, the old woman fell into a heavy swoon, for it was like the grasping the hand of a spirit, knowing that the young woman had died and had actually been buried. After the three had greeted and wept over each other, all mounted their horses and moved on to the camp of the people.

It was late in the afternoon when they entered the camp. They were received in the most touching manner by all of the people and wept over. Many fell into a faint when they touched the hand of the young woman, for they did not quickly overcome the notion that they were grasping the hand of a spirit.

For a long time, the people did not tire of hearing the young man tell the story of his coming back to life, and they were greatly interested in the song of the spirits who for four nights visited him in their efforts to get back to this life. Some of the songs are remembered even to this day. It was suggested at one time that the songs be used in the *non'-hon-zhin-ga* [rite of vigil] rites, but the young man objected to it, and so it was that the songs of the spirit ceremonies were not taken seriously and embodied in the tribal rites.

Thi-ta-zhin-ga, Little Dove, was the name given to the young man by the spirits, and this name was frequently used in many of the songs that they sang in all their nightly processions.

2.29 The Little People (Tho'-xi Zhin-ga)[103]

My father took me to school,[104] and as he put me there he said, "You must not come back until I come for you. If you run away and start home alone, the *mi'-wa-gthu-shka* [little people][105] will catch you and take you to their home. I will come after you every Saturday."

I knew nothing about the *mi'-wa-gthu-shka*, but from the warning given me by my father I imagined it to be some kind of a malicious spirit given to the habit of doing harm to people, particularly to children, and although I did not like the school and often yearned to go home, I heeded the warning and never attempted to go home alone.

My father took me home one Saturday morning, and I spent the afternoon with my dog, hunting rabbits along a rail fence that was not very far from our house. I carried a little ax with which to dig out the rabbits if they should flee into holes in the ground or into hollow trees.

While hunting along the rail fence, my dog suddenly attacked something that at the moment was entirely invisible to me and then rushed back as though in terror. The dog made another attack [and] then at the place from which he fled back to me a little mist arose that gradually took the form of a little naked man with a bushy head. I was stricken with fear. The dog, standing by my side, kept barking furiously, while, literally paralyzed with fear, I stood unable to move. I was also powerless to withdraw my gaze from the little man. With mischievous grimaces he beckoned me repeatedly with a stick he used in beating a little drum that he hugged tightly under his left arm.

My mother, hearing the barking of the dog and thinking that some danger was threatening me, ran up to me and took me in her arms. She tried at first to see what was plain to the dog and to myself, the little man with his mischievous grimaces and his beckoning drum stick, but she could not. She could not hear the sounds of the drum, which also had in turn an enticing and mischievous influence. She tried to drag me away, but I fell down and could not rise. Then she called to my father for help, telling him that I was under the spell of a *mi'-wa-gthu-shka*. My father hurried to us with a little tin pail filled with ashes. He bent over me and spoke to me, but I could not reply because I was unable to make my lips meet and I was voiceless.

My father pressed my eyelids together and then dashed a handful of ashes upon my forehead. Then, picking me up, he carried me to the house. Then I was bathed in hot water and made to smell the smoke of burning cedar fronds. Then the mischievous sounds of that little drum slowly died away, and I began to feel the power of motion coming back to my legs and arms, and I could talk.

When I got well and could go about, I saw that my father had made a ring of ashes around our house to prevent the wicked little *mi'-wa-gthu-shka* from coming near me. He never bothered me anymore, but I could hear the sounds of his little drum sometimes on a quiet evening coming from a certain high cliff.

—

2.30 The Demon Animal (Ben Wheeler)[106]

Wherever there is a hill that is separated from all others and [that] stands all by itself in a level place, these animals are to be found there. Of all the known demons, this one is feared the most because it hardly ever fails to overtake any animal or man that it pursues. It has a body like that of a weasel and is much larger. The entrances to their dens are always surrounded with the bones of animals the[y] [have] destroyed.

At one time there were two young men who thought of going on a deer hunt. The deer trails led them toward a lonely hill. When the dogs that they had with them got halfway up the hill, they suddenly lowered their tails and came stealthily down toward their masters as though in great terror. The two young men looked around the see what had frightened the dogs, and they themselves became terror stricken when they beheld a number of *we-ts'a-ta-zhon-gle-shka* lying around the entrance of their den, asleep. The men and their dogs retreated as quietly and as speedily as they could toward the river because it was known that these creatures were afraid of water, and a stream of water was the only place of safety from their attack. The two young men with their dogs had not gone very far when the demons awoke and sprang up to chase them. When they saw this, the men urged their horses forward, and their pursuers were close upon them when they splashed into the water and were safe. The screams and the roaring of the demons when they saw that they could not get at the men was terrible, and although the young men knew that they were safe, they continued their flight until they got out of hearing of the sounds.

At one time the two men went in search of their horses that had strayed away. They came to a level place along the river, where they found the horses feeding. They approached the horses without any suspicion of danger when one of them saw the head of an animal thrust up above the tall grass. The man in frightened whisper gave the warning to his companion. They looked cautiously around and saw other heads peering over the tall grass and that their horses were being surrounded by the *we-ts'a-ta-zhon-gle-shka* and were about to be attacked by them. The demons all at once rushed forward to attack the horses, and then the two young men fled, but two of the creatures saw them and turned to give them chase. The men made for the river and plunged into the water, . . . their pursuers . . . close upon the heels of the horses. The two young men gave the alarm, and all the warriors [came?] with guns and bows and arrows went out to fight the demons. They came upon them when they were devouring the horse they had killed, and the fight began. The demons did not mind the arrows that were shot at them, but the bullets that were shot at them proved deadly to them. They retreated toward their den in the side of a hill that stood in the middle of a level tract of land, fighting fiercely. Before they came to their den they succeeded in kill[ing] three of the Osages. Finally they fled into their cave, not being able to stand the guns, and then the men hastily gathered grass, and stuffing it into the entrance of the cave, [they] set fire to it. They stuffed more and more of the grass into the cave and kept up a hot fire. The cries of the beasts, at first, were frightful, but as the fire became unbearable in the cave their noises grew fainter until they became altogether silent. The men raked the ashes from the cave and found that one of the beasts had come close to the entrance when it died from heat and suffocation. The other also died of suffocation from the smoke. Since that time the *we-ts'a-ta-zhon-gle-shka* [have] never [been] heard of again.

Part Three

Animal Stories

3.1 The Squirrel Maidens[1]

"Let us go to the squirrel maidens [*cin-ga-ga-con-ci*] and make love to them," said Rabbit [Mon-shtin'-ge] to Buffalo Bull [Tse-dto'-ga].

"Yes," replied Buffalo Bull gladly, "let's go and make love to the squirrel maidens." And so it was that Rabbit and Buffalo Bull went to the home of the squirrel maidens in the black forest, way beyond the blue hills. The arrival of two strangers was indeed cause for great excitement and wonder among the squirrel maidens. They had never before been visited by men, and the sudden appearance of two enlivened the hitherto dull life of the squirrel maidens. Each one strove to appear attractive to Buffalo Bull by brightening up her personal adornments, for each one admired his massive size, his strength of limbs, the manner of his walk, and his dignified bearing. Rabbit received not the slightest attention from the squirrel maidens, and he felt lonely, although the forest was alive with maidens. With hidden and suppressed jealousy he watched the amorous attentions of the squirrel maidens to Buffalo Bull, and though [he was] outwardly quiet his mind was active with plans for stealing the affections of the squirrel maidens from his friend and companion. Buffalo Bull felt not the slightest concern for his friend's discomfort, for like his own kind he was satisfied to have all the maidens all to himself.

It so happened that for a time Buffalo Bull had to be absent, and it was in that time that Rabbit took occasion to set his plans in motion. For lack of better company the squirrel maidens gathered around Rabbit and began to talk to him in loving praise of Buffalo Bull, who they longed again to see. Rabbit listened quietly and coldly and jealously to the chattering of the squirrel maidens and gave not a word of reply to them until they had settled down to sober quietness. Then he said to them: "You admire and love Buffalo Bull because he is large and strong and good looking, but if you knew, as I do, that he is only a servant and is not his own master, you would have no love for him."

"You speak not the truth," cried all the squirrel maidens in one voice. "We know that Buffalo Bull is a great man and is master of himself."

"Words alone cannot convince the love stricken of the truth," said Rabbit, suppressing his anger with effort, "but you will know that what I have told you is true when you see, yourselves, Buffalo Bull, the great man, bridled and saddled and mounted by his master."

It was not long after this that Buffalo Bull came to Rabbit's wigwam and said to him, "Friend, let us go again to see the squirrel maidens and make love to them."

"I'm very sick and cannot go with you this time," replied Rabbit in a feeble voice, pressing his bandaged head with both hands. He breathed fast and hard and groaned as though in real pain and tossed from side to side in his bed.

"Oh, you wouldn't need to walk," said Buffalo Bull. "I can carry you there and back. You can saddle and bridle me and be very comfortable."

Buffalo Bull was very much puffed up with conceit; he was not satisfied only with winning the love of the maidens but must have someone witness his wooing, and that was to be his undoing.

It was difficult for Rabbit to suppress the smile that lurked in the corners of his mouth as he made answer, accepting the offer, and to maintain the part he was playing, but he successfully carried it through by making a groan and a grunt follow each word of his answer.

On the following morning, Rabbit bridled and saddled Buffalo Bull. The bridle was beautifully beaded and adorned with fluttering feathers of the golden eagle. No less beautiful was the saddle in its make and the ornamentation. It was made of real elk horn covered with white rawhide and was trimmed with deerskin, soft and yellow. The flaps of the crupper were handsomely beaded and from the lower edges flowed long, wavy white fringes. Rabbit, wrapped in his finest beaded blanket and dressed in fine deerskin leggings, jacket, and moccasins, mounted. A large eagle feather fastened in his scalp lock set off his shaved and roached head,[2] and in his right hand he carried a fan made of the tail of the golden eagle. Mounted and dressed in this manner Rabbit entered the village of the squirrel maidens. Whichever way he moved the air became fragrant with the odor of *mon'-bi-xon*,[3] the leaves of a sweet-smelling weed he had liberally rubbed into his blanket. The maidens came to the doors of their wigwams, paused a moment to see, and then all gathered admiringly around Rabbit. Some brought him water to quench his thirst and others brought him food to refresh him. The change of attitude toward him was complete. He had completely won their admiration and love, and there was not one who gave even as much as a look to Buffalo Bull. Rabbit did not deign to dismount but sat there on Buffalo Bull's back, fanning himself with his great eagle feather fan.

It did not take long for Buffalo Bull to notice the transfer of the admiration of the maidens, and it was not long before his jealousy and anger began to rise within him. This was clearly indicated by the erection and the trembling of his little tail and his pawing of the earth. Then with startling suddenness he plunged forward, bucking and kicking in the true fashion of a bucking horse, bellowing loudly at every jump and kick. The squirrel maidens fled to the trees as fast as they could go, for they were in real danger. Rabbit grasped the pommel of the saddle and hung on as long as he could, but the girth broke as Buffalo Bull made a desperate leap upward, and he came down in a heap with all his finery to the ground and Buffalo Bull came at him with lowered horns. With remarkable agility Rabbit plunged into a briar thicket and was out of harm's reach.

And it was thus that the wooing of the squirrel maidens by Rabbit and Buffalo Bull came to an end.

3.2 The Hawk and the Horned Owl[4] (Tho'-xi Zhin-ga)

The horned owl (*i'-ton*) and the hawk (*gthe-don*) met one evening and engaged in a fight with each other that lasted the whole night long. Both fought with equal courage, but the hawk, [was] unable to see very well in the dark [and thus] was at great disadvantage, while the sight of the owl strengthened with the approach of darkness. Toward morning the hawk became so exhausted that he was no longer aggressive and fought only to defend himself.

It happened that on that very night, and close to the scene of the conflict, a man sat with arms folded around his knees [and] in his hands held a little pipe that he used in his supplications to the unseen power. He had fasted six days and was in the sixth night when he heard the noises of the combat all around him. All night long the man sat listening to the cries of the combatants, to the sound of their wings as they chased each other through the air about him. He knew from the cries what birds these were that were using all their strength and courage to destroy each other. In some of their flights they passed so close to him that he could feel the air driven by their wings against him.

The morning star arose with the struggle still going on, and the faster was about to again put moistened earth upon his forehead when again he heard the sound of wings coming swiftly toward him. Then, suddenly one of the birds shot under his arms and the other, the owl, sped on with loud and curious cries. After a moment he returned and alighted upon the ground near the man. With anger in his voice he spoke:

"Give up that person to me," he demanded, but the man sat silent and unmoved.

"Listen not to him," the hawk said. "He has baffled me in this night's conflict, for his strength is in the darkness of the night, but protect me till the coming of the dawn. In the light of the day is my strength; keep me till its coming and I will reward you. You have enemies; I will give you power to overcome them in the broad light of the day even though they have with you the equal advantage of seeing where to strike."

The man's spirit leaned in sympathy toward the hawk, but he neither spoke nor moved.

Again the owl spoke in a voice angrier than before:

"Give up that person to me," he said. "I also have the power to give rewards. In the darkness of the night is my strength. My enemy hears not my coming when I attack nor sees me when I strike. Give up that person to me while yet it is night, and I will give to you the same power that I have, the power to see in the night as well as you can see in the day. Your enemies shall fall an easy prey to you when you attack them in the darkness of the night."

The man raised his head as though to speak, when he beheld the pale light of the early dawn upon the eastern horizon. The owl, also seeing this, spread his wings and lifted himself to the limb of a tree nearby where he alighted. It was then that the hawk moved and spoke:

"My strength revives; you have rendered me a service," he said to the man, "and I shall reward you. Pluck from my left wing the shortest feather you find there. Keep it always upon you, and if ever there comes to you a moment of dire distress it will remind you of this scene and you shall have both strength and courage to meet the danger. You shall fall upon your foe with the same courage and strength with which I shall now fall upon mine."

The hawk shook himself, [and] then arose in the air, uttering a cry that he [makes] when about to fall upon his prey. With the unsteady beating of wings the owl took to flight; then like an arrow swiftly descending, the hawk shot down; he struck the fleeing owl with a cracking sound, and the bird of the night fell fluttering to the earth in death.

The fasting man feebly arose to his feet and gazing upon the red glow of the dawn spoke, saying, "Thus the light of day falls upon and overcomes the darkness of night."

3.3 The Four Coyotes and the Persimmons[5] (Tho'-xi Zhin-ga)

Four brother coyotes went on the warpath. They [had] traveled for many days when they came to a river that was too deep for them to cross by wading and too wide to swim over, and so they traveled up the stream in single file, the oldest one leading, in search of a shallow place where they could cross safely.

So intent were the brothers upon crossing the river that they gave all their attention to the water and looked neither upward nor toward the land. Suddenly all saw in the water at the same time *cta'-in-gi* (persimmons) in great bunches. This was a welcome sight to them, for they had not eaten anything for two days and were very hungry. "They are down in the water," they all said at the same time. The oldest one said, "Tie a stone to my neck and let me down, and I will gather some of the fruit and bring them up to you."

The three younger brothers ran round hunting for a stone and found one. They tied it to the neck of the oldest one and let him down. He was down for some little time when some bubbles rose to the surface of the water. Then one of the three said, "How selfish he is; he is eating the persimmons all alone and is giving us no thought. Tie a stone to my neck, and I will go down."

A stone was tied to the second eldest one, and he was let down into the water. After a little time had passed some bubbles arose to the surface, and there was no further sign of the second oldest brother. Then the next one said, "Younger brother, tie a stone to my neck and let me down. Our brothers do not seem to desire to let us share in the persimmons. I will go down."

This was done, and the third of the eldest brothers went down into the deep water to get persimmons. When the rings of ripples died away and the surface became smooth again, a bunch of bubbles shot to the surface, and there were no more signs of the last diver.

The last coyote was hunting along the lower edges of the bank for a stone so that he might let himself down into the water, when a strong breeze disturbed the leaves of the persimmon tree hanging over the edge of the bank. Hearing the rustling of the leaves, the last coyote looked upward and there above him were the persimmons hanging down in great bunches. He looked to the ground and saw scattered all about him the wind-fallen persimmons. The youngest and the only remaining coyote warrior then fell to eating the wind-fallen persimmons without giving any thought to his elder brothers.

3.4 The Coyote and the Woodpecker[6]

The coyote made a visit to the red-headed woodpecker. The woodpecker welcomed his visitor and then said to him:

"My friend you have come just at a time when we are all out of provisions, but I will do what I can to properly entertain you."

The woodpecker then flew to a dead tree nearby and began to peck at it with his bill. In a short time he had a good-size pile of dust on the ground from his pecking. He had his wife put this into a wooden bowl and set it before the coyote. The dust as soon as it was put into the bowl turned into pounded buffalo meat, which the coyote heartily enjoyed.

When the coyote had finished eating, he said to his host: "You have beautiful red feathers on the top of your head; how did you get them? They look like fire."

"I was born with them," the woodpecker replied. "My father and his father and his father had them and my son and his son and his son will have them. All my descendants will have them."

"How beautiful," said the coyote. "But I want you to come and see me in three days. Be sure and do this, for it will give me great pleasure to see you at my house."

"I will do so," the woodpecker said in a hesitant way. "In three days I will be at your house."

Upon the third day after this visit the woodpecker went to the coyote's house. With expressions of gladness the coyote greeted his friend and invited him to take a seat in the middle of the house usually assigned to an honored guest. The coyote was dressed in a very peculiar manner. He had taken a burning brand from his fireplace and fastened it to the back of his head, and the dead trunk of a tree had been planted in the house near his side. The woodpecker noticed the queer headdress of his host, but like a well-bred person, he refrained from making any allusions to it. After the formal greeting and a few complimentary remarks the coyote said:

"My friend, you have come just at a time when we are all out of provisions, but I will do what I can to properly entertain you."

The coyote then leaned toward the dead tree and pecked it with his nose. In doing so the flames from the firebrand tied to his head struck the side of the house, which was made of grass, and set fire to it. The fire burned fiercely, and the woodpecker barely escaped with his life by flying swiftly out through the smoke hole. The coyote was caught in the flames and burned to death.

3.5 The Coyote and the Fawn[7]

The coyote in his restless wanderings over the earth suddenly met the fawn and was struck with the beauty of the little round spots on his back. "What beautiful spots you have on your back," said the coyote. "How did you get them?"

"It is easy to get them," replied the fawn. "I got my pretty white spots from hot fire. I hunted for a hollow log, and when I found one I stuffed it with dry grass and leaves and then set fire to it. When the fire became very hot I sat with my back close against it until the pretty white spots came."

The coyote made no further remarks but went on his way, looking back every now and then to see if the fawn was watching him. When he thought he was far enough away from the fawn and could not be seen by him, the coyote hunted around for a hollow log. He soon found one and gathered dry leaves and grass and stuffed the log [in and] then set fire to it. When the fire became very hot the coyote sat with his back close against it and waited for the pretty white spots to come. The fawn had forgotten about the talk with the coyote so was surprised when he suddenly came upon him seated with his back against a hot fire.

"Why do you sit with your back against so hot a fire?" asked the fawn. "You will surely get scorched."

"Keep still, keep still," said the coyote. "I feel the spots coming. I'm going to have as many pretty spots on my back as you have on yours."

The fire began to [get] hotter and hotter, and the coyote's eyes began to bulge outward, [and] then suddenly they both popped out with a big noise. The fawn sprang forward and gave chase to the flying eyes and caught them. Instead of bringing back the eyes to the coyote, the fawn ran on singing mischievously:

The da'-don in-shta'don, the a'-bthin a-thin he,
Shon'-ton-xo'-dse shta-don a'-bthin a-thin he.

(Here, what eyes are these that I have as I run?
Gray-wolf's eyes I have as I run.)

"Listen," cried one of a number of coyotes who heard the fawn's song as he was passing by. "What is the fawn singing?"

"He says he has our brother's eyes," exclaimed another, "and he is running away with them."

"Quick," cried the leader of the coyotes. "Cin'-tso-k'e (Hairless Tail), you give chase and bring back our brother's eyes."

The leader of the coyotes knew that the fawn was the fleetest of all animals, so he selected the best of his runners to give chase to the fawn. Cin'-tso-k'e put all his strength into the pursuit, but the best that he could do was to snap at the fawn's legs. When he gave out, the leader cried: "You, Cin'-tse-ga-ha-xpon (Bushy Tail), take up the chase and bring back our brother's eyes."

Down the valleys and up the hills, Cin'-tse-ga-ha-xpon chased the fawn. With his utmost effort Cin'-tse-ga-ha-xpon overtook the fawn, but all he could do was snap at and bite off the fawn's tail. The fawn did not give up the coyote's eyes but went on, bewailing the loss of his own beautiful tail:

Wa-non-xe-a-ba cin-tse on-thi sdu-dsa da tha
Wi'-cin-dsa!

(The ghosts have pulled out my tail,
My tail!)

In his flight, the fawn happened to come across the rabbit. The rabbit was touched by the distressing cry of the fawn and in true sympathy asked: "What are you crying for, my brother?"

"The ghosts have pulled out my tail," replied the fawn. "That's what I am crying for."

"Don't cry," said the rabbit in a kindly voice. "I will lend you my tail."

"Thanks, brother, thanks." replied the fawn in gratitude. "I will wear it but a short time and then come back and return it to you. In truth, you show me pity and kindness."

The rabbit pulled off his pretty tail, leaving only the fluffy little bunch at the root and handed it over to the fawn. The fawn, still profuse with his thanks, took the tail and put it on. Then over the hills he went still having the coyote's eyes and wearing the rabbit's tail. The fawn never came back to return the rabbit's tail, and he is wearing it to this day, while the rabbit goes about with only the little fluffy bunch of hair he had left when he parted with his tail.

Notes

Preface

1. See Bailey 1995:18–19 and Bailey and Swan 2004:109–23 and 137–49.
2. Fletcher and La Flesche Papers.
3. La Flesche 1905:12.
4. For biographical data on La Flesche, see Liberty 1978, Mark 1982 and 1988, and Bailey 1995.

Chapter 1

1. While *The Omaha Tribe* appears in the *Annual Report of the Bureau of American Ethnology* for 1905–6, the volume was not published until 1911.
2. The 1914 manuscript was not published until 1921. See La Flesche 1921.
3. For additional biographical information, see Bailey 1995:11–29, Alexander 1933, Liberty 1978, and Mark 1988.
4. La Flesche 1930:533.
5. Bailey 1995:77–84.
6. See La Flesche 1932:359–403.
7. Clan priesthoods were divided into seven different degrees of which the Ni'-ki was one. The precise importance of these degrees is unknown.
8. La Flesche 1932:60.
9. See Bailey 1995:17–26.
10. See La Flesche 1932.
11. See Tinker 1957.
12. See Bailey 1995:36–40 for clans and known life symbols.
13. See La Flesche 1932:65.
14. See La Flesche 1932:208.

Chapter 2

1. This is a very brief summary of Osage history. For a more in-depth account, see Bailey 1973:3–75, Bailey and Swan 2004:3–10, Rollings 1992, Din and Nasatir 1983, and Burns 1989:73–459.

2. Most of the tribes along the Mississippi and Missouri raided the Caddoan tribes for captives to trade to the French. As a result, so many of the Indian slaves in Louisiana were Caddoan speakers that the name "Pani" or Pawnee became the word for "Indian slave" in the local French dialect (Hyde 1951:15).

3. Although the French government outlawed Indian slavery in Louisiana in 1720, the law was ignored (see Nasatir 1952:1.11, 19).

4. The Spanish outlawed the trade in horses because many of the horses were taken in raids on Spanish settlements in New Mexico and Texas (Bolton 1914:1.71).

5. Nasatir 1952:1, 50.

6. Mayhall 1962:26–27.

7. Although they controlled most of Arkansas, southern Missouri, eastern Oklahoma, and southeastern Kansas, in 1800 the Osage numbered less than ten thousand. This figure is based on the estimates of eighteen hundred "warriors" in 1800 (Flint 1904:294), of twelve hundred "warriors" in 1802 (DuLac 1807:56), and fifteen hundred "warriors" in 1811 (Brackenridge 1904:60).

8. The "Indian territory" was not a formally organized territory of the United States but rather referred to a specific region designated as occupied by Indians.

9. See Farnham 1906:121.

10. Quoted in Bailey 1973:58.

11. Ponziglione Ms.:267.

12. See Office of Indian Affairs 1875:276.

13. See White 1965:202.

14. For a more detailed discussion of Osage religion, see Bailey 1995:29–35, 61–75, and Bailey and Swan 2004:27–38.

15. The Osage word term for this was *wa-thi'-gethon*, "the power to search with the mind" (see La Flesche 1930:530).

16. See Bailey 1995:47.

17. See Bailey and Swan 2004:49–67.

18. For a list of clans and their known life symbols, see Bailey 1995:36–40.

19. For a list of known subclans, see Burns 1984a:32–42.

20. La Flesche 1921:45 and Mathews 1961:143–48.

21. During the early decades of the nineteenth century, villages continued to fragment. Burns (1984a:10–14) offers a list of thirty-two villages that existed between 1847 and 1861 and the band with which each was associated.

22. See Burns 1989:128–45 for a discussion of these and other Osage trails. These trails and campsites were well known to hostile tribes. Their enemies, particularly the Pawnee, would frequently hide along them in the hope of ambushing any stragglers from the main party.

23. Fletcher and La Flesche 1911:58.

24. Fletcher and La Flesche 1911:58.

25. Only certain men were used as criers. How formalized this position was is unknown.

26. At the turn of the twentieth century only one such bundle was known to have still existed. The bundle priest had died, and the bundle was thought to have been buried with him (La Flesche 1921:70).

27. For a description of the initiation rite used for this priesthood, see La Flesche 1921 and Bailey 1995:222–76.

28. For a fuller description of this bundle, see La Flesche 1921:72.

29. See La Flesche 1939:201–55 for a description of this ceremony.

30. La Flesche 1928:29–95 discusses two versions of the child-naming rite.

31. For lists of personal names by clan, see La Flesche 1928:122–64 and Burns 1984a:45–110.

32. See story 1.5, "Earth Names and Sky Names."

33. Very little is known of the different clan haircuts of the Osage, but Fletcher and La Flesche (1911) supply illustrations of the different clan haircuts of the closely related Omaha.

34. La Flesche 1932:223–24.

35. La Flesche (1932:108) defines *ni'-ka don'-he* as "a grandee; good man; illustrious; a hero; distinguished; a prosperous man; a man honored by his people." Pipe priests were also referred to by this term. It is assumed that while all pipe priests were called *ni'-ka don'-he* that not all *ni'-ka don'-he* were pipe priests.

36. La Flesche 1932:121.

Part 1

1. This was not told as a single story. Taking stories told by four different priests, La Flesche put them together to construct a single narrative outlining the development of tribal religious and political organization. This story was published (see La Flesche 1921:59–71). I have made some changes in La Flesche's published text; I have removed his summary statements, deleted redundant paragraphs, moved some of the paragraphs to better fit the chronology of events, and divided the narrative into six named parts.

2. Every clan had its own version of coming to earth. See stories 1.2, 1.3, and 1.8 for the origin stories of the Wolf, Black Bear, and Gentle Sky clans.

3. The pipe symbolized unity.

4. In this case the leader of Wa-zha'-zhe meant that they were part of the Hon-ga moiety.

5. The phrases "new country" or "move to a new country," which appear several times in this narrative, do not refer to a geographical move. La Flesche (1921:62) explains it as "a term expressive of a slow movement that preceded a change in the government of the tribe."

6. See story 1.4, 49–51, for additional information.

7. This paragraph has been moved from its original place in La Flesche's published version and inserted at this point.

8. The pipe also symbolized a prayer to Wa-kon'-da (see La Flesche 1930:578–79).

9. The phrase "made a pipe of his body" refers to the pipe being a life symbol of the Wa-zha'-zhe tribal division.

10. The "red boulder" is a life symbol of the Hon'-ga division. The red boulder was

symbolic of endurance as well as of the sun. The sun in turn was symbol of never-ending life (La Flesche 1921:61).

11. The Tsi'-zhu were also present, and the Wa-zha'-zhe offered them a pipe as well, which they accepted (La Flesche 1921:62).

12. See story 1.11. The sacred foods are corn and water lily root.

13. The sacred earthen pot. "The common belief concerning this . . . is that some mysterious power is given the food cooked in this sacred earthen pot, a power that can reach the enemy and render them incapable of resistance when attacked" (La Flesche 1932:161).

14. See story 1.4 for more discussion of the specific plants.

15. By this phrase they meant that all of the clans agreed to this by symbolically "placing within the house their life symbols." This was symbolically accomplished by the priests of each of the clans reciting their clan *wi'-gi-e* that named their life symbols. See the last part of story 1.7 for this ritual. I have deleted the last part of the paragraph that discusses this.

16. At this time the Osage reorganized around the four groups (the Water, Earth, Isolated Hon'-ga, and Sky peoples).

17. The organization of a *don-don-ton-ga*, or tribal war party, involved long and elaborate rituals that could take the better part of two weeks.

18. The difference between the first two types of war parties is not clear.

19. *Tsi'-ga-xa* probably means "outside the house of mystery," while *do-don'* means "war party." Thus it means a war party organized outside the House of Mystery (La Flesche 1921:66).

20. A paragraph has been deleted here, and it and the preceding paragraph have been moved forward.

21. The hawk was the symbol of the warrior.

22. *Wa-xo'-be* means any item consecrated for ritual use and thus that is sacred. In this case it means the clan or hawk bundles.

23. "At an initiation of a member of one of the various clans into the mysteries of the war rite, the hereditary caretaker of the *wa-xo'-be*, who belongs to the Ni'-ka Wa-kon-da-gi clan . . . is given the bird to redecorate, an act equivalent to its recon-secration for the benefit of the initiate. If the hereditary caretaker happens to be absent from the initiation, this duty is performed by the second official caretaker, who belongs to the Tho'-xe clan" (La Flesche 1921:65).

24. In La Flesche's original text, four other paragraphs appeared at this point. Three of these paragraphs have been moved forward and one paragraph has been deleted.

25. For another discussion of the vision of the Sky chief, see story 1.17.

26. Also called ginseng root.

27. The roots were used to create a new bundle, the *mon-kon ton-ga wa-xo'-be*, or great medicine bundle.

28. The story of this vision is given in three *wi'-gi-e*: "Non'-zhin-zhon Wi'-gi-e" ("Wi'gi-e of the Vigil"), "Hon'-ga Wa-gthin Ts'a-ge" ("The Aged Eagle"), and the "Mon'-ce Wi'-gi-e" ("Metal Wi'-gi-e"). See La Flesche 1921:70 and 84–91 for the text of these *wi'-gi-e*. For another narrative on the vision of the Earth chief, see story 1.7.

29. This bundle was called the *wa-xo'-be ton-ga*, or great bundle, and was used in the tattooing rite.

30. Published in La Flesche 1921:272–74 as the "Ni'ki Wi'-gi-e of the Cin-dse-a-gthe." La Flesche recorded the narrative of this *wi'-gi-e* but not the *wi'-gi-e* itself.

31. Because unlike other trees, the willow remains green all year, it became a symbol of everlasting life.

32. These names do not appear in the list of names for the Buffalo Bull Face clan or any other clan in La Flesche 1928. Thus his list of clan personal names is incomplete.

33. These names do not appear in La Flesche 1928.

34. This is the "path of life" from east to west.

35. These names do not appear in La Flesche 1928.

36. Originally entitled "Genesis of the Osage"; see the handwritten field notes in Fletcher and La Flesche Papers 4558 (78). What Bacon Rind related was a very brief narrative version of the Bear Clan's *ni'ki wi'-gi-e*. This is a long *wi'-gi-e*, 577 lines, and he has left out many parts (see La Flesche 1921:220–37 for the full text of this *wi'-gi-e*). Every clan had its own version of the *ni'-ki wi'-gi-e*, and each mentions different events in the past. La Flesche (1921:219–20) discusses the differences between the Bear clan version and that of the closely related Puma clan. Another interesting point about the narrative versions of *wi'-gi-e* is that it appears that they could be altered depending on the specific point or points the teller wished to emphasize. In this telling Bacon Rind seems to be explaining why the Bear clan people have personal names that refer to the swan, the buffalo, and Little Chief, and only certain parts of the *wi'-gi-e* are relevant to this point. Bacon Rind could have focused on the life symbols of the clan, which would have involved discussing still other parts of the *wi'-gi-e*.

37. This is a metaphorical reference to the Gentle Ponca clan.

38. This name and the other two names are Earth names; see story 1.5.

39. This is a metaphorical reference to the Elk clan (see La Flesche 1921:225–26).

40. Only four were named.

41. Originally entitled "The Tsi' Wa-kon'-da-gi." See typescript of field notes in Fletcher and La Flesche Papers 4558 (83). This story is based on the *pe-xe thu-ce wi'-gi-e* and the *ho-be-cu wi'-gi-e*.

42. By this statement they meant that the Wa-zha'-zhe were part of the Earth people moiety.

43. By this they meant collective the three original groups, the Water, Land, and Earth peoples.

44. Clans.

45. Sparganium (La Flesche 1932:67).

46. *Nymphaea advena* (La Flesche 1932:30), or yellow pond lily (Gilmore 1919:79).

47. *Sagittaria latifolia* (La Flesche 1932:30), or arrowleaf (Gilmore 1919:143).

48. Bean seed, or *Falata comosa* (La Flesche 1932:65), also called ground bean (Gilmore 1919:141).

49. Children were the future; to destroy the young women of the enemy tribe was thus to destroy their future.

50. See note 48

51. Published in La Flesche 1928:49. This narrative was constructed by drawing on information from several different *wi'-gi-e*.

52. For other Earth names of the Bear clan, see story 1.3.

53. Field notes in Fletcher and La Flesche Papers, Dec. 1, 1910, "Story of Origin," 4558

(90). This story appears to have been taken from several *wi'-gi-e*. Part of the story is found in lines 1447–1542 of the *ni'-ki wi'-gi-e* of the Puma (mountain lion) clan (see La Flesche 1921:209–11), and another part of the story is found in the *hi'-ca-da wi'-gi-e* (see La Flesche 1921:212–19). Still other parts must have been from other *wi'-gi-e*.

54. Typescript in Fletcher and La Flesche Papers 4558. The story was told in response to La Flesche's question as to why a yard of calico was tied to the left arm of the *sho'-ka*. The calico was symbolic of the slave status of the *sho'-ka*. Saucy Calf added that originally the left arm was tied with the hide of a bull snake and that the calico was a recent innovation because snake hides were not always easy to find.

55. The original text called them a "sub-clan of the Wa-zha'-zhe clan," which means they were a clan of the Wa-zha'-zhe phratry.

56. This part is another telling of "Vision of the Sky Chief" in story 1.1.

57. This is another telling of "Vision of the Earth Chief" in story 1.1.

58. Charles Wah-hre-she was a member of the Puma clan priesthood. During the ceremony, the priests would recite their clan *wi'-gi-e* simultaneously, making it difficult for others to know what they were saying. Obviously Wah-hre-she had some knowledge of clan *wi'-gi-e* other than his own. La Flesche (1921:92–139) was able to collect a number of clan *wi'-gi-e* from Wah-hre-she. However, Wah-hre-she lacked the authority to give any information concerning *wi'-gi-e* of other clans. In his narrative summaries of clan *wi'-gi-e* he does not include summaries of all of the clan *wi'-gi-e* he knew, and in many cases his summary is extremely brief, touching only on part of the story. It may well have been that while he knew the wi'-gi-e he did not fully understand its meaning. Interestingly, he did not give a summary narrative concerning his own clan (Puma) *wi'-gi-e*.

59. This appears to be a general statement of the Water phratry and not that of a clan.

60. For the text of the *wi'-gi-e* of the Elder Water clan (Wa-zha'-zhe Wa-non), see La Flesche 1921:92–93.

61. For the text of the *wigi-e* of the White Water clan (Wa-zha'-zhe Cka), see La Flesche 1921:94.

62. La Flesche (1932:81) defines this word as "cavity; or roof of the mouth."

63. For the text of the *wi'-gi-e* of the Bow clan, see La Flesche 1921:98–101.

64. See La Flesche (1932:41).

65. For the text of the *wi'-gi-e* of the Deer clan, see La Flesche 1921:95–98.

66. For the text of the *wi'-gi-e* of the Eagle clan (Hon-ga A-Hiu-ton), see La Flesche 1921:104–5.

67. For the text of the *wi'-gi-e* of the Elk clan, see La Flesche 1921:112–15.

68. It is not certain if this is a narrative version of the *wi'-gi-e* of the Gentle Sky clan or a more general narrative covering several clan *wi'-gi-e* of the Sky moiety.

69. This is the only known appearance of this Osage term.

70. This term appears to refer any white flower and not a particular plant (see La Flesche 1932:219).

71. See La Flesche 1932:219.

72. For the text of the *wi'-gi-e* of the Night clan, see La Flesche 1921:123–24.

73. La Flesche (1932:108) defines this term as "a people" and states that it is a ritual term.

74. This part includes information not found in the *wi'-gi-e* of these two clans. For the text of their *wi'-gi-e*, see La Flesche 1921:133–39.

75. *Tse'-xo-be*, "a spider" (La Flesche 1932:161); *wa-ga'-xe*, "a picture of; a symbol of" (La Flesche 1932:188). This story is taken from the *wi'-gi-e* of the Red Eagle (La Flesche 1928:90–91).

76. In this instance "Wa-zha'-zhe" refers to the Water, Land, and Sky clans. The name Wa-zha'-zhe can be used as a collective term for all the Osage. In fact the word "Osage" is a French corruption of Wa-zha'-zhe.

77. Originally entitled "Haircut of the Tsi'zhu Wa-shta-ge Clan." Published in La Flesche 1928:89.

78. Also called *Ratibida columnaris*, or coneflower.

79. Published in La Flesche 1939:89–92. La Flesche did not note the *wi'-gi-e* from which this story was derived.

80. These were not *sho'-ka* in the later sense of the term; rather they were clans (see story 1.5).

81. This is one of the few times that the term Hon-ga Wa-non is used as a clan name. It probably refers to the Eagle clan since the term *wa-non* (elder) usually designates the first in the ordering of seven clan groups.

82. The Crawfish people are one of the clans of the Earth people.

83. The Elk people became one of the clans of the Earth people.

84. The *wi'-gi-e* from which this story is taken is *a'-hon-btha-bi*. Saucy Calf had not recited this particular *wi'-gi-e* for a long time, and his memory of it was indistinct. So instead of giving the *wi-gi-e*, he told La Flesche the narrative story of the *wi'-gi-e* instead. Published in La Flesche 1930:610–14. When a war party was being organized the leader of the party, the *do-don'-hon'-ga*, undertook the rite of vigil for seven days. During this time he asked for Wa-kon'-da's blessings and aid. It was important for the man to keep his thoughts focused. This *wi'-gi-e* speaks of those things on which the man had to keep his thoughts focused.

85. A better translation of this term might have been "there is in it no purpose." The Osage emphasized that nothing one did should be without purpose.

86. By the phrase the stranger means that the man's thoughts have not been selfish; he has rather thought of others.

87. Pipes symbolize the ideal man and of the unity of human thought in communicating with Wa-kon'-da.

88. This is a metaphorical reference to the passage of life from sunrise (birth) to sunset (death).

89. The sacred birds were hawks. Hawks symbolized courage and were the primary sacred object in the clan medicine bundles.

90. The sunrise is symbolic of birth. In this case the color crimson is probably a metaphorical reference to children, which were considered the greatest of all blessings.

91. This reference to all animals was probably a metaphorical reference not just to food, leather, and hides but also to the behavior of animals that humans could use as a model for their own behavior.

92. This refers to the blessing of old age that every human desired.

93. The sweat house and seat house were means of spiritually purifying the body.

94. The war club symbolized war and the destruction of human enemies.

95. These crooked necked staffs, covered with swan skin, deer skins, and eagle feathers, were the main symbol of war.

96. Published in La Flesche 1928:54–55.

97. Water lily.

98. Originally entitled "Instructions to the Wife of the Singer." Published in La Flesche 1925:192–94.

99. These instructions continue and include "Instructions to the Mother" (story 1.11) and "Instructions in the Painting of the Sacred Robes" (story 1.13). I have deleted these last parts because they would be redundant.

100. Published in La Flesche 1925:270–71. The instructions to the wife of a new priest appear to have varied both by clan and individuals. In some cases the "Instructions to the Mother" were also included. In this case the priest in charge is giving the wife and the other women present the ritual authority to paint robes. Red, the color put on the robe, is the sacred color of the Elder Sky clan. Red symbolizes the fire and the sun. Hlu-ah-wah-tah was a Elder Sky priest who died in 1915. Could only a priest of the Elder Sky clan bestow this authority on the wife? Did this only take place during an initiation in the Ni'-ki rite degree or with other degrees as well? These questions have to remain unanswered.

101. The *o'-don* are not listed in any of the *wi'-gi-e*. The only time the *o'-don* were formally noted appears to have been when a *wa-don-be* listed his honors as part of a ritual. Published in La Flesche 1925:179–81. I have dropped the Osage names of these *o'don* except in the case of one, for which the meaning is uncertain.

102. The meaning of this term is vague. It was one of the least important of the war honors (see La Flesche 1932:205).

Part 2

1. Handwritten field notes in Fletcher and La Flesche Papers 4558 (78).

2. This sentence has been moved. In the original field notes it came after the two following sentences.

3. This is the only known reference to this ceremony. By the nineteenth century it must have been abandoned.

4. Priest of the Deer clan.

5. In the original handwritten notes, this paragraph was followed by two redundant paragraphs that have been deleted since they would only serve to confuse the reader.

6. The Quapaw would appear to be the logical identity of this second group. However, Pa-nee-wa-with-tah for some reason did not identify them with this group.

7. Typescript in Fletcher and La Flesche Papers 4558 (78).

8. An *o'-xta* was "a favored person" (see La Flesche 1932:124).

9. A person with supernatural power.

10. This story is found in what appears to have been the notes of an informal storytelling session. Handwritten field notes in Fletcher and La Flesche Papers 4558 (77). No source given.

11. La Flesche gave no title to this story, which was published as part of his description of the war ceremony (La Flesche 1939:9–11). This appears to be the adult version of the animal story "The Hawk and the Horned Owl" told by Tho'-xi Zhin-ga (see story 3.2).

12. Typescript in Fletcher and La Flesche Papers 4558 (83). No source given.

13. Sororal polygyny, in which a man married sisters, was the ideal form of polygyny for the Osages.

14. Bears were usually hunted in the late winter.

15. Originally entitled "Pa-hiu'-gthon-ge Wa-xo'-be" ("Hair Bundle"). Typescript in Fletcher and La Flesche Papers 4558 (78). Charles Wa-hre-she's account of this story was also published in La Flesche 1932:404–6.

16. Sometime before 1719, the Little Osage moved their village to the Missouri River, settling near the village of the Missouri tribe. In the 1770s, the Little Osage moved back to the Osage River. See Chapman 1959 and Margry 1886:6.311.

17. The Sun Carrier clan was one of the clans of the Sky moiety.

18. See story 1.1 on the dwelling of the chief as a sanctuary.

19. Any type of war party required the support of the clan priests.

20. Without a *wa-xo'-be*, or clan bundle, the war party was not sanctified by the priesthood and the men of the party could not claim war honors for their actions. In most cases, the refusal of a clan bundle to the leader would cause the party to disband.

21. Charles Wah-hre-she's farm was north and east of Hominy, Oklahoma. The Pawnee and other Caddoan-speaking peoples abandoned their villages in this area during the 1770s owing to Osage attacks. Thus this story must date to 1770 or before.

22. Charles Wah-hre-she told La Flesche substantially the same story with one major difference. In Wah-hre-she's account, the war party killed an enemy warrior who was wearing a scalp or scalps on his shoulders as decoration. It was this scalp that was used. This bundle is in the Smithsonian and is made from pieces of a number of different scalps. This *wa-xo'-be* belonged to the Mik'in' Wa-non (Sun Carrier) and Hon I-ni-ki-shi-ga (Night) clans (La Flesche 1932:406).

23. Published in La Flesche 1932:403–4. No source given.

24. This was highly usual in that the Osages placed a great deal of emphasis on relative birth order and the older sibling was always in charge.

25. It appears that this war party was not sanctioned by a priest and had no bundle. Thus they made a new clan bundle. In speaking of this bundle, Charles Wah-hre-she added that one of the enemy warriors was carrying a reed whistle, which the brothers made part of the *wa-xo'-be*—thus its name. This *wa-xo'-be* is in the Smithsonian (La Flesche 1932:404).

26. Published in La Flesche 1939:87–88.

27. See La Flesche 1939:86–144 for a description of the mourning rite.

28. *Wa-sha'-be a-tin*, or war rite, was the ceremony used for organizing a tribal war party (see La Flesche 1939:3–85). An abbreviated form was used in the mourning dance (see La Flesche 1939:86–139).

29. The original title was "The Story of a Warrior." Handwritten field notes in Fletcher and La Flesche Papers 4558 (83).

30. The original title was "Osage Woman Taken Captive by Pawnee." No source indicated. Typescript of field notes in Fletcher and La Flesche Papers 4558 (83).

31. He did not literally have possession of a *wa-xo'-be*, or clan bundle. He was a candidate for the priesthood and had just about collected all of the items needed for his initiation.

32. Osage hunting trails and their regular camp site were well known to the Pawnee and other enemy tribes. As a result, the village usually traveled to the plains and back as a group. However, as in this case, on the return trip some families would leave the main body to hunt on their own.

33. "Brother-in-law" is *i-ta'-hon* (see La Flesche 1932:238).

34. This is one of the important lessons of this story. The Osage stressed that it was better to be overly cautious when they saw something they did not fully understand. Another Osage story, not in this collection, tells of a scout who found footprints and raised an alarm in the camp. A group of armed men went out and followed the footprints back to the camp. A boy then told them that he had been walking in that area but had not mentioned this because he could not be certain the footprints were his. The boy had acted correctly. What if the footprints had been those of an enemy and not the boy?

35. Originally entitled "The Boy Driven from Home by His Father." Typescript of field notes in Fletcher and La Flesche Papers 4558 (83). No source given.

36. In this case, the brother-in-law is assuming the role of the father in helping the young boy.

37. The Osage considered banishing children to be totally inappropriate behavior on the part of fathers and mothers.

38. The tribe is not mentioned; however, the form of marriage described here is very different from the more formal marriages of the Osage.

39. The fact that an adopted and/or intermarried man from another tribe should become chief is not surprising. White Plume, a Kansa chief during the early nineteenth century, was an intermarried Osage (see Urau 1971:119). Joseph La Flesche, the father of Francis La Flesche, was half French and half Ponca. Adopted by the Omaha chief Big Elk, he succeeded Big Elk as chief on his death (see Bailey 1995:14).

40. What they are referring to is the peace, or calumet, ceremony discussed in chapter 2.

41. The basic form of wealth was horses, and Osage families generally had few if any horses.

42. Originally entitled "Story Told by Tho'-xi Zhin-ga." Typescript of field notes in Fletcher and La Flesche Papers 4558 (78).

43. This is the rite of vigil.

44. A mourning war party needed only two captains.

45. There is no mention of the ritual preparations used in organizing a mourning war party, and the assumption is that there were none. As a result, this party was probably not sanctioned by a clan priest.

46. It was necessary for the men to have their faces painted black so that they could later claim any *o'-don*, or war honors, that they won, even though here there is no mention of a bundle.

47. The leader of a war party was entitled to everything captured.

48. A *wa-je'-pa-in*, or crier, was a secular messenger, while a *sho'-ka* was a messenger used in rituals.

49. Originally titled "Wa-zha'-xa-in and Ga-hi'-ge-wa-tse-xi." Typescript of field notes in Fletcher and La Flesche Papers 4558 (78). No source given.

50. The Osage had "Omaha"-type kinship terms. In these systems, the father's brother is called by the same term as the father. The mother's brother is called by a different term, which may be translated as "mother's brother" or "uncle." Thus the girl's uncle would have been her mother's brother.

51. Maternal uncles had to approve the marriages of their nieces. In this case, acting on his own authority, he declared his niece divorced and remarried. This is the only known case of a maternal uncle having done so. Had he not publically done such, the husband would have had the right to kill his wife and her lover because they had committed adultery.

52. A large family was considered a sign of Wa-kon'-da's approval of the marriage.

53. This indicates that the community fully accepted the marriage of this couple, which is unusual given the fact that she had left her first husband.

54. A happy old age, surrounded by children and grandchildren, would be an indication of Wa-kon'-da's blessing.

55. Although they lived to be old, the fact that they were childless and friendless would be indications of Wa-kon'-da's disapproval.

56. Originally titled "A Love Story." Typescript field notes in Fletcher and La Flesche Papers 4558 (78).

57. Osage buried individuals in the ground and covered them with a mound of rocks.

58. The host of a feast always prepared more food than the guests could eat, and guests were expected to take the uneaten food home.

59. In this case, the husband had the right to kill his wife and her lover.

60. Originally entitled "Mourning Customs." Typescript field notes in Fletcher and La Flesche Papers 4558 (83).

61. The very same name was given to a regular war ceremony as to a mourning ceremony. There were, however, many important differences. See La Flesche 1939:86–143.

62. A form of the rite of vigil.

63. See La Flesche 1939:19 for a description of the standard.

64. Originally entitled "The Story of Two Young Men Who Mourned for Their Father while He Was Yet Living." Handwritten field notes in Fletcher and La Flesche Papers 4558 (83). Some of the words were difficult to read.

65. Little is known concerning Osage clowns or jesters other than that they existed.

66. Typed field notes in Fletcher and La Flesche Papers 4558 (78). No source indicated.

67. The original title of this story was "Pa-thi Wa-kon'-da-gi." *Pa-thi* was the term used by the Osage to refer to tribes not related to the Osages (see La Flesche 1932:126). Thus "Strange Medicine Man." Typescript in Fletcher and La Flesche Papers 4558 (78). No source indicated.

68. La Flesche added that this was like the Pebble Society of the Omaha. For a discussion of this society, see Fletcher and La Flesche 1911:530, 537, 565–78.

69. Wa-ce-to Zhin-ga was the name of Louis Pryor (1879–1934). When Moonhead

was building Black Dog's peyote fireplace at the turn of the twentieth century, he was attacked by a *wa-kon'-da-gi* who attempted to "shoot" him with mecal beans. This *wa-kon'-da-gi* may have been Louis Pryor's father (Bailey field notes).

70. There were two men and a young boy by the name of To-wah-ehe listed on the 1906 roll. One of the men died in 1910 and the other in 1916.

71. He died in 1914. Pah-nee-wah-with-tah, meaning "Annoyer-of-the-enemy," was a war name of the Elder Sky clan (La Flesche 1928:144).

72. He was born in 1840 and died in 1923.

73. Birth date unknown; he died 1913.

74. This would mean that he probably died in the 1850s.

75. An adulterous wife could be killed by her husband. This happens in story 2.14.

76. *Xu'be* refers to a "holy" or "supernatural power" (La Flesche 1932:221), and *wa-tsi'* means "dance" (La Flesche 1932:206). This is the only reference to such a dance.

77. A centipede (see La Flesche 1932:88).

78. This story was originally entitled "Ton'-won-ga-xe and Ki-ba'-xra-hi." Ton'-won-ga-xe, or Village Maker, is a name of the Gentle Sky clan (La Flesche 1928:149), while Ki'-ba-xra-hi is an early transcription of Gi-wa'-xthi-zhi or "Not Stingy," a name belonging to the Isolated Earth clan (La Flesche 1928:132). No source given. Typescript in Fletcher and La Flesche Papers 4558 (78).

79. La Flesche added that this story is "somewhat like" the killing of Blackbird of the Omaha (see Fletcher and La Flesche 1911:82).

80. This story was originally entitled "Wa-ca'-be ton-ga and Ni-ka-ki-ba-non." *Wa-ca'-be* means "bear," while *ton-ga* means "large," "big," or "great"; thus the translation "Big Bear." This name is not found in La Flesche's (1928) list of clan names. Ni'-ka-ki-ba-non, or, more correctly, Ni'-ka-a-ki-ba-non, meaning "Runs-to-meet-men," is a clan name of the Night people (La Flesche 1928:155). Typescript in Fletcher and La Flesche Papers 4558 (78). No source given.

81. This was a magical "arrow," not a real arrow.

82. Originally entitled "I-tsin'-ke and Wa-hon-i-zhin-ge." *Wa-hon-i-zhin-ge* means "orphan." Typescript in Fletcher and La Flesche Papers 4558 (78). The story of I-tsin'-ke was found not just among the Osage but also the Omaha, Ponca, and other Siouan peoples (La Flesche 1932:81). Thus it is undoubtedly an extremely old story.

83. I have no idea why the terms for these animals were translated as "tiger" and "lion." In the Southeast, pumas were sometimes called "tigers," which accounts for why there was a Tiger clan among some of the Muskogean peoples.

84. Originally entitled "Wa-da'-in-ga." Handwritten field notes in Fletcher and La Flesche Papers 4558 (78). I have substituted the more standardized spelling of Wa-da'-in-ga's name throughout this story. Wah-ti-an-kah was the most famous of the Osage prophets and visionaries as well as a major political leader. He died in the 1880s. Mathews (1932:49–56) provides an interesting description of and story about him. This story was given by Bacon Rind, who was his grandson.

85. The rite of vigil lasts until the morning of the seventh day. Wah-ti-an-kah had extended his vigil for two additional days.

86. Handwritten field notes in Fletcher and La Flesche Papers 4558 (78).

87. Short for *wa-sha'-be a-thin wa-tsi*, or carrying-the-charcoal dance. This was probably a mourning dance.

88. This was probably before he was married. Later in life he married into an Upland Forest family and lived with them.

89. The term means "isolated bundle" or "sacred object."

90. See story 1.14.

91. La Flesche gives two translations for this term: "first to strike while on the march" (La Flesche 1932:104) and "striking of an enemy in the open country," which was the sixth of the seven (Hon'-ga) o'-don (La Flesche 1925:180).

92. I have changed the title of this story. La Flesche originally entitled it "E'-zhi-ga-xthi," a personal name meaning "Slew-the-wrong-man" (La Flesche 1932:42). The relationship of this person to the story is unknown. This may have been the man who gave him the story. Typescript in Fletcher and La Flesche Papers 4558 (78).

93. Handwritten field notes in Fletcher and La Flesche Papers 4558 (78).

94. Kettle carriers, or *tse'-xe-k'in non-non*, were the "privates," or common men, of a war party.

95. This is a description of a regular wedding.

96. This was told as a *u'-tha-ge*, or true story. Handwritten field notes in Fletcher and La Flesche Papers 4558 (78).

97. Typescript in Fletcher and La Flesche Papers 4558 (78). No source given. This appears to be a very old story, since Washington Irving (1956:164–65) recorded a slightly different version of it in 1832.

98. A man taking a wife to his home would have been unusual, since Osage families were usually matrilocal.

99. The original title was "Little Dove." Typescript in Fletcher and La Flesche Papers 4558 (78). This story was told as a true story.

100. The Osages would frequently cache heavier objects, such as the mat coverings for wigwams, in trees near the camp so that they could be used by the family on their return.

101. Osage camps had a fixed arrangement of dwellings by clans and families of the clan.

102. Osage houses had two fireplaces.

103. This story originally had no title. Handwritten field notes in Fletcher and La Flesche Papers 4558 (78).

104. Although there were some schools for the Osage prior to their removal to Indian Territory in 1872, this story probably is from the post-1872 period. Little people stories are still told, and many individuals believe in their existence. Most people who have had encounters with little people say that they are dressed like "old-time" Indians. However, one individual stated that he had seen little people who looked like white men. Little people are said to frequent certain places and travel on old trails, some of which today pass through houses. Many think that little people are invisible unless they wish to be seen or caught unawares. Dogs are said to be able to sense them even if humans cannot see them (Bailey field notes).

105. La Flesche 1932:93 translated the term as "elf" or "fairy." Today the Osages translate the term as "little people."

106. The original title was "We-tsʹa-ta-zhon-gle-shka." Typescript in Fletcher and La Flesche Papers 4558 (78). This animal has not been identified. *We-tsʹa-ta* means "snake" or "reptile" (La Flesche 1932:215), while *zhon* means "tree" or "wood" (La Flesche 1932:224).

Part 3

1. Typed field notes in Fletcher and La Flesche Papers 4558 (78). No source indicated. Dorsey (1904:9) also recorded this story and calls it "The Buffalo and the Rabbit."

2. Osage men shaved their heads, leaving only a small roach on top.

3. Refers to perfume. The Osage used columbine and other sweet-smelling seeds (see La Flesche 1932:95).

4. The story was originally entitled "Conflict between Gthe-do and I-to." Typescript field notes in Fletcher and La Flesche Papers 4558 (78). This appears to be a children's version of story 2.4, "The Vision of a War Leader," told by Charles Wah-hre-she.

5. Handwritten field notes in Fletcher and La Flesche Papers 4558 (78). The moral of this story is be certain before you act. Story 2.10 concerns a man who was not cautious.

6. Typescript field notes in Fletcher and La Flesche Papers 4558 (78).

7. Typescript field notes in Fletcher and La Flesche Papers 4558 (78).

References

Osage Sources

When known, the spelling of personal names and birth and death dates are given as they appear on the Osage tribal roll (see Tinker 1957).

Andrew Jackson (Osage Name: Hon-mon-in [Traveling Night]), ?–1918

Bacon Rind (Osage name: Wa-tse-mon-in [He-who-wins-war-honors]), 1860–1932

Ben Wheeler (Osage name: Hu-lah-pa? [Eagle Head?]), 1876–1937

Black Dog (Shon-ton-ca-be), ?–1910

Charles Wah-hre-she (transcribed by La Flesche as Wa-xthi-zhi [Generous]), ?–1923

Hlu-ah-wah-tah (transcribed by La Flesche as Xu-tha'-wa-ton-in [Eagle-plainly-seen]), ?–1915

Me-ke-wah-ti-an-kah (Playful Sun Carrier), 1857–1931

Pah-nee-wah-with-tah (transcribed by La Flesche as Pa'-thin-wa-we-xta [Annoyer-of-the-enemy]), ?–1914

Saucy Calf (Osage name Tsa-shin-kah-wah-ti-an-kah [Playful Calf]), ?–1912

Shun-kah-mo-lah (Walking Dog), ?–1919

Tho'-xi Zhin-ga (Little Bull), unidentified

Secondary Sources

Alexander, Hartley. "Francis La Flesche." *American Anthropologist* 35.2: 321–28.

Bailey, Garrick A. 1973. *Changes in Osage Social Organization, 1673–1906.*

University of Oregon Anthropological Papers 5.

———. 1995. *The Osage and the Invisible World: From the Works of Francis La Flesche.* Norman: University of Oklahoma Press.

———. 2001. "Osage." In *Handbook of North American Indians.* Vol. 13, pt. 1, 476–96.

Bailey, Garrick, and Dan Swan. 2004 *Art of the Osage.* Seattle: University of Washington Press and Saint Louis Art Museum.

Bolton, Herbert E. (ed.). 1914. *Athanase de Mezieres and the Louisiana-Texas Frontier, 1768–1780.* Cleveland: Arthur H. Cark.

Brackenridge, H. M. 1904. *Journal of a Voyage up the River Missouri Performed in Eighteen Hundred and Eleven.* Cleveland: Arthur H. Clark.

Burns, Louis F. 1984a. *Osage Indian Bands and Clans.* Fallbrook, CA: Ciga Press.

———. 1984b. *Osage Indian Customs and Myths.* Fallbrook, CA: Ciga Press.

———. 1989. *A History of the Osage People.* Fallbrook, CA: Ciga Press.

Chapman, Carl H. 1959. "The Little Osage and Missouri Indian Village Sites, ca. 1717–1777 AD." *The Missouri Archaeologist* 21:1-67.

Din, Gilbert C., and Abraham P. Nasatir. 1983. *The Imperial Osages: Spanish-Indian Diplomacy in the Mississippi Valley.* Norman: University of Oklahoma Press.

Dorsey, George A. 1904. *Traditions of the Osage.* Field Columbian Museum Publication 88.

DuLac, M. Perrin. 1807. *Travels through the Two Louisianas and among the Savage Nations of the Missouri: Also in the United States, along the Ohio, and Adjacent Provinces, in 1801, 1802, and 1803.* London: Richard Phillips.

Farnham, Thomas J. 1906. *Travels in the Great Western Prairies, the Anahauc and Rocky Mountains, and the Oregon Territory.* 1843. Cleveland: Arthur H. Clark.

Fletcher and La Flesche Papers. National Anthropological Archives, National Museum of Natural History, Smithsonian Institution, Washington D.C.

Fletcher, Alice C., and Francis La Flesche. 1911. "The Omaha Tribe." *Twenty-seventh Annual Report of the Bureau of American Ethnology (1905–06)*: 17–660.

Flint, James. 1904. *Letters from America, Containing Observations on the Climate and Agriculture of the Western States.* Cleveland: Arthur H. Clark.

Gilmore, Melvin Randolph. 1919. "Uses of Plants by the Indians of the Missouri River Region." *Thirty-third Annual Report of the Bureau of American Ethnology (1911–12)*: 53–154.

Hyde, George E. 1951. *Pawnee Indians.* Denver: University of Denver Press.

Irving, Washington. 1956. *A Tour on the Prairies.* Norman: University of Oklahoma Press.

La Flesche, Francis. 1906. *Who Was the Medicine Man?* Hampton, VA: Hampton Institute Press.

———. 1915. "Omaha and Osage Traditions of Separation." *Proceedings of the International Congress of Americanists* 19:459–62.

———. 1918. "Researches Among the Osage." *Smithsonian Miscellaneous Collections* 70.2:110–13, 118–19.

———. 1921. "The Osage Tribe: Rite of the Chiefs; Sayings of the Ancient Men." *Thirty-sixth Annual Report of the Bureau of American Ethnology (1914–15)*: 35–604.

———. 1925. "The Osage Tribe: Rite of Vigil." *Thirty-ninth Annual Report of the Bureau of American Ethnology (1917–18)*: 31–630.

———. 1928. "The Osage Tribe: Two Versions of the Child Naming Rite." *Forty-third Annual Report of the Bureau of American Ethnology (1925–26)*: 23–164. Washington, D.C.

———. 1930. "Osage Tribe: Rite of the *Wa-xo'-be*." *Forty-fifth Annual Report of the Bureau of American Ethnology (1927–28)*: 529–833.

———. 1932. *A Dictionary of the Osage Language*. Bureau of American Ethnology Bulletin 59.

———. 1939. *War Ceremony and Peace Ceremony of the Osage Indians*. Bureau of American Ethnology Bulletin 101.

Liberty, Margot. 1978. "Francis La Flesche: The Osage Odyssey." In *American Indian Intellectuals*, ed. Margot Liberty, 44–59. St. Paul, MN: West Publishing.

Margry, Pierre. 1876–86. *Découvertes et établissements des français*. 6 vols. Paris: D. Jouaust.

Mathews, John Joseph. 1932. *Wah'kon-tah: The Osage and the White Man's Road*. Norman: University of Oklahoma Press.

———. 1961. *The Osages: Children of the Middle Waters*. Norman: University of Oklahoma Press.

Mark, Joan. 1982. "Francis La Flesche: The American Indian as Anthropologist." *Isis* 73.4:487–510.

———. 1988. *A Stranger in Her Own Land: Alice Fletcher and the American Indians*. Lincoln: University of Nebraska Press.

Mayhall, Mildred. 1962. *The Kiowas*. Norman: University of Oklahoma Press.

Nasatir, A. P. (ed.). 1952. *Before Lewis and Clark: Documents Illustrating the History of Missouri, 1785–1804*. 2 vols. St. Louis: St. Louis Historical Documents Foundation.

Ponziglione, Paul. "Father Schoenmaker and the Osage." Unpublished manuscript. St. Louis University Library, St. Louis.

Office of Indian Affairs. 1875. *Report of the Commissioner of Indian Affairs*. Washington, D.C.: GPO.

Rollings, Willard H. 1992. *The Osage: An Ethnohistorical Study of the Hegemony on the Prairie-Plains*. Columbia: University of Missouri Press.

Tinker, Sylvester. 1957. *Osage Indian Roll Book*. Pawhuska, OK: Sam McClain.

Urau, William E. 1971. *The Kansa Indians: A History of the Wind People, 1673–1873*. Norman: University of Oklahoma Press.

White, E. E. 1965. *Experiences of a Special Indian Agent*. Norman: University of Oklahoma Press.

Index

invisible world, 24; marriage, 100; naming, 4, 5, 23, 26, 28, 65; peace, 22–23, 24; of sending (*wa-the'-the*), 54; songs of spirit, 136; of tattooing, 58–59; for visible world, 23; warfare and, 23, 40. *See also* ritual(s)

charcoal, 55–56, 97, 123

Cherokee, 10, 11

Cheyenne, 10

chief(s) (*ga-hi'-ge*), 8, 16; choice of, 53; creation of, 42–44; duties of, 20, 42–43; fireplace of, 44; house of, 43, 44, 83; protection by, 43, 83; soldiers of, 43; succession and, 44. *See also specific chiefs*

child(ren), 6, 31, 33; banishing, 89–94, 160n37; as blessing, 15, 26, 34, 157n90; favored, 76–77; naming ceremony for, 4, 5, 23, 26, 28, 40, 65; neglect of, 89–90; nurturing of, 66; sacred food for, 66; sacred robe for, 33, 65–66, 69–70; safety for, 52; young woman with, 27. *See also* honored little one (*zhin-ga'-o-xta*)

Chouteau, Pierre, 12

ci-ge/a-cin-ga (third daughter), 26, 102

Civil War, 12

clan(s), 3, 4, 8, 16–17, 26; life symbols (*aho'-i-the*) of, 16, 27; names and, 7, 26; organization, 17; totems, 55–58; *wi'-gi-e*, 55–58. *See also specific clans*

clan bundles, 17, 21–22; origin of, 41–42

clan priest, 21–22, 23

clay: blue, 61; for face painting, 60; red, 61, 69; yellow, 61

club: sacred, 46–47; war, 62, 65, 158n94

color(s), 69; finding four, 59–62; red on head, 66, 67, 68

Comanche, 10

conceit, 144

contact, European, 9, 13

corn, 8, 26, 33, 58, 89, 100, 102, 154n12

cosmos. *See* Wa-kon'-da

courage, 6, 15, 31, 41, 67, 97, 118, 145, 146;

sending, 68; test of, 78; true, 80

coyote, 146–50

cradle board, 28, 106

crawfish, 60, 61

Crawfish people, 4

creation: ability for, 13; beneficial/dangerous, 14–15; of chief, 42–44; of house of mysteries (*tsi'-wa-kon'-da-gi*), 49–50; meaning of, 14, 15; purpose of, 15.

criers (*wa-je-pa-in*), 21, 95, 100, 152n25

culture, xi, xii, 8

customs: mourning, 109–10, 111–12; of tattoos, 52–53

dance, 132; captive, 28; mystery, 115; pipe, 24; standard bearer, 110, 129; war, 123. *See also* mourning dance

daughter, 26, 27, 102

day, 57, 58, 66; power of, 80, 145, 146

death, 14, 25, 35–36, 127; accompanying spirit and, 86–87, 96, 129; hardened against, 55, 57; of husband, 30; of old warrior, 80–82; return from, 129–36; sentence, 42; village of, 39; of wife, 129–30

deer, 75, 78, 138

Deer clan (*Dta' I-ni-gka-shi-ga*), 55, 75, 76

demons, animal, 137–39

Dhegiha Siouans, 9

dignity, 118

divorce, 29–30

do-don'-hon'-ga. See war party(ies): leader

dogwood, 57

Dorsey, George, xi, xii, 6

dreamer(s), 122–24; woman, 124–25

dreams, 62–65; coming true of, 122–24; magical powers through, 116–17

Dwellers Below (I-u-dse'-ta), 18

eagle, 45, 46, 54, 59

Eagle clan, 56

Early Risen, 32

earth, 4, 16, 58; descent to, 4, 46, 48, 49, 51, 59; honoring, 53, 54; house (*hon'-ga tsi'*), 40; names, 26, 51–52; surface of, 14, 56

Earth chief, 20, 25, 54; vision of, 45–46

Earth people. *See* Hon'-ga

education, 27

eighteenth century, 9–10, 31

elder tree, 59

Elder Water clan, 55

elk: great (*o'-pon ton-ga*), 51, 60–61; symbolism of, 56, 61

Elk clan (O'pxon), 4, 56, 58

enemy(ies), 31, 41, 68; attack on, 146; destruction of, 51, 57, 61, 64, 65; striking of, 70; taking head of, 71, 72

E-non' min-dse-dton, 55

envy, 147–48

equality, 30

face paint, 23–24, 61, 68, 97; clay for, 60

fall hunt, 18–19

famine, 76

fasting, 25, 49, 61, 78–79, 86, 95, 97, 112, 127. *See also* rite of vigil

father, 27, 31, 111–12

fear, 42; of medicine men, 120

feathers, 54, 65, 75, 77, 80

fields, 8

fire, 15, 58; blessing of, 102, 103

fireplace, 50; of chief, 44; four stones in, 40–41; sanctity of, 102, 103, 105; symbolism of, 40

fish, 55

fleetness, 56

La Flesche, Francis, xi, xii, 1, 3, 6–7, 25

Fletcher, Alice, 1, 2

flood, 18

Flower people, 58

folk stories, xii–xiii, 2; categories of, 5; *hi'-go* (fictional), 5; purpose of, 6; true (*u'tha-ge*), 5, 36

food, 58; animals providing, 61–62; sacred, for child, 66; search for, 56

France, 9

French and Indian War, 9

friendship, 24, 40, 43

furs, 9

ga-hi'-ge. See chief(s)

game, 75; abundant, 56; securing of, 58

generosity, 94

Gentle Ponca clan (Wa'-tse-tsi Wa-shta'-ge), 53, 54

Gentle Sky clan (Tsi'-zhu Wa-shta'-ge), 53, 57, 58; haircut of, 59

ghost, 36, 127–29

gifts, 22, 26, 28, 29, 35, 94; sacred, 54

gkon-ha u-thishte, 57

good man (*ni'-ka don'-he*), 29, 31, 152*n*35

grass, 56, 102

gratitude, 66

great bundle, 22, 23, 24, 154*n*29

Great Plains, 9–10

greed, 146–47, 150

grief, 127

guests, 24, 28, 100, 132

guidance, 25; supernatural, 53

guns, 9, 138

hair bundle, origin of, 82–85

haircut, 4, 27, 152*n*33; of Gentle Sky clan, 59

hawk, 31, 41, 79–80, 97, 145–46, 157*n*89

Heart Stays (Non'-dse-wa-cpe), 18

heaven, 46, 66

heredity, 21, 26, 43–44

hides, 9, 10, 75, 96

history, xiii, 8; of tribal organization, 3

Hlu-lah-wah-tah, 59

ho'-e-ga (surface of earth), 14, 56

hon'-ga, 4; definition of, 7

Hon'-ga (Earth people), 3, 4, 7, 16, 17, 44, 60; Wa-zha'-zhe and, 40

Hon'-ga U-ta-na-dsi, 49, 52

Hon'-ga U-ta-non-dsi (Isolated Hon'-ga), 16, 19, 39, 40, 58, 59

Hon'-ga Wa-tse-ga-wa, 51, 52

Hon'-ga Wa'-tse-gi-tsi, 51, 52

honored little one (*zhin-ga'-o-xta*), 28

horned owl, 145–46

horse(s), 9, 94, 131, 160*n*41; mourning dance for, 109–11; riding, 90–91; trade, 152*n*4

hospitality, 103

house: bad, 59; building of, 101; of chief, 43, 44, 83; earth (*hon'-ga tsi'*), 40; sacred (*tsi'wa-kon'-da-gi*), 50, 51; sweat, 65, 157*n*93; symbolism of, 40

house of mysteries (*tsi'-wa-kon'-da-gi*), 40, 41, 70; creation of, 49–50

humiliation, 53

hunt(ing), 9, 23, 30, 56; bison, 9, 12–13, 24; black bear, 81; buffalo, 1, 77, 82, 83, 90, 95–96; camps, 19; ceremony for, season, 75; deer, 78, 138; expansion of, ground, 9–10; fall, 18–19; loss of, ground, 12; summer, 18–19; violating rule of, 75–76

husband: abusive, 30; death of, 30; responsibility of, 29; role of, 30–31; wife leaving, 101, 102

identity, preservation of, 56

Indian, xii, xiii; outlaw of, slavery, 9; policy, 9

Indian Removal Act (1830), 12

Indian Territory, 9, 12, 13, 152*n*8

in-gthon (eldest son), 26, 27

insult, 117–18

Isolated Hon'-ga. *See* Hon'-ga U-ta-non-dsi

I-tsin'-ke, orphan and, 120–21

Jackson, Andrew, 111–12

jealousy, 101, 143, 144

Judas tree, 57

Kansa, 9

Kansas, 12

ka'-zhin-ga (third son), 26

kindness, 103, 150

kinship, 28, 161*n*50

Kiowa, 10

knife, sacred (*mon'-hin-i-ba-btho-ga*), 46

knowledge: encyclopedia of, 3; as power, 15; ritual, 21

kshon'-ga (second son), 26

language, 1, 9; dictionary of Osage, 2, 7; imagery of, xii

leader(ship), 26, 53; political, 20–21; religious, 20; of ritual, 23; of war party, 23, 25, 71, 78–80, 110; woman war, 95–101

leech, white/dark, 51, 59, 60

life: coming back to, 129–36; journey, 55, 56, 57, 58; long, 53, 54, 56, 57, 58, 66; symbols of long, 106

life cycle, 15, 25

life symbols (*aho'-i-the*), 17, 26, 41, 59, 154*n*15; of clan, 16, 27

linguistics, xii, 1

literature, oral, xii

Little Dove (Th-t-zhin-ga), 136

Little Earth, 49

Little Osages. *See* Dwellers Below (I-u-dse'-ta)

Little People (*mi'-wa-gthu-shka*), 136–37, 163*n*104

living beings, 13; meaning/purpose of, 14

Louisiana, 9, 10

maize, 67

man medicine (*mon-kon ni'-ka-shi-ga*), 45, 53, 58

marriage, 93, 127, 161*n*51; categories of, 28; ceremony, 100; new, 104–5; proposal, 98

meaning: of creation, 14, 15; of *wi'-gi-e*, 3

medicine, 45, 53, 58

medicine man (men) (*wa-kon'-da-ge*), 34–35; Big Bear, 119–20; fear of, 120; I-tsin'-ke, 120–21; Not Stingy, 117–18; power of, 112–14, 115–18; Runs-to-meet-men, 119–20; society of, 114; strange, 114–17; Village Maker, 117–18; war party and, 112–13

Me-ke-wah-ti-an-kah, 82–85

men: role of, 30; war and, 28; young, 62
Men of Mystery/Thunder clan (Ni'-ka
    Wa-kon'-da-gi), 42, 43, 58
Me-she-tsa-he, Charles, *30*
Mi-k'in' clan, 82
mi-na (eldest daughter), 26, 27
mind, 12; healing, 35, 127; power of, 152*n*15
Mississippi River, 75
Missouri, 8, 12
Missouri River, 82
mnemonic device, 2, 3
Mon-zhon'-ga-xe (Earth Maker), 56
moon, 57
mother, 26; instructions to, 65–67; role of,
    4–5, 33
mourning, 25, 35, 86, 95, 96, 127; customs,
    109–10, 111–12; period, 107
mourning dance, 23, 25, 35, 129; for horse,
    109–11; origin of, 86–87
murder, 42
mussel, 55
myths, xii; origin, 17

name(s): clan, 7, 26; earth, 26, 51–52; giv-
    ing, 4, 5, 23, 26, 28, 40, 65; origin of, 26,
    47, 48–49; sky, 26, 51–52
neglect, of child, 89–90
new country, move to, 39, 42, 153*n*5
night (*hon*), 57, 66; power of, 80, 145, 146
Night clan, 57–58
ni'-ka don'-he. *See* good man
non'-hon-zhin-ga. See priest(s)
Not Stingy, 117–18
nurturing, 30, 33; of child, 66

oak tree, 59
obedience, to teachings, 107
o'don. See war honors
oil, exploration, 13
Omaha, 1, 9, 76; departure of, 75
ornamentation, 62
Osage Allotment Act, 13
Osage River, 8
Ozarks, 10

Pah-nee-wah-with-tah, 75–76, 107–9
Pa-thi Wa-kon'-da-gi, 114
Pawnee, 9, 31, 87–89, 152*n*2, 152*n*22
peace, 21, 51, 59; ceremony, 22–23, 24
pelican, 45, 54, 58
pelts, 10
Peyote church, xi
phratry(ies), 16, 17
pipe, 39, 64, 65, 76, 87, 113; dance, 24; priest
    (*non'-hon-zhin-ga*), 22–23, 24, 152*n*35;
    symbolism of, 153*n*3, 153*n*8, 153*n*9
pity, 150
plant: *cin*, 50, 51; *cin-mon-non-ta*, 50, 51;
    hon-bthin'-cu, 50, 51; *ho'-xthon ta-xe*,
    50, 51
polygyny, sororal, 29
Ponca clan (Wa'-tse-tsi), 9, 44, 76
pot, sacred (*tse-xe ni-ka-pu*), 50, 51, 154*n*13
power: balance between tribes, 9; of day/
    night, 80, 145, 146; killing, 48; knowl-
    edge as, 15; magical, through dream,
    116–17; of medicine man, 112–14,
    115–18; of mind, 152*n*15; of priests, 21;
    supernatural, 34–35, 76–77, 113, 127; of
    Wa-kon'-da, 15
prayer, 15
priest(s) (*non'-hon-zhin-ga*), 17, 26, 41,
    42, 75; becoming, 22; distinctions
    between, 21–22; duty of, 20, 21; great
    bundle, 22, 23, 24; instructions to
    wife of, 67–68; pipe, 22–23, 24, 152*n*35;
    power of, 21; ritual for becoming, 22;
    wife of, 5, 34, 158*n*100. *See also* clan
    priest; *sho'-ka* (messenger of priests);
    tribal priest
priesthood(s), 2, 3, 21; candidate for, 22,
    24; Ni'-ki degree of, 5; types of, 22
protection, 66, 79–80; by chief, 43, 83
Pryor, Louis, 114
puma (*in-gthon'-ga*), 52, 57
Puma clan (Wa-tse-ga-wa/In-gthon'-ga),
    4, 43, 49, 50
purity, 157*n*93
purpose, 69, 157*n*85; of creation, 15; of

folk stories, 6; of living beings, 14; of religious rituals, 2; strength and, 62; warfare and, 31

Quapaw, 9
quarrel, 42, 81

rabbit, 143–45, 149–50
raids, 10, 11
reason, 13
Red River War, 12
relationships, xii, 21
religion, xi, 2, 8, 13–16, 20, 23–25
reproduction, 51
reservations, 9, 11–12, 13
residence, matrilocal, 29, 33
respect, 31; self, 118
responsibility: for actions, 13–14; of husband, 29
retreat, 130
revenge, 86, 109
reverence, 102, 103
rite of vigil, 24–25, 35, 49, 53, 68, 77, 78–79, 86, 97, 122, 128. *See also* fasting
ritual(s), xi, xii, 1, 15, 24–25; for becoming priest, 22; elements of, 2; knowledge, 21; leader of, 23; objects, 17; of painting (*ki'-non*), 69; purpose of religious, 2; women and, 34. *See also* ceremony(ies)
Runs-to-meet-men, 119–20

sacred bundle (*wa-xo'-be*), 16, 46, 53, 54, 55–58, 67, 68, 88, 154*n*22; definition of, 7; origin of hair bundle, 82–85; origin of whistle bundle, 86; war party and, 34, 41–42, 70–72, 85, 112, 123, 124, 159*n*20, 159*n*25. *See also* clan bundles; great bundle; tribal bundles
sacred robe: for child, 33, 65–66, 69–70; instruction in painting, 68–70; symbolism of, 66
sacred teachings, 2–3, 17; characteristics

of, 4–5; obedience to, 107; socioreligious structure and, 8
Saucy Calf, 2, 52, 62–65, 67–68, 87–88, 109
scalp, 85, 98
school, 136, 163*n*104
sho'-ka (messenger of priests), 23, 42, 59, 76, 156*n*54; origin of, 52
Shun-kah-mo-lah, 59, 70, 122–24
sky, 4, 14, 16, 17, 55, 57, 58; names, 26, 51–52
Sky chief, 21, 25, 53; vision of, 44–45
Sky people. *See* Tsi'-zhu
slavery, 152*n*2, 152*n*3, 156*n*54; outlaw of Indian, 9
snakes, 5
social status, 25–26, 28, 29, 34
socioreligious structure, 8
soil, 61, 68, 79; rubbed on head, 53, 54, 95, 110, 128; symbolic, 49
soldiers (*a'-ki-da*), 21; of chief, 43
solitude, 102
son, 92; eldest, 26, 27
songs, 2; of spirit ceremony, 136; victory, 123
Spain, 9
spider (*dtse-xo-be*), 51, 58
spirit, 14, 36, 113, 132, 135; death and accompanying, 86–87, 96, 129; songs of, ceremony, 136; woman, 125–27
spouse, choice of, 28
spring, blossoms of, 57
squash, 58
squirrel maidens, 143–45
standard, 65, 71; bearer dance, 110, 129
star, 57
Star chief, 49
story(ies), xi; date of, 13; origin, 3–4; origin, of Bear clan, 48–49; origin, of Wolf clan, 46–48. *See also* animal stories; folk stories
storytelling, 27
strength, 61, 67, 146; purpose and, 62
summer hunt, 18–19
sun, 15, 55, 58; rays, 57, 59; rise, 157*n*90

Wheeler, Ben, 127–29, 137–39
whistle bundle, origin of, 86
White, E. E., 13
White Water clan, 55
Wichita, 9
widows, 28, 95
wife: authority over, 29–30; death of,
    129–30; instructions to, of priest,
    67–68; leaving husband, 101, 102; of
    priest, 5, 34, 158*n*100; role of, 30, 33;
    unfaithful, 107–9
wi'-gi-e (poem), 2, 4, 54, 85, 154*n*15, 155*n*36,
    156*n*58; clan, 55–58; definition of, 3;
    Wa-zha'-zhe, 55
wigwam, 18
wi'-he (second daughter), 26
willow tree, 46, 66; evergreen, 57–58;
    symbolism of, 155*n*31
Wind clan, 35

winds: four, 39; killing with, 58, 59
winter, 5, 9
wolf, 86, 97
Wolf clan (Pah-nee-wah-with-tah), origin
    story of, 46–48
woman(en): abuse of, 101; dreamer,
    124–25; expectations of, 33; instruc-
    tions to, 4; planting/gathering by,
    8–9; rituals and, 34; role of, 30; spirit,
    125–27; tattooing of, *33*; war leader,
    95–101; young, with child, 27
woman medicine, 45, 53, 58
woods, four sacred, 57
world: upper/lower, 59; visible/invisible,
    13, 14, 21, 23, 24, 34, 36

xthe'-ts'a-ge (commander), of war parties,
    23, 110

zhin-ga'-oxta. See honored little one

www.ingramcontent.com/pod-product-compliance
Lightning Source LLC
Chambersburg PA
CBHW030844270326
41928CB00007B/1214